ORTHODOX CHRISTIAN BIOETHICS

ORTHODOX CHRISTIAN BIOETHICS

The Role of Hospitality (*philoxenia*),
Dignity, and Vulnerability in Global Bioethics

Rabee Toumi

◥PICKWICK *Publications* · Eugene, Oregon

ORTHODOX CHRISTIAN BIOETHICS
The Role of Hospitality (*philoxenia*), Dignity, and Vulnerability in Global Bioethics

Copyright © 2020 Rabee Toumi. All rights reserved. Except for brief quotations in critical publications or reviews, no part of this book may be reproduced in any manner without prior written permission from the publisher. Write: Permissions, Wipf and Stock Publishers, 199 W. 8th Ave., Suite 3, Eugene, OR 97401.

Pickwick Publications
An Imprint of Wipf and Stock Publishers
199 W. 8th Ave., Suite 3
Eugene, OR 97401

www.wipfandstock.com

PAPERBACK ISBN: 978-1-7252-5369-8
HARDCOVER ISBN: 978-1-7252-5370-4
EBOOK ISBN: 978-1-7252-5371-1

Cataloguing-in-Publication data:

Names: Toumi, Rabee, author.

Title: Orthodox christian bioethics : the role of hospitality (*philoxenia*), dignity, and vulnerability in global bioethics / Rabee Toumi.

Description: Eugene, OR : Pickwick Publications, 2020 | Includes bibliographical references.

Identifiers: ISBN 978-1-7252-5369-8 (paperback) | ISBN 978-1-7252-5370-4 (hardcover) | ISBN 978-1-7252-5371-1 (ebook)

Subjects: LCSH: Orthodox Eastern Church—Doctrines. | Bioethics—Religious aspects—Orthodox Eastern Church. | Medical ethics—Religious aspects—Orthodox Eastern Church. | Spiritual life—Orthodox Eastern Church

Classification: R725.56 .T68 2020 (print) | R725.56 .T68 (ebook)

Manufactured in the U.S.A.   OCTOBER 1, 2020

To Rezanne, Julia, and Lydia
Without you, this could not be achieved, or even bear meaning.

Contents

Preface and Acknowledgments ix

Abbreviations xii

1. Introduction 1

2. The Hermeneutics of Orthodox Theology 5

3. The Interpretive Context of Pluralism in Bioethics 47

4. The Meaning of Human Dignity: A Systematic Interpretation 98

5. The Meaning of Human Vulnerability: A Systematic Interpretation 139

6. The Application of Dignity and Vulnerability to Hospitality: End of Life Care in Global Bioethics 183

7. Conclusion 229

Bibliography 241

Preface and Acknowledgments

This book began as a PhD dissertation at Duquesne University's Center for Healthcare Ethics. The deep discussions and international perspectives offered during my classes at Duquesne inspired many of the perspectives included in this book.

As a deacon in the Antiochian Orthodox Church of North America at the time, I was challenged to formulate a relevant perspective on evolving bioethical issues while still being rooted in an authentic Orthodox Christian mindset. Coming from the Church of Antioch, where the disciples were first called Christians (Acts 11:26), I took the challenge of bioethics a step further than other Orthodox Christian bioethicists; not only was I interested in what is unique about Orthodox bioethics, but I also wanted to find the common ground with other value systems, religious or otherwise. In Antioch, and since the dawn of Christianity, Christians were the bridge between different civilizations, cultures, and religions. Without being intimidated for being a minority for more than fifteen centuries, Christians in Antioch created hospitable niches to discuss their commonalities with the different neighbor and accepted any challenges to their perspectives—even when it led to their martyrdom. They continue to be inspirational even today.

My academic career may seem unusual to an outside observer. I left my medical training in internal medicine after a year at Damascus University to pursue theological training at the University of Balamand (UOB). To combine my two backgrounds, in medicine and in theology, I was offered the possibility of pursuing further graduate theological training in the US, thanks to the generosity of Mr. Diya Obeid, to whom I will always be indebted. I am also grateful for the trust and encouragement of the faculty at St. John of Damascus Institute of Theology (UOB); Metropolitan Isaac Barakat, Drs. George Nahhas and Daniel Ayuch, and Frs.

Porpherios Georgy and Ramy Wannous were exceptional mentors at a demanding time of my personal formation.

At the Holy Cross Greek Orthodox Seminary in Brookline, Massachusetts, many professors helped me grow as a person and a scholar; I am especially appreciative of the support and friendship of Drs. Timothy Patitsas and Philip Mamalakis.

This book would not have materialized without the inspiration and support of the faculty at the Center for Healthcare Ethics at Duquesne University. Perhaps because they believed in my ability to produce something authentically novel and relevant, I was admitted to the PhD program and was offered a generous scholarship for three years. I want to thank my dissertation advisor, Prof. Gerard Magill, for his encouragement and valuable insights throughout the process of writing the dissertation and beyond. I am also grateful to Prof. Henk ten Have for being such an inspirational figure in my life; his unusual career and life brought hope when I doubted my own academic choices. At the Center, Mrs. Glory Smith is the example of true Christian hospitality to every student, regardless of their background. I am indebted to her and her husband, Tom, for adopting me and my little family while we lived in Pittsburgh—and beyond. While in Pittsburgh, the prayers and friendship of bishop John Abdalah and Fr. Bogdan Bucur, along with many of the faithful at St. George Cathedral in Pittsburgh and St. Mary Church in Hunt Valley, Maryland, lifted me up when an internal anguish to succeed coincided with a war that tore my home country for years.

My extended family and several friends were always there to support my growing family. I am especially indebted to my lifelong friend, brother, and now-concelebrant Fr. Damaskinos Elias Issa. My ultimate gratitude befits my little family. My daughters, Julia and Lydia, grew rapidly while I was writing my dissertation. Their laughter and hugs gave me the courage and motivation to keep going when life challenges were creeping around. My wife, Rezanne, shaped my dissertation and this book in so many ways. During the writing process, she was pursuing her graduate medical training in internal and then geriatric medicine. That was not an easy time for both of us. However, many of her encounters with patients and struggles with colleagues are invisibly knitted into this book. Her kindness, dedication, and care for her patients inspired me all along. She is the reason I continue to smile.

My existential gratitude befits the Lord who was crucified and has risen indeed out of his love and philanthropy toward all humankind.

Through this volume, I hope to have given a glimpse of his love to a broken world which is in dire need of more love.

Rabee Toumi, MD, PhD
Rockville, MD
March 2020

Abbreviations

AJOB	*American Journal of Bioethics*
BMJ	*British Medical Journal*
JAMA	*Journal of American Medical Association*
NEJM	*New England Journal of Medicine*

1

Introduction

Bioethics is an interdisciplinary academic venture that has developed over the past few decades. Although the study of ethics is an integral component of systematic theology and philosophy, rapid advances in medicine have raised serious moral dilemmas that can only be addressed on a global scale. The development of medicine accompanied new world politics and economics and brought about unprecedented broad consequences. Furthermore, since the scientific breakthroughs took place in Western countries, ethical deliberations were shaped by the prevailing Western mindset and its premises.

In the West, Orthodox Christian scholars and theologians are polarized between their own Eastern mindset and worldview and the Western context where medicine is shaped and practiced. Further, within the current global context of medical practice, Orthodox Christian bioethicists ought to address the global repercussions of modern medicine and the predominant disparities in health in developed and developing countries. Global bioethics is a dynamic movement that is striving to build a genuine consensus around the increased complexities of moral issues related to health while realistically addressing the particularities of diverse human communities.

One notable exception to the general thrust of contemporary bioethics is the highly respected Orthodox philosopher and bioethicist Tristram Engelhardt. Early in his academic career, Engelhardt supported the possibility of nurturing a common rational morality building on the Enlightenment project. However, after converting to Orthodox Christianity, he adamantly opposed any possibility of bridging the moral gap that separates various value systems. Contrary to his position, this book explores the theological foundations on which an inclusive and sustainable global bioethics is possible. Rather than discovering this common ground using—exclusively—human rationality, this book highlights the commonalities in the human condition and experiences (mainly mortality) and their anthropological repercussions; thus, it uncovers a global bioethics agenda distilled through the tenets of Orthodox Christian anthropology.

Unlike Engelhardt, Stanley Harakas approached rising ethical dilemmas, social and medical, from a pastoral perspective addressing Orthodox Christian faithful who live in the West. As a prolific author, he did not directly engage in discussing the philosophical and theological premises of other Western authors; he primarily depicted an Orthodox Christian way of living that is unique to that tradition. Besides, Harakas, like many other theologians, recognizes the global salvific mission of Orthodox Christianity within a church typology that humbly embraces the entire world.

Building on that inclusive typology, this book presents and analyzes several theological themes to assist Orthodox Christian theologians and bioethicists in finding a common ground with other value systems adding a block toward building a substantive global bioethics. The premise of this work is that the human condition and experiences, understood within the advocated Orthodox Christian hermeneutics, motivates a critical engagement with other value-systems, disciplines, and a broad array of literature to establish the advocated common ground. Without compromising the dogmatic and anthropological heritage of Orthodoxy, this book takes the inspiration from the truth of Jesus Christ as the personal savior of humankind and attempts to advance his mission in addressing human suffering and mortality.

To identify the advocated middle ground, this book discusses the core relation between hospitality, dignity, and vulnerability. Based on Orthodox Christian theology and hermeneutics, an anthropocentric approach to bioethics is presented. More specifically, in the context of medical practice, healthcare workers and patients meet as ultimate strangers; thus, hospitality (*philoxenia*: the love of the stranger) is the core value to bridge the gap that separates them. Hospitable medical practice is presented as a constructive answer to human anguish especially at the end of life since hospitality, as experienced in Orthodoxy, takes seriously the dignity and vulnerability of all human beings.

This book explores the hermeneutical apparatus derived from Orthodox Christian theology (chapter 2) to unfold the dimensions of the human condition and experiences within the contemporary pluralistic and global context of bioethics (chapter 3). Building on the suggested hermeneutics, a fresh theological *phronema* (mindset) justifies the possibility of an anthropocentric ground for an inclusive and substantive moral discourse which evolves around human dignity and vulnerability. The relationship between hospitality, dignity, and vulnerability in Orthodox hermeneutics, it will be suggested, derives from the three-fold christological mission of priesthood, kinghood and prophethood, respectively. To reveal this relationship, the meaning of human dignity (chapter 4) and human vulnerability (chapter 5) will be explored at the theoretical/theological level and at the applicable global levels. In the final chapter (chapter 6), the relation of dignity and vulnerability to hospitality (*philoxenia*) will be illustrated with end of life care. The discussion will unveil the role of gratitude, compassion, and solidarity—as they hinge on the discussed concepts, respectively—in shaping the education and practice of medicine in a globalized world.

Although the suggested moral discourse derives from Orthodox Christian theology and anthropology, it garners support among non-Orthodox, whether they are religious or secular. Human dignity and vulnerability will be briefly examined in both theological and secular frameworks to highlight the centrality of gratitude and compassion in the medical encounter. Approaching dignified but vulnerable humanity with hospitality, therefore, paves the road for an authentic anthropocentric medical care. In medical practice, ultimate strangers meet; they are not only moral strangers who have different worldviews, but they are ultimate strangers who, more often than not, belong to different worlds. Thus, human dignity and vulnerability, as common attributes among all humans, will be examined through their relationship to hospitality and solidarity in medical practice, especially at the end of life. This will highlight hospitality, and its derivative, solidarity, as fundamental to navigate bioethical inquiries globally.

At this point, it is warranted to provide a brief understanding of *phronema* as a concept that is central to the argument of this book. *Phronema* is understood to represent the mindset within which the Orthodox Church connects her faith to her practice of that faith. The fundamental connection between *orthodoxia* (the right faith) and *orthopraxis* (the right worship) is achieved within a certain mindset that is handed within the ecclesiastical community. This mindset is ecclesiastical in that it is experienced daily inside the community of believers rather than being rationally expressed in exclusively dogmatic formulations.[1] Therefore, the advocated mindset is necessarily communal in that it highlights the human experience within the broader social context rather than as an isolated individualistic experience. Moreover, this *phronema* builds on the contemporary human condition (fallen as it is) and experiences while taking the redeemed humanity (in the person of Jesus Christ) as its compass. Therefore, the advocated *phronema* is anthropocentric in that it considers the human experience in its totality rather than as a one-sided emphasis on human rationality. The writings of Olivier Clément are inspirational in this regard.[2]

This book is not meant, in its entirety, for everyone. Those who are interested in the theological basis of the argument may read only the relevant sections. Due to the limitations of this book, the theological component of the argument is not meant to be comprehensive and inclusive of all the primary theological resources, such as biblical texts and patristic resources. Rather, the theological argument builds on the work of other contemporary theologians for the sake of brevity. Detailed research into the biblical and patristic underpinnings of the argument of this book is warranted but is left to future publications. Readers who belong to a different religious tradition, Christian or non-Christian, are invited to reflect on how the theological argument of this book may resonate with their own respective tradition.

Nonetheless, those who are interested in the practical implications of the argument may choose to read the relevant chapters. They are invited to critically reflect on how the discussed concepts may have practical implications in their approach to healthcare policy, the practice of medicine, and medical education.

The argument of this book is very ambitious in that it attempts to bring together relevant concepts using different disciplinary approaches. It is only a beginning!

---

1. Florovsky, *Bible, Church, Tradition*, 73–92, 93–103; Casiday, "Church Fathers and the Shaping of Orthodox Theology," 167–87; Breck, "Orthodox Bioethics in the Encounter between Science and Religion," 119–30.

2. Especially his book, Clément, *On Human Being*.

2

The Hermeneutics of Orthodox Theology

This chapter discusses the hermeneutics on which Orthodox theology can actively engage in bioethical issues at the global level. Although hermeneutics as a discipline was started in Reformation circles, Orthodox theologians adopted this discipline to develop a patristic *phronema* that is relevant to the daily life of the faithful and to minister to their needs.[1]

This chapter explores the theological foundations on which the Orthodox Church should engage in the current global bioethics discourse. Building on an inclusive theological anthropology, the Orthodox Church bears the responsibility to find a common ground with other groups, regardless of how different they may seem in their ethos. This responsibility derives from the Church's eschatological-eucharistic identity and mission.

Theological Foundations in Orthodox Theology

To explore the advocated common ground for a substantive global discourse in bioethics, this section will explore the relevant theological themes in Orthodox Christianity at two dimensions. The first dimension pertains to the historical encounter between Orthodoxy and (post-)modernity which shaped contemporary perceptions toward health and medical practice in the West. The second dimension explores the theological basis for an active involvement in global bioethics discourse.

---

1. Kattan, "Hermeneutics," 47–57.

Orthodox Christianity at New Frontiers

Orthodoxy in Western Countries

Orthodox Christianity has only established its presence in Western countries close to the end of the second millennia. Contemporary Orthodox parishes in Western Europe and North America are comprised of immigrants who moved at various times from Orthodoxy's homeland east of the Adriatic along with a few generations of their offspring. In many places, however, Orthodoxy has flourished among native Westerners of various religious backgrounds who embraced Orthodoxy after serious searching for a more traditional version of Christianity compared to their previous tradition.[2] Since the end of the nineteenth century, the immigration of lay Orthodox faithful to the West created a need for clergymen to move from the old countries to minister to their compatriots. Over the passage of years, monasteries and seminaries were established to effectively address the growing needs of these emigrants and their families. In a new culture with a different religious ethos, Orthodox believers needed a special help to reconcile the ethos within which they grew in their old countries (or within their households in a new homeland) with the new environment. At the same time, Orthodox theologians who immigrated to different Western countries, especially to Paris and New York, were actively involved in academic circles and ecumenical meetings which shaped their relation to modern (and then post-modern) society and challenged their understanding of the Orthodox tradition.

This book situates the Orthodox Christian encounter with modern and post-modern society within the tradition of those pioneer Orthodox theologians who actively engaged in an enriching discourse with their peers of various religious backgrounds. The premise of this enterprise is that Orthodox Christianity can provide a fresh but traditional perspective to post-Christian societies, especially is regards to disturbing bioethical dilemmas. This perspective is not only relevant to Orthodox faithful in the West but is also formative to Orthodox communities everywhere. An authentic Orthodox Christian involvement in global bioethics extends the traditional and catholic (universal) mission of the church to contemporary post-Christian communities that differ from its originally eastern context.[3]

---

2. Andreopoulos, "A Modern Orthodox Approach to Spirituality," 10–23.

3. Agadjanian and Roudometof, "Introduction: Eastern Orthodoxy in a Global Age," 1–26.

To unfold the advocated Orthodox *phronema*, it is first warranted to briefly illustrate the historical experience of Orthodox Christians over the past two millennia using a very broad brush.

Brief History[4]

For two millennia, Orthodox Christians have lived on the land of the Eastern side of the Roman Empire (also known as Byzantium) comprised of the Southern and Eastern shores of the Mediterranean. Outside the geographical boundaries of Byzantium, other ethnic groups embraced Orthodox Christianity, especially the Slavs of Eastern Europe. Despite their geographical distance, the faithful of either side of the Roman Empire and those outside its boundaries exchanged their ideas, including theological ones, throughout their history. However, this exchange was not without confusion or misunderstanding at times, possibly partly due to linguistic differences.

Arguably, contemporary exchange of ideas between East and West is partly shaped by the past historical patterns of this exchange. Although contemporary Western societies are post-modern and post-Christian, current exchange between Orthodox Christianity and the West is still shaped by previous theological encounters between the two cultures. It is also necessary to keep in mind that Easterners have not experienced the Protestant Reformation and the Enlightenment movement firsthand. Easterners have migrated to Western societies after those movements have resulted in a compartmentalization of religion outside "secular" public life. Such a stark separation between religion (the church) and public life (while respecting various religious beliefs) is unknown in Orthodoxy's heartland, as will be further explained shortly.

Therefore, although the following brief historical illustration may not be directly related to the discussion of this book, it is necessary to keep in mind, simply because history plays an important role in shaping Orthodox Christian identity, ethos and worldview.[5] For instance, on various feast days, Orthodox hymnology frequently uses the adverb "*Today…*" to commemorate various biblical or historical events.[6] Hence,

---

4. Cunningham and Theokritoff, "Who Are the Orthodox Christians?," 1–18.

5. Casiday, "Church Fathers and the Shaping of Orthodox Theology," 167–87.

6. Harakas, *Health and Medicine*, 3–11; similar referrals are made in Bucur, "'Feet That Eve Heard,'" 3–26.

events in history are not just shadows of a bygone era: they are mystically shaping the here and now and the Orthodox worldview.

Byzantium

During the first three centuries of Christianity, scores of faithful were persecuted and many executed for being members of the nascent religion. They were especially perceived as a threat to the Roman Empire because of their adamant refusal to submit to the assumed divine authority of the Roman Emperor and the Pantheon. Despite this persecution, many people joined the emerging Christian community and missionary work bore the good news of the gospel to communities outside the Empire. However, the promulgation of the Edict of Milan in AD 313 changed the church's relationship to political authorities and guaranteed a peaceful environment for the believers to live their faith and spread the word. Under the auspices of the emperors, many ecumenical councils were convened to define the Orthodox faith in dogmatic formulations.

Notwithstanding the benefits of a supportive political system, the conversion of the Roman Emperor, Constantine, and the adoption of Christianity as the Empire's official religion had untoward consequences on the new faith. For instance, many people nominally converted to Christianity to climb the political and social ladder. Besides, some of the dogmatic controversies attracted political meddling to preserve the unity of the empire rather than to discern the truth. As a reaction to corrupting political life, the monastic movement (also known as the white—i.e., bloodless—martyrdom) flourished among the faithful. Monks fled imperial urban centers to live a simple spiritual life of asceticism to attain holiness. Arguably, this same movement is what preserved the authentic meaning of Christian life and its daily strife to encounter God.[7]

Because of church-state symphony, many Christian communities of the East were left outside mainstream Christianity for centuries. Some of these communities were outside the physical borders of Byzantium, such as the Armenians and the Church of the East (also known as the Nestorian Church). Others were excluded partly because of the state's support of certain linguistic dogmatic formulae in Greek rather than in their respective languages (such as the Syrian-Jacobite Church and the Coptic Church). The division among these Christian communities (and others,

---

7. Clément, *On Human Being*, 69–90.

including the Melkites who emerged after 1724 because of Western missionaries to the East) continues to this day in contemporary nation-states around the Mediterranean. However, these historical differences are usually downplayed in public discourse due to the minority status of these communities within their current political-social milieu.[8]

Western Christianity

Unlike its Eastern side, the Western side of the Roman Empire did not experience similar divisions among Christians during the first millennia. Under the authority of the bishop of Rome (traditionally called the Pope of Rome, similar to the Pope of Alexandria), the church participated in the seven ecumenical councils convened in Byzantium and endorsed their dogmatic formulations. However, several factors drifted the Western church away from its Eastern counterpart during the first millennia which culminated in the mutual excommunications of 1054. These factors include: the language differences between the Latin west and the Greek east; the Germanic control of Rome after 476; the growing authority of the Pope of Rome contrary to the conciliarity of bishops traditionally practiced in the East; the addition of the "filioque" (and from the Son) to the Nicaea-Constantinople creed; the banning of clergy marriage; the missionary work outside the Christian empire, especially among the Slavs; the adoption of the doctrine of the purgatory; and the use of unleavened bread in celebrating the Eucharist.[9]

Encounters between the East and the West

Although the 1054 excommunications targeted the church hierarchies of Constantinople and Rome, several events that followed grew the faithful themselves apart. Some of the consequences of these events linger to this day in the collective memory of the Orthodox and other Christians of the East. The Crusades are one significant example. Many economic and theological reasons motivated Westerners to free the Holy Land, including Jerusalem and the surrounding area, from the control of the rising Islamic Empire. However, this seemingly noble mission has, since then, disadvantaged those Christian communities who lived under the rule of

---

8. Cunningham and Theokritoff, "Who Are the Orthodox Christians?," 1–18.
9. Cunningham and Theokritoff, "Who Are the Orthodox Christians?," 1–18.

Islam. Since then, Eastern Christians have perceived with distrust the motivations of Western intervention in their lives.[10]

European crusaders and their leaders dethroned numerous Orthodox bishops of Eastern cities and uncanonically enthroned Latin bishops, particularly in the established Latin states of Antioch and Jerusalem for instance. Moreover, Muslims of Greater Syria distrusted their Christian compatriots for being co-religionists with the European invaders (an issue that lingers to this day in international relations). Even worse, in 1204, the crusaders of the fourth campaign invaded Constantinople—which was not under the Islamic rule at that time—and desecrated its churches in a way that was not seen when the city later fell to the Muslim Turks.

The distrust between Easterners and Westerners reached its apex when Constantinople was under siege by the Turks in 1453. Because of constant Turkish attacks, the rulers of shrinking Byzantium were compelled to seek the help of Western Christians. However, during the meetings convened in Florence and Ferrara in 1438–39, the envoys to Rome were mistreated and asked to submit to the papal authority through unitary agreements in exchange for military help that never arrived. In the end, Constantinople fell to the Turks and most of the geographical territory of the once Byzantine Empire became under the control of Muslim rulers. For the following four centuries, Muslim Turks controlled four of the five historical patriarchates: Constantinople, Antioch, Jerusalem, and Alexandria—the fifth being Rome. During these centuries, Christian communities lived among their Muslim compatriots as second-class citizens (under the millet system) and many were forced to convert to Islam.[11]

The Turkish yolk over the former Byzantine Empire was finally lifted at various times and in various ways. Unlike the experience in Greece and the Balkans where Orthodox Christians were the majority, for the Arabic Middle East it was the rise of secular nationalist states that brought to Christians the hope of equal citizenship. Thus, Antiochian Orthodox Christians, at home and in the diaspora, actively participated in the Arab renaissance and nationalistic movement to establish secular states to guarantee their equal citizenship.[12] Among many Orthodox Christians around the Mediterranean, nostalgia toward the glory of Byzantium still

---

10. Abou Mrad, "The Witness," 246–60.
11. Cunningham and Theokritoff, "Who Are the Orthodox Christians?," 1–18.
12. Abou Mrad, "The Witness," 246–60.

lingers. Although theologically unjustifiable, such a collective experience has a similar parallel among the Christians of "Holy" Russia who ruminate on the glory of Orthodoxy before the Bolshevik revolution and subsequent atheistic communism.

Orthodoxy in Russia

The experience of Orthodox Christians in Russian territory was different from those mentioned above. A mass conversion of the Russian Empire took place in 988 after the delegates of Prince Vladimir of Kiev experienced the majesty of the celebrated liturgy in Agia Sophia of Constantinople—an event that holds a dear place in the hearts of many Orthodox faithful. In organizing the political and public life henceforth, Russian Emperors imitated the Byzantine symphony between church and state. This symphony tickled the imagination of some Russian authorities and theologians to consider Moscow the Third Rome of the emerging Christian Empire of Russia. However, too much involvement by political authorities in church life bore unfavorable consequences at times.[13] For instance, in 1689, Tsar Peter the Great enforced a "modernizing" paradigm on the Russian Church similar to the Western Reformed churches. Peter's paradigm of church reformation exposes the still-relevant dilemma: how to encounter modern and post-modern social reality without betraying the apostolic heritage of the Orthodox Church. A contrast exists between those who wish to literally preserve the holy tradition and those who perceive this tradition as a dynamic way of life.[14] As will be further explained next, by perceiving the tradition in terms of a dynamic experience, the faithful would be better equipped to stay loyal to the spirit of the Orthodox tradition.

Encountering Modernity: Two Schools of Thought

Among Orthodox theologians mainly of Russian descent, two schools of thoughts emerged to address the encounter of Orthodox Christianity with modern and post-modern society. These two schools, Russian philosophical and neo-patristic, parallel the historical-institutional and

---

13. Cunningham and Theokritoff, "Who Are the Orthodox Christians?," 1–18.
14. Harakas, *Health and Medicine*, 3–11.

philosophical-ontological responses to modernity, respectively.[15] While earlier encounters with modernity happened from afar, these thinkers had to move and live in modern Western societies around the beginning of the twentieth century. Not only did they have to discuss modern ideas away from home, but they lived in modern societies whose ethos was drastically different from their own Orthodox communities.[16] Their writings influenced how the Orthodox diaspora lived in their new home and fostered a theological renaissance in Orthodoxy's heartland when those communities were ready.[17]

Theologians of Russian decent led both schools of thought, Russian philosophical and neo-patristic, in discourse with modernity. These theologians experienced a spiritual, monastic renaissance in Russia that dates back to the nineteenth century. This renaissance was rooted in Athonite monasticism but was flourishing in Russia's monasteries. Although Mount Athos, a community of twenty monasteries housed on a peninsula in contemporary Greece, has had monastic life since the tenth century, its influence on public spirituality was limited partly because of the burden of the Ottoman occupation.[18] However, in 1782, St Makarios of Corinth and St Nikodimos of Athos published the *Philokalia* ("the love of beauty"), a compilation on spirituality and constant prayer written by several church fathers. This compilation influenced the spiritual life outside of Mount Athos.[19]

After its translation to Slavonic, the Philokalia was influential in reviving monastic life in Russia, especially in the Optina monastery near Kiev, around the beginnings of the nineteenth century. It was arguably more influential among the Slavs than among Orthodox Christians close to the Mediterranean at that time. Although theologians of the above schools of thought may have not directly drawn from contemporary monastic resources, flourishing monasticism arguably shaped their worldview and mindset (*phronema*)—a mindset that actively engaged the modern world, though using different methodologies.[20]

---

15. Stöckl, "Modernity and Its Critique," 243–69.
16. Schmemann, "Task of Orthodox Theology," 180–88.
17. Plekon, "Russian Religious Revival," 203–17.
18. Cunningham and Theokritoff, "Who Are the Orthodox Christians?," 1–18.
19. Louth, "Patristic Revival," 188–202.
20. Cunningham and Theokritoff, "Who Are the Orthodox Christians?," 1–18.

An anecdotal example shows the influence of Optina monasticism on public conscience and spirituality at that time, namely the writings of Fyodor Dostoevsky. Many contemporary Christian ethicists use Dostoevsky to discuss Christian morality of the nineteenth century and its implications today. In *The Brothers Karamazov* for instance, Starz (elder) Zosima represents one of the spiritual elders of Optina and his influence on the broader community beyond the monastery.[21] However, after the 1917 revolution, thriving Russian monasticism withered and many figures of the intelligentsia migrated to the West, including the theologians who pioneered the Russian philosophical and neo-patristic schools. In Paris, these theologians found a home at the St Serge Institute of Orthodox Theology (established in 1926) where their interactions, among themselves and with other Christian theologians, fostered a broad Orthodox renaissance.[22]

The Russian Philosophical School

Theologians of the Russian philosophical school approached modernity using a Christian philosophy. In the late nineteenth century, Sergei Bulgakov (1871–1944), Nikolai Berdyaev (1874–1948), and Pavel Florensky (1882–1937) among others explored a "theology of engagement with the secular world" of modernity.[23] They used a philosophical language to engage the prevalent approaches in and toward modernity. They criticized secular humanism inasmuch as they shunned sectarian "traditional" theological thought: for them, both approaches denied the active presence of God in the world. Secular humanism has rationally excluded God from the created world; similarly, "traditional" theology was sectarian in that it denied the presence of God outside the church.[24] Due to the condemnation of Bulgakov's sophiology as heretical in the 1930s,[25] (despite its importance in shaping modern Orthodox theology),[26] it is thought that the Russian school has withered away, leaving it to the neo-patristic school to flourish in Orthodox circles. Nonetheless, the spirit of the

---

21. Valliere, "Russian Religious Thought," 227–41.
22. Cunningham and Theokritoff, "Who Are the Orthodox Christians?," 1–18.
23. Valliere, "Russian Religious Thought," 227–41.
24. Valliere, "Russian Religious Thought," 227–41.
25. Louth, "Patristic Revival," 188–202.
26. Cunningham and Theokritoff, "Who Are the Orthodox Christians?," 1–18.

Russian philosophical school has seemingly lived through the activism of several theologians in Europe. Paul Evdokimov (1900–1970), Lev Gillet (1893–1980), Mother Maria Skobtsova (1891–1945), Elizabeth Behr-Sigel (1907–2005), and Olivier Clément (1921–2009) among others took the social mission of the church, or "Christian socialism" according to Bulgakov, very seriously. Through their life and theological contribution, they embodied the so-called "the sacrament of the brother [and sister]" (taken from St John Chrysostom) which shaped modern Orthodox renaissance in Europe and elsewhere.[27]

The Neo-Patristic School

Contrary to the Russian school's approach to modernity, the protagonists of the neo-patristic school avoided using a philosophical language to engage modernity. Starting in Paris then moving to New York, George Florovsky (1893–1979) and Vladimir Lossky (1903–1958) advocated for a patristic *phronema* to promote a unique Orthodox language to converse with modernity. Citing patristic resources, they noted, was not enough to make a modern theology patristic.[28] They benefitted from a growing interest in patristics among academicians of Roman Catholic and Protestant backgrounds who convened in Oxford every four years since 1951 for the International Conference on Patristics.[29] While pioneering a neo-patristic synthesis to address modernity, Florovsky did not draw a clear path to achieve his synthesis. Further, he unjustifiably condemned the Russian school's approach as being captive to Western scholastic methodologies, particularly the sophiology of Bulgakov.[30] Yet, his own approach was limited in its ability to address the wide range of issues raised by modernity.[31] Generally, the patristic heritage of Orthodoxy, these theologians frequently emphasized, is embedded in dynamic and lively writings that are inherently heterogeneous; this leaves room to differentiate between personal theological opinions-*theologomena* (by each

---

27. Plekon, "Russian Religious Revival," 203–17; Clément, "Purification by Atheism," 22–39; Stöckl, "Modernity and Its Critique," 243–69.

28. Ware, "Orthodox Theology Today," 105–21; Clément, *On Human Being*, 91–107.

29. Louth, "Patristic Revival," 188–202.

30. Louth, "Patristic Revival," 188–202.

31. Ware, "Orthodox Theology Today," 105–21.

specific church author), and unnegotiable and widely accepted doctrinal formulations.[32]

In a few words, both schools of thought did not promote Orthodox Christian estrangement from the world; however, they engaged the world on different grounds. Theologians of the Russian school actively conversed with secular humanism using contemporaneous religious philosophy to advance a "Christian humanism." However, neo-patristic theologians delved into patristic resources to extract the essence of an authentic answer to modern dilemmas.[33]

Although these schools may seem to have a salient contrast in their methodologies, generations of theologians since their founders have used fundamental elements from both approaches to foster an Orthodox spiritual and theological renaissance, in the diaspora and in Antioch (Syria and Lebanon) for instance.[34] More important, by avoiding polemical dogmatic discourse, many contemporary theologians focus on uncovering the uniqueness of Orthodox theology and its relevance to present-day Christians wherever they live. The elaboration of an authentic Orthodox ecclesiology, for instance, has influenced–through dialogue–the ecclesiology(ies) of other Christian communities regardless of their backgrounds.[35]

Unfortunately, theological anthropology has yet to be fully developed in the writings of contemporary Orthodox theologians.[36] Several theologians have used available scientific or humanist disciplines to articulate an Orthodox anthropology relevant to postmodern dilemmas. However, emerging globalization, environmental crises, and bioethical dilemmas have recently fueled an interest in Orthodox anthropology.[37]

It is because of these same issues that this book advocates an active involvement of the Orthodox Church in global bioethics discourse. An

---

32. Casiday, "Church Fathers," 167–87; Louth, "Patristic Revival," 188–202.

33. Stöckl, "Modernity and Its Critique," 243–69.

34. Abou Mrad, "The Witness," 246–60.

35. Ware, "Orthodox Theology Today," 105–21.

36. Harrison, "Human Person," 78–92; Andreopoulos, "Modern Orthodox," 10–23; Lubardic, "Orthodox Theology of Personhood: A Critical Overview (Part 1)," 521–30; Lubardic, "Orthodox Theology of Personhood: A Critical Overview (Part 2)," 573–81; Clapsis, "Challenge of a Global World," 47–66.

37. Theokritoff, "Creator and Creation," 63–77; Harakas, *Living the Faith*, 215–21; Wirzba, "A Priestly Approach," 354–62; Ware, "Orthodox Theology Today," 105–21; Harrison, *God's Many-Splendored Image*, 1–8, 185–94.

inclusive and philanthropic mission to save humankind is well-rooted in Orthodox hermeneutics and theology.

Theological Themes for Contemporary Discussions

Since this book is advocating a certain theological *phronema* to advance a substantive discourse in global bioethics, it is warranted to briefly delineate the relevant theological themes. "*Phronema*" in this context refers to the hermeneutics of the divine salvific providence. *Phronema* is the mindset which shapes the worldview of Orthodox Christians, the role of God in the world and in their own lives, and the way they should engage the world to continue the divine redemptive plan as a church—the living body of Christ (Colossians 1:24).[38]

An Orthodox Phronema beyond Doctrines

The advocated *phronema* is not limited to the dogmatic tenets formulated throughout the centuries; it is rather inclusive of the ethos that shapes the Christian community in its daily strife to encounter a personal God.[39] Thus, doctrinal formulations are valued because they facilitate the human communion with God rather than because of their literally interpreted ideological tenets.[40] Dogmas, for Orthodox Christian theology, aim at healing humanity of its fallenness and alienation through re-establishing an authentic communion with God. Inseparable, then, are the mystical-spiritual experiences and the dogmatic formulations in an authentic Orthodox *phronema*; this is contrary to the scholastic compartmentalization of spirituality away from dogmas (although Orthodox theology has been influenced by scholasticism at times).[41] Evagrius Ponticus (c. 346–399) is frequently quoted since he recapitulates this organic relationship between spirituality and dogmatic theology by saying: "If you are a theologian, you will pray truly, and if you pray truly you will be a theologian."[42] By the same token, theological opinions (*theologomena*)

---

38. Steenberg, "The Church," 121–35; Harakas, *Health and Medicine*, 12–21.
39. Harakas, *Living the Faith*, 344–92; Papanikolaou, "Orthodoxy, Postmodernity, and Ecumenism," 527–47.
40. Casiday, "Church Fathers," 167–87.
41. Lossky, *Mystical Theology*, 7–22.
42. As quoted in Casiday, "Church Fathers," 173.

on non-dogmatic issues do not impede the recognition of the holiness of a church writer; this highlights that church fathers are not monolithic in their theological writings. Rather, their unhindered enthusiasm to be united with God is what draws attention to their work.[43]

In a book that is dedicated to the discussion of health and medicine in the Orthodox Church, Fr Stanley Harakas illustrates an Orthodox *phronema* that transcends ethnic, social, and historical backgrounds of various Orthodox communities.[44] This *phronema* is founded on a dynamic antinomy (paradox) between the two realms of the divine and created realities; it provokes the following senses. At the edge between Godhead and creation, Orthodox Christians cherish *a sense of the holy* that simultaneously embraces, without confusion, the transcendent and the immanent.[45] The faithful also experience *a sense of the incarnation* which unites the spiritual and the material and excludes the Cartesian duality in perceiving the world. Further, they encounter the world with *a transfigurational sense*, a sense that balances between the permanence of a tradition inherited from the Apostles and the necessity of change to address the evolving life of humankind. The same transfigurational sensibility refers to the eschatological transfiguration of the entire created reality to a reality beyond human imagination: "A new heaven and a new earth" (Revelation 21:1).[46]

Furthermore, this Orthodox *phronema* is realistic in its recognition of *the evil and sin* committed by humanity. Yet, human fallenness is not perceived within a legalistic framework; rather it is a state of being which does affect human beings and has considerable repercussions on the entire creation.[47]

Notwithstanding human fallenness, an Orthodox *phronema* highlights the *ultimate victory of Christ over death* which is celebrated in Pascha (Easter) and on every Sunday (Kyriaki in Greek, the Lord's Day). This sense of victory is epitomized in the paschal hymn of resurrection: "Christ is risen from the dead, trampling down death by death, and unto those in the tombs bestowing life." Therefore, in acquiring this *phronema*, Orthodox Christians recognize that Christ's sacrifice in not a legalistic

43. Casiday, "Church Fathers," 167–87.
44. Harakas, *Health and Medicine*, 12–21.
45. Also in Theokritoff, "Creator and Creation," 63–77.
46. Steenberg, "The Church," 121–35.
47. Louth, *Introducing Eastern Orthodox Theology*, 66–81; Yannaras, *Freedom of Morality*, 29–48.

ransom to human misdemeanor but a philanthropic act of compassion by the persons of the Trinity. Eventually, what saves humanity from its alienation from God is God's love for humankind (*philanthropy*): a theme that is frequently mentioned in Orthodox hymnology.[48]

Relevant Theological Themes

After illustrating the *phronema* with which Orthodox Christians encounter the world, it is warranted to briefly explore the theological themes that stand behind this worldview. Unlike scholastic theology, Orthodox theological reflection avoids compartmentalizing those themes. Therefore, to unfold an Orthodox anthropology that tackles post-modern dilemmas, it is necessary to briefly explore the relevant tenets of trinitarian, christological-soteriological, and ecclesiological theology(ies).

The Holy Trinity

God was revealed to humanity in the three persons (*prosopon-prosopa, hypostasis*) of the Holy Trinity who share the same divine essence-nature (*ousia-physis*) but each has one's own personal will and attributes.[49] Since the divine revelation was through and in the persons of the Holy Trinity, personhood plays a central role in Orthodox theology despite some possible controversies on applying modern thoughts to old patristic writings.[50] Moreover, Orthodox Christian experience of the Godhead occurs only in relation with those persons, rather than through an experience of an amorphous divine essence. Those persons are known to be God the Father who is the origin of the other two persons before all times; God the Son who incarnated in the person of Jesus Christ from the Virgin Mary and bridged the gap which separates God from the created world; and God the Holy Spirit who proceeds from the Father only (John 15:26) (unlike the later addition in the West of the *filioque*: "and [from] the Son,"

---

48. Plekon, "Russian Religious Revival," 203–17; Harakas, *Health and Medicine*, 59–68.

49. Louth, *Introducing Eastern Orthodox Theology*, 16–32.

50. Louth, "Patristic Revival," 188–202; Papanikolaou, "Personhood and Its Exponents," 232–45; Lubardic, "Orthodox Theology of Personhood: A Critical Overview (Part 1)," 521–30; Lubardic, "Orthodox Theology of Personhood: A Critical Overview (Part 2)," 573–81; Clément, *On Human Being*, 25–42.

to the Creed) and who sustains the church in its worldly mission until the second coming.[51]

Despite the transcendence of God, God is still actively present in the created world.[52] Early church fathers (such as Clement of Alexandria (150–215), the Cappadocian fathers (fourth century), and Athanasius (296–373))[53] and recent fathers (including Gregory Palamas, fourteenth century) agree on the difference between the divine essence-nature and the divine uncreated energies (powers, *energeia*).[54] While divine essence is not accessible to human speculation, God's energies are actively sustaining the created world and are subject to theological reflection. Because of this differentiation, humans are not able to know God in who God is but through the divine attributes which interact with the creation. This dynamic differentiation between what is accessible—and what is not—in the divine persons establishes the basis for two different but intertwined ways of doing Orthodox theology: *cataphatic* and *apophatic* theology.[55] This same dynamic differentiation has significant implications for all other theological themes including anthropology (as will be explained shortly).

In terms of *cataphatic theology*, various aspects of divinity are knowable to the world through divine energies and are therefore explicable in positive terminology. Terms such as, "God is merciful and loving," fall under this category. However, using *apophatic theology*, humans are able to express in negative terminology the ineffable and unfathomable elements of the Godhead. These elements can be experienced through a personal and mystical relationship with God: mystical as related to the church sacraments, where encountering a personal God is possible but unfathomable.[56] Eventually, the only remaining tool to elaborate on that encounter is a negative language. Hence, in the previous example, while God is merciful and loving, a mystical personal experience of God's mercy and love unveils that those attributes are beyond any human

---

51. Bobrinskoy, "God in Trinity," 49–62.
52. Costache, "Christian Worldview," 21–56.
53. Theokritoff, "Creator and Creation," 63–77.
54. Lossky, *Mystical Theology*, 44–66, 67–90.
55. Lossky, *Mystical Theology*, 23–43.
56. Louth, "Patristic Revival," 188–202.

understanding of those attributes.⁵⁷ In a few words, any human linguistic expression is an imperfect attempt to articulate the human encounter with God.⁵⁸

Writing theology using *cataphatic* and *apophatic* terminologies may look paradoxical (*antinomical*) for an outsider. However, this does not disturb Orthodox theologians who emphasize that rationality does not lead the theological enterprise; rather, it is the mystical personal relationship with God which inspires theological reflections.⁵⁹ The antinomy is clearest in the person of Jesus Christ as a God and a man at the same time. In his person, the realms of divinity and humanity are united, which may be very difficult to comprehend within a rational frame of mind. Attempts to use pure reason to understand this paradox/antinomy led to the rise of many controversies and heresies throughout the history of Christianity. Similarly, the crucifixion of Jesus Christ unveils a contradiction between his divine omnipotence and his ultimate vulnerability when submitting to death for the sake of the entire world (John 3:17). Further, while God is omnipotent and has created the entire world from nothingness (*ex nihilo*), God is not willing to violate human freedom and to force humans to submit to his authority. God, thus emphasized many church fathers, prefers that humans would freely seek him and develop a genuine sense of what freedom means, rather than to force the divine will on them.⁶⁰

Human Fall, Christology, and Soteriology

This same dynamic relationship between *cataphatic* and *apophatic* trinitarian theology shapes other themes in Orthodox theological reflection including Christology (tenets pertinent to the person of Jesus Christ) and Soteriology (the salvific providence of God). However, to understand the christological mission, it is warranted to first illustrate how the church fathers understood the sin committed by Adam and Eve and their fall. The ancestral sin does not mean sin in the legal sense of an offence or crime (against a prescribed normative rule). God created Adam and Eve to live

---

57. Casiday, "Church Fathers," 167–87.

58. Kattan, *Shiraa' Fi Uyoun Mustadira*, 43–56; Avakian, "Mystery of Divine Love," 39–68.

59. Ware, "Orthodox Theology Today," 105–21.

60. Clément, "Purification," 22–39; Clément, *On Human Being*, 25–42.

in communion with him; they were still growing in communion when they disobeyed God. The human condition in paradise, church fathers contended, was far from perfect. Paradise was meant to be a place for humankind to become God-like (achieve *theosis*, divinization, deification) through constant communion with God.[61]

When Adam and Eve disobeyed God's commandment, they broke their communion with the divine persons; even worse, they aspired to become gods on their own by following the serpent's advice to eat from "the tree of the knowledge of good and evil" (Gen 2:17; 3:25). The result of breaking communion with God was a separation from the only source of life, which allowed corruption and death to afflict the entire universe.[62] In a few words, the result of breaking the divine commandment was not a punishment commensurable to the offense; rather it was a natural (though actually unnatural per the divine plan) result of breaking away from God. Death, the new ontological reality, has afflict both humanity and the entire created world since then.[63]

As a divine answer to address the new universal reality of death, the second person of the Holy Trinity assumed to his person everything that is in the human nature (through incarnation) and re-established the lost communion between the Creator and the creation. Gregory of Nazianzus (329–389) put it this way: "That which is unassumed [by Christ] is unhealed." Christ's salvific (soteriological) intervention in human history, thus contended many church fathers, was not a bloody ransom paid to assuage an angry Godhead; rather, it was an atonement (at-*one*-ment) that mended the alienation between God and humankind.[64] The triumphant resurrection of Christ from among the dead annulled death and stripped it of its authority over humans. Christ has thus highlighted the true meaning of death as breaching the communion with God (so it is spiritual and physical death), and that the only remedy for its inevitability is communion with God and others.[65]

Church fathers used various ways to illustrate the soteriological mission of Christ; they all concur that *theosis* is the ultimate goal of humanity—which was attainable because of Christ bridging the gap between

---

61. Theokritoff, "Creator and Creation," 63–77.
62. Pentiuc, *Jesus the Messiah*, 25–33.
63. Harakas, *Health and Medicine*, 35–44.
64. Bouteneff, "Christ and Salvation," 93–106.
65. Harrison, *God's Many-Splendored Image*, 29–45.

God and humanity.[66] However, for the sake of this book, a threefold vocation model of Christ's mission is adopted to unfold a similar threefold vocation for humanity to address emerging ethical dilemmas at the global level. Early church authors (as early as Eusebius of Caesarea (263–339) drawing on earlier Jewish writings) along with recent ones (including John Calvin (1509–1564)) contend that Christ assumes three callings pertinent to his soteriological economy: he is the King, the Prophet, and the Priest.[67] In what follows, these callings will be briefly discussed in their pertinence to Christ; however, in the subsequent chapters, they will be further elaborated on to illustrate a model for Orthodox Christian encounter with a post-Christian world and its ethical dilemmas.

Christ the King

The kinghood of Christ manifests in his consubstantial unity with God the Father. He is a divine person who has the same divine essence as God the Father and God the Holy Spirit. He is thought of, allegorically, as being one of two hands (the Holy Spirit being the other one) with which God the Father has created the entire universe. Several church fathers contend that Adam and Eve were created according to the image and likeness of Christ himself. That is why Byzantine icons of Adam and Eve before the fall show facial similarity to Christ. When incarnated from the Virgin Mary, God the Son assumed the human nature. He assumed all that was human to make it possible for humans to acquire that which is God's. In other words, Jesus Christ was fully God and fully human, so that human beings may grow in their likeness to God—to become God-like. He mended human alienation from God and through his sacrifice emphasized the original dignity of humans.

Christ the Prophet

The prophethood of Christ manifested in two stages and is related to an authentic knowledge of God and the created reality.[68] In the Old Testament, God chose several prophets to announce, through them, his

---

66. Bouteneff, "Christ and Salvation," 93–106; Lossky, *Mystical Theology*, 135–55.

67. Bouteneff, "Christ and Salvation," 93–106. Yannaras, *Freedom of Morality*, 89–107.

68. Bouteneff, "Christ and Salvation," 93–106.

divine word to the chosen people. Announcing his word did not mean the foretelling of the future; it rather centered around situating the daily experience of the faithful, whether positive or negative, within the divine economy.[69] Old Testament prophets repeatedly reminded the chosen people how God has called and saved them and how without his philanthropy (love toward humankind) they would perish. Without the only giver of life, the chosen people would wither away.

Similarly, through the incarnation of Christ, himself being the Word of God (John 1), the word of God was fully announced in his person. This announcement reiterated the message of the Old Testament prophets emphasizing the mortality of humankind. By acquiring the human nature, Christ declares that humanity is condemned to death unless a divine savior intervenes to change the *status quo*. In his philanthropic death, Christ has shown the vulnerability of God since he loved the world to the extent of dying on the cross. Nonetheless, Christ's love is what saves humanity from death: by his death, he trampled down death and stripped the existential human enemy of its thorn. In a few words, what shows as vulnerability in submitting to death on the cross becomes a way to defeat human mortality through God's philanthropy. True love defeats death.[70]

Christ the Priest

The priesthood of Christ is epitomized in his universal mission to restore communion between God and the entire creation. Through his incarnation, Christ unites divinity and humanity in his person: he bridges the gap which separates the created world from God. In the liturgy, he is unambiguously the one who offers and who is being offered for the salvation of the world (the prayer of the Cherubic hymn in the Orthodox Liturgy).[71] Put differently, Christ revives the mission—originally assigned to humankind—of being the microcosm who bridges the existential gap between the creator and the created world (as understood in the writings of St Maximus the Confessor (580–662), for instance).

---

69. Schmemann, "Task of Orthodox Theology," 180–88.

70. Bouteneff, "Christ and Salvation," 93–106; Clément, *On Human Being*, 43–58; Louth, *Introducing Eastern Orthodox Theology*, 50–65.

71. Bouteneff, "Christ and Salvation," 93–106; Meyendorff, "Unity of the Church," 30–46.

These three callings, substantiated in the person of Jesus Christ, shape the mission of humanity in general, and particularly the mission of the faithful believers who belong to the "One Holy and Apostolic Church." However, before illustrating the particular mission of the church in today's world, it is necessary to briefly discuss the mission of humanity in general, as the church fathers have understood it, i.e., the anthropological implications of the advocated Orthodox *phronema*. Derived from the above discussion, two issues are to stay in mind. First, God is still working in the world outside the boundaries of the church through his own mystical methods. Second, in the church, God has fully revealed his divine economy, in words and in deeds, which puts more responsibility on the shoulders of the faithful when engaging the world outside the church.[72]

Anthropological Implication of Orthodox Theology

Building on the above theological foundations, this section will discuss the ramifications of Orthodox theology at the practical-human experience level in today's globalized world. Several anthropological tenets will be discussed to understand humanity's mission in the world while taking into consideration the fallen human condition. Anthropology will be understood here as reflecting on who the human being is and how this fits into the divine salvific providence. This reflection will bring practical insights to the study of global bioethics.

The Divine Image and Likeness in Humans

Following the advocated *phronema*, several anthropological elements arise especially the multi-dimensional understanding of the human being.[73] Unlike the modernist narrow emphasis on rational human faculties, an authentic Orthodox *phronema* realizes a broader anthropocentric common ground in moral discourse; such common ground is morally substantive since it is founded on universal human experiences, namely, those related to suffering and dying.

---

72. Trakatellis, "Orthodox Churches in a Pluralistic World," 1–10; Clément, *On Human Being*, 108–25.

73. Ware, "Orthodox Theology Today," 105–21; Louth, *Introducing Eastern Orthodox Theology*, 82–95.

Genesis as a Source for Anthropology[74]

In the first three chapters of the book of Genesis, many contemporary Orthodox theologians find a major source to reflect on anthropology. They follow the conclusions of many church fathers whose exegesis reflects a worldview (cosmology) that centers on God. In the creation narrative, Adam, the first human being, was created in the image and according to the likeness of God (Gen 1:26); this model of creation has shaped Orthodox anthropology for centuries. Several lessons derive from this narrative and are pertinent to the argument of this book.

The first lesson pertains to the origin of humanity. "Adam" is not actually a name but rather derives from "*adama*" in Semitic languages which refers to the dust of the ground (Gen 2:7). As the ancestor of the entire humanity, Adam's name underscores the common origin of human beings which is only dust.[75] However lowly this origin may be, God created Adam in a way different from all other creatures. God, allegorically, used his divine hands to form the first human and breathed into his nostrils to give him life (Gen 2:7).[76] The dominion over the rest of creation, given to Adam (Gen 1:26), illustrates the unique position of humans in God's plan. Many church authors understood the authority assigned to humanity as a stewardship: a responsibility toward God through caring for the universe, rather than as a recklessly selfish exploitation of its resources.[77]

The second lesson pertains to the relationship between man and woman and how that affects the human relationship with God. The creation narrative comes in two versions. In the initial story, "So God made man; in the image of God He made him; male and female He made them" (Gen 1:27). The second version mentions the creation of Eve from the side of Adam (Gen 2:21). In symphony, these versions emphasize the common origin of all humans, men and women, created from dust (*adama*), rather than allude to any difference in dignity between Adam and Eve. The incarnation of Jesus Christ, the New Adam (Gal 3.28), further emphasized this commonality and equality. Also, several Byzantine hymns refer to the Virgin Mary as the New Eve, thus recognizing the

---

74. Pentiuc, *Jesus the Messiah*, 5–24.
75. Harrison, "Human Person," 78–92.
76. Harrison, "Human Person," 78–92.
77. Harrison, "Human Person," 78–92; Theokritoff, "Creator and Creation," 63–77; Pentiuc, *Jesus the Messiah*,10–14.

central role of women in the divine salvific providence. Without the "yes" uttered by Mary on the day of the Annunciation, the incarnation would not have taken place.[78]

Equally important is the reason for creating Eve: "It is not good for man to be alone. I will make him a helper comparable to him" (Gen 2:18). The divine rationale was to create an equal to Adam, a soulmate, to be in communion, instead of the company of all other creatures. This rationale highlights that God has consecrated human unity within diversity. While the bodily difference between man and woman did not hinder their unity, other differences do not necessarily hinder reaching unity among humans, either.[79] Nonetheless, the blessed diversity of the human ancestors was intended to be experienced in communion rather than as a self-centered, individualistic diversity.

The third lesson from the creation narrative pertains to the consequences of disobedience. After Adam and Eve broke God's commandment, they lost their communion with him and among each other as peers. The outcome of the serpent's advice concords with the nature of the devil itself, *dia-bolos* (*dia*: separate, *bolos*: will; i.e., the divider).[80] Following the devil's advice, Adam and Eve broke their communion with God. Similarly, but not surprisingly, their own communion shattered as a result and they started to blame each other and the serpent for their disobedience (Gen 3:12–13). Since they discovered their nakedness (Gen 3:7), human ancestors entered a new state of alienation with God and with each other.

Finally, the plural used by God in the narrative is a frequently visited theme in the creation narrative. Adam and Eve were created "in Our image, according to Our likeness" (Gen 1:26). The plurality of persons in the Godhead attracted the attention of church authors as an early indication to the trinitarian personhood in God.[81] That trinitarian communion inspires genuine communion among human beings to overcome their inherited state of estrangement since the fall.

---

78. Clément, *On Human Being*, 25–42.
79. Harrison, "Human Person," 78–92.
80. Bouteneff, "Christ and Salvation," 93–106.
81. Harrison, "Human Person," 78–92.

In the Divine Image, According to the Divine Likeness

In regard to the meaning of the image of and likeness to God, several opinions among church fathers exist; however, they all highlight a *dynamic* understanding of the divine image and likeness.[82] Notwithstanding the possibility of mere literary emphasis by saying the same thing twice: image *and* likeness (similar literary emphasis happens frequently in Arabic, for instance), church fathers have speculated on the possible difference between the two concepts.[83]

Divine Image

"In the image" (*kat'eikona*) of God (Gen 1:27) refers to a static human makeup that shares many attributes with God. It is a multidimensional makeup endowed on every human being and analogous (to some extent) to certain divine attributes. However, none of these attributes, on its own, can recapitulate and limit the divine image in any given human being. Some of the similarities between God and humans include: freedom and responsibility, spiritual perception (*nous*) and relationship with God and other humans (communion), excellence of character and holiness (virtues), royal dignity, creativity and rationality manifesting in human arts, sciences, and various cultural products (humans acting as co-creators).[84] Among all these attributes, modern culture narrowly emphasizes human rationality and freedom. However, church fathers and contemporary Orthodox theologians have underlined that these two attributes are open to misuse (as was clear in the story of the fall), especially if they are not understood within the broad mission of humanity.

In patristic understanding of rationality, human reasoning springs from a higher intellectual faculty, the *nous*, which is considered the "focal point of the divine image." As a faculty, it does not arise from logical-reasonable mental processes; however, it emerges from a spiritual perception ("spiritual," i.e., that is according to the Holy Spirit, as understood in Orthodox Christian spirituality; more explanation will follow).

---

82. Lossky, *Mystical Theology*, 114–34.
83. Harrison, "Human Person," 78–92.
84. Harrison, "Human Person," 78–92; Harakas, *Health and Medicine*, 59–68.

A perception that is according to the Holy Spirit penetrates beyond the visible and tangible and reaches the innermost realities of things.[85]

For example, using a clear noetic perception, the beholder can see the spiritual realities depicted on icons (more on icons will follow).[86] With an open spiritual eye (and illumined *nous*), a faithful beholder is invited not to merely stand in front of the icon as a passive-objective spectator but to actively participate in those depicted divine realities.[87] However, to be able to actively engage in this iconic presence, the noetic eye of the beholder needs to be trained to do so; inasmuch as the noetic eye actively engages that presence, the eye becomes illumined by God, and the human being comes closer to the aspired God-like status (to which the discussion will turn next).

This same noetic perception is equally quintessential to perceive the divine image in other human beings, regardless of where they stand in their spiritual journey.[88] The responsibility is therefore the beholder's to see the image (*eikona*-icon) of God imprinted in every other human being. In the liturgical practices of the Orthodox Church, the priest (as well the deacon and bishop if present) censes with reverence every attendant of the prayer service in a way similar to censing the icons adorning the church building. This practice emphasizes that the iconic reality of every attending person (whether they belong to the community or they are just visiting) derives from the Godhead who created her rather than from any tangential human attribute.[89]

Divine Likeness

"According to Our likeness" (Gen 1:27) refers to *theosis* (deification, divinization) toward which every human being should strive with the help of God's grace.[90] A frequently cited phrase from St Athanasius (296–373) recapitulates the divine economy in this regard: "He became human that

---

85. Harrison, "Human Person," 78–92; Harakas, *Health and Medicine*, 59–68.
86. Harrison, "Human Person," 78–92.
87. Fortounatto and Cunningham, "Theology of the Icon," 136–49; Chryssavgis, "World of the Icon," 35–43.
88. Harrison, "Human Person," 78–92; Clément, *On Human Being*, 126–43.
89. Chryssavgis, "World of the Icon," 35–43.
90. Louth, *Introducing Eastern Orthodox Theology*, 82–95.

we might be made divine."[91] Moreover, since Christ, the Son of God, has revealed himself to be the true image of God (Col 1:15), human beings, many church fathers believe, are made according to Christ's image and aspire to become Christ-like.[92] However, Christ, the New Adam, has materialized in his person the prototype of humanity to mend the estrangement of Adam and Eve. Whatever vocations Christ has assumed to redeem the fallen world, humankind should adopt to restore its communion with God and to continue the divine economy under the auspices of the Holy Spirit. By so doing, the existential gap between God and creation will be bridged and the loving reign of God on earth will be established (as sought in the "Our Father" prayer).

Human Fallenness

Notwithstanding the creation of humanity in the image and after the likeness of God, the ancestral disobedience has changed the human condition since then. As discussed above, many church fathers have perceived this change within a communal mindset which contrasts a legalistic understanding of the ancestral sin.[93] The new fallen state of humanity did not efface the divine image imprinted in every human being; it rather disrupted the human ability to achieve the God-likeness.[94] More particular, Adam and Eve became able to know the good and the evil (because they ate of the fruit of that tree) but while sustaining a state of alienation from God because of their disobedience. Thus, whatever divine-like attributes humans enjoyed before the fall were not retracted because of their sin; rather, the noetic eye became fogged leaving human beings deprived of a clear perspective to achieve their Godlikeness. This lost perspective warped their inclination toward communion with God; instead, human beings worshiped other gods (including themselves) toward which they directed their existence.

Although they have lost the clarity of their spiritual perception, human beings preserved their genuine predisposition toward communion with God, regardless of their belonging to any religious or philosophical

---

91. Casiday, "Church Fathers," 167–87.
92. Harrison, "Human Person," 78–92.
93. Yannaras, *Freedom of Morality*, 29–48.
94. Meyendorff, "Unity of the Church," 30–46; Lossky, *Mystical Theology*, 114–34.

belief system.⁹⁵ They have also preserved their ability to be co-creators like God through their cultural and aesthetic creativity, although they have sometimes used their creativity in evil manners. In a few words, the image of God was preserved in humanity but veiled because of human fallenness; thus, the incarnation of Christ was necessary to re-introduce the divine perspective and re-establish the lost communion between God and the creation.

In bringing this section to a conclusion, it is important to reiterate those aspects of the advocated Orthodox Christian anthropology which will have ramifications on the argument of this book. Although human beings are rational and free creatures, their rationality and freedom cannot be perceived outside a holistic understanding of the divine image imprinted in every person. Human beings cannot be reduced to their rational and free choices which, if deprived of the spiritual noetic perception, are open to corruption.

However clouded the human spiritual perception may be because of fallenness, humans' innermost desires continue to seek an authentic communion with God regardless of their religious or belief system.⁹⁶ Therefore, an authentic anthropocentric Christian engagement with secular and post-modern humanism should highlight the failure of the latter's anthropology(ies) to realistically address the [fallen] human condition.⁹⁷ Both impersonal collective communism and individualistic capitalism, for instance, derive from distorted anthropologies which condemn them to failure. They fail to satisfy the human innermost desire to unite with each other and with God.

Next, this chapter will reiterate humanity's mission as assigned by God since its creation to explore how Orthodox Christian theology and spirituality have established the way to achieve it.

Humanity's Mission

Theosis, Spirituality, Asceticism

The ultimate mission of humanity is to achieve *theosis* (deification): to become God-like. This can only be achieved through communion with

---

95. Louth, *Introducing Eastern Orthodox Theology*, 82–95.

96. Avakian, "Mystery of Divine Love," 39–68; Khodr, "Church and the World," 33–51.

97. Harrison, "Human Person," 78–92.

God and the entire universe. Although human ancestors were in communion with God before their fall, their status in Paradise was a project-in-the-making to achieve the aspired *theosis*. When humans become God-like, the resulting transfiguration does not only affect humanity itself, but also manifests in a transfigured universe (contrary to the result of the disobedience by Adam and Eve).

Practically speaking, becoming God-like entails a divine-human synergy (*synergeia*, cooperation/co-working). This is a necessarily two-directional relationship which extends the redemptive work of God into the daily lives of the faithful.[98] On the side of God, divine grace, i.e., divine uncreated energies, nurtures and supports human effort to become God-like. However, on the side of humans, asceticism/mysticism is central to this effort according to Orthodox Christian spirituality.[99] Orthodox Christian spirituality is understood through its relationship to, and cooperation with, the Holy Spirit rather than as being a vague spiritual experience or elusive pietism.[100]

Central to this understanding of spirituality, Orthodox Christian resources highlight the fundamental importance of asceticism (*askesis*) to any genuine spiritual experience. Ascetic practices do not aim at the mortification of the human body, simply because the body is part of the divine image imprinted in humans.[101] Similarly, asceticism does not deny the material needs of humans, such as food or drink. Rather, by denying oneself the pleasures or necessities of life, one transforms her spiritual mindset. Ascetical practices change the meaning of those same pleasures and needs and gradually transfigure the faithful to a God-like being.[102]

Asceticism on the Way to Transfiguration

When the entire universe, including human beings, are transfigured through communion with God, the divine meaning (*logos*) of the universe will be revealed: a meaning that was meant by God since the very

---

98. Steenberg, "The Church," 121–35.

99. Chryssavgis, "Spiritual Way," 150–63.

100. Yannaras, *Freedom of Morality*, 119–36; Andreopoulos, "Modern Orthodox," 10–23.

101. Harakas, *Health and Medicine*, 25–34; Yannaras, *Freedom of Morality*, 109–17.

102. Chryssavgis, "Spiritual Way," 150–63; Theokritoff, "Creator and Creation," 63–77.

beginning. Furthermore, the meanings (*logoi*) of every created thing/person will find its ultimate fulfillment in the Logos: the Word of God (John 1), the second person of the Holy Trinity, the Logos of the entire creation.[103] This dialectic between the *logoi* (pl. of *logos*, meanings or principles) of every created thing/person and the Logos who unites them in himself refers to Stoic philosophy.

St Maximus the Confessor (580–662) christianized these philosophical tenets to emphasize the unity of all created reality in the person of Christ.[104] That is what made St Maximus perceive the human being as a microcosm in whom the created and uncreated worlds come to interact. Humans are the only species who have the necessary noetic-spiritual perception to recognize the spiritual realities and *logoi* of creation. Dumitru Staniloae (1903–1993), one of the leading theologians of the twentieth century, developed St Maximus's ideas to emphasize that not only humans are microcosms but also that the cosmos is "*macranthropos*," the human writ-large. Staniloae highlights in this concept the human responsibility toward the cosmos.[105]

Furthermore, to have access to the *logoi* of creation, and to perceive them as embedded in the Logos, the faithful should have access to the eschatological realities of the creation. Using an illumined spiritual-noetic eye, humans may then understand the eschatological meaning of the entire creation as it was assigned by God since the very beginning. (More on the importance of eschatology in perceiving the world and properly engaging it will follow).

Monasticism Leading Spirituality: Death, Vulnerability, and Compassion

On a practical level, asceticism-mysticism should be the practice of every devout Orthodox Christian. Usually, ascetic-mystical practices are linked to monastic communities in their life of constant prayer and fasting. However, the mystical experience of God through *askesis* is also available

---

103. As understood by Staniloae for instant, in Louth, "Patristic Revival," 188–202; Theokritoff, "Creator and Creation," 63–77; Louth, *Introducing Eastern Orthodox Theology*, 33–49.

104. Bouteneff, "Christ and Salvation," 93–106.

105. Louth, "Patristic Revival," 188–202; Harrison, "Human Person," 78–92; Abou Mrad, "The Witness," 246–60; Avakian, "Mystery of Divine Love," 39–68.

to clergy and laity who live in the world (i.e., outside monasteries).[106] One important ascetical exercise is the silent remembrance of death. Although this exercise is constantly practiced among monastics, it can shape the spiritual practices of the faithful in general.

The first part of this exercise is silence (*Hesychasm*). In monastic life, this practice aims at self-knowledge, specifically a knowledge of the human need for the other. One does not only rely on others to provide the material needs for everyday life, but more importantly, one needs others to know one's own self. In a monastic community, every person (monk or nun) needs the brethren and a spiritual mentor (father or mother) to achieve *theosis*.

The second part of this exercise, constant remembrance of death, is fundamental. Arguably, all other monastic ascetical practices revolve around this one theme: the recognition of one's own mortality. Although this might sound like a morbid fixation on death, it has been practiced in Orthodox monasticism (and perhaps other ascetic traditions, Christian or not) as a joyful venture embedded in a frequent celebration of the triumphant resurrection of Jesus Christ in weekly and yearly liturgical cycles.[107] In short, monastics live what they believe is the model to confront human mortality; by embracing one's own vulnerability and inevitable mortality, one recognizes the fragility of every human life and embraces those who are suffering with sincere compassion and solidarity.[108]

Humanity's mission may then be modeled using the kind of knowledge experienced in monastic communities. When human beings become comfortable with their own vulnerable and mortal existence, they can authentically (though not effortlessly) recognize that which unites them as human beings. It is the recognition of the frailty of their mortal existence that brings human beings together rather than an impeccable rational consensus.

Moreover, Orthodox monasticism emphasizes one more important thing about human vulnerability. Human beings are not only physically vulnerable in confronting disease and death; they are weak in facing their sinful spiritual passions. Passions in English may have a positive connotation such as when saying, "I have a passion for painting." However, in Orthodox monastic literature, passion translates *pathos*, which bears

---

106. Chryssavgis, "Spiritual Way," 150–63.
107. Clément, *On Human Being*, 9–24.
108. Chryssavgis, "Spiritual Way," 150–63; Harakas, *Health and Medicine*, 45–55.

a negative connotation referring to distorted/sinful use of human emotions, such as anger, selfishness, and lust for power. These passions are meant to serve a lofty goal, specifically to unveil the innermost "passionate" love toward God and "com-passion" for the entire creation.[109] These passions are best summarized in the work of St John Climacus ("of the ladder"), a monk from the seventh century. He described the spiritual journey toward God as climbing a ladder while transforming human passions to virtues at every rung.[110] Therefore, to grow spiritually, a sincere recognition of one's own vulnerability would nurture a Christ-like desire to assume the vulnerabilities of others and to strive to bear with them the burdens of their lives (Gal 6:2). In other words, standing by other humans in solidarity is cardinal to knowing oneself and one's own vulnerability, and is an unavoidable part of growing spiritually and becoming God-like.[111]

In the same vein, embracing one's own vulnerability highlights, in Orthodox spirituality, a cherished meaning of repentance. Repentance translates *metanoia* in Greek which means *"meta-"* change, and *"noia"* from *nous*: mind. As the central call by St John the Baptist in the beginning of the Synoptic gospels (Matt 3:2; Mark 1:4; Luke 3:3), repentance invites the people of God to have a new mindset. Likewise, the faithful today are invited to acquire the same new mindset through constant repentance. Hence, repentance in Orthodox spirituality is not only about confessing one's sins (as if they were legal offences to be absolved); rather, it is about changing one's mindset to be re-integrated into the community of believers, against whose communion sins are committed.[112]

Perhaps, this communal re-integration can be further expanded to include the entire human community. In other words, through repentance, one is not only reconciled into the Christian community to which she belongs, but also, she is reconciled into the entire human community (for whose salvation, God has sent his only begotten Son (1 John 4:14)). One can only grow spiritually when she is re-integrated into the universal divine economy to save the whole world.

To summarize, Orthodox spirituality thrives on asceticism not as an individualist and escapist disciplining of one's fallen desires; nor does it flourish on idealist and angelic paradigms which ignore the fallen human

---

109. Chryssavgis, "Spiritual Way," 150–63.
110. Hamalis and Papanikolaou, "Toward a Godly Mode of Being," 271–80.
111. Chryssavgis, "Spiritual Way," 150–63.
112. Chryssavgis, "Spiritual Way," 150–63.

condition. Rather, Orthodox spirituality is perceived and practiced as a social discipline which is lived within a church community but that is open to the entire world.[113] Moreover, asceticism seeks a mystical encounter with God not through the mortification of the human body but through the transfiguration of the person, the community, and ultimately the entire universe.

Transfiguration demands an avowal of one's own vulnerability and mortality as a step toward embracing the vulnerability and mortality of other human beings. By so doing, one acquires a new unifying mindset: however different humans may seem in their philosophical beliefs and reasoning, they all are vulnerable and mortal. They are therefore worthy of sincere Christ-like philanthropic compassion.[114] A Christ-like mission toward the entire universe entails a *metanoic* perspective that is inclusive and centered on bearing the burdens of others with compassion and solidarity regardless of their religious convictions.[115] Lastly, the Orthodox Church, to which the discussion will turn now, can only fulfill her mission to divinize humanity inasmuch as she follows the example of Christ "the only philanthropist," as liturgical hymnology frequently describes him.

Eschatology as the Interpretive Lens for Orthodox Theology and Anthropology

Lastly, this section will discuss how the advocated *phronema* should shape the Orthodox Church's responsibility toward the world on a daily basis. The liturgical experience of the *eschata* (the last things) defines the Orthodox Church and thus opens the door to a dynamic understanding of her mission in the world. The economy of the Holy Spirit inspires this mission to continue the salvific mission of Jesus Christ toward the entire creation.

A Holistic Eschatological Mindset

The Eucharist is central to the mission of the Orthodox Church in the world. It is the manifestation of the pneumatological (related to the

---

113. Louth, "Patristic Revival," 188–202.

114. Harakas, "Orthodox Christianity in American Public Life," 377–97.

115. Harakas, *Health and Medicine*, 59–68; Clapsis, "Challenge of a Global World," 47–66.

Holy Spirit) economy which continues the christological-soteriological mission. Moreover, the Church's ecclesiology (her self-perception as an institution and a community of believers) is shaped within incarnational and trinitarian theology.[116] In the Eucharist, the church becomes aware of her own identity, not as an entity in opposition to an inimical world, but as a missionary that works in the world to bring the entire creation back to God.[117] It is the liturgy—the work of the people—which substantiates this mission on a daily basis.

Economy of the Holy Spirit

The salvific mission of Jesus Christ continues to this day in the mission of the Holy Spirit, both inside and outside the church. The Spirit sustains the church through the many talents and blessings bestowed upon the believers; the Spirit also sustains the world and mystically works in the world to bring it back to God. To understand the mission of the Holy Spirit in the world and inside the church, it is important to explore what happened on the day of Pentecost as was understood by church fathers and many recent theologians. Many theologians justifiably believed that the church started her mission on the day of Pentecost; however, dating her birth back to Paradise, as some authors did, is not unreasonable if the church's mission (as a community, not only as an institution) is centered in the communion between God and humanity.

The descent of the Holy Spirit (Acts 2:4–11), thus understood the church fathers, was meant to reverse the sin of those who built the tower of Babel (Gen 11). This is best expressed in the Byzantine hymnology of the feast of the Pentecost.[118] The *Kontakion* of the feast reads as follows:

> When the Most High came down and confounded tongues of men at Babel, He divided the nations. When He dispensed the tongues of fire, He called all to unity, and with one voice we glorify the Most Holy Spirit.

The sin of the Babylonians is not different from that of Adam and Eve. They wanted to reach heaven, or become gods, on their own by

---

116. Steenberg, "The Church," 121–35.

117. Harakas, "Church and the Secular World," 167–99; Khodr, "Church and the World," 33–51.

118. A similar use of Byzantine hymnology as a source of theology is frequently encountered in Orthodox theological writings; see for instance, Bucur, "Feet that Eve Heard," 3–26.

building a tower using man-made material. Because of that, not only their communion with God was broken (similar to what happened with Adam and Eve) but also the communication (comm-uni-cation, comm-uni-on) among themselves was severed. Because of that sin, various nations (ethnic groups)—which spoke different languages—emerged. Not surprisingly, as a result of broken communion with God, communion among human beings was shattered. In contrast to Babel's splintering of the nations, at Pentecost, language barriers were overcome by the powers of the Holy Spirit. At Pentecost, the possibility of communion despite language differences was restored. To reverse the sin of Babel, the divine events did not erase history and "go back" to a "symbolic" one language of the pre-tower era (if at all that language existed). Nor was post-Pentecostal communication in the language of the apostles (whether Greek or Syriac-Aramaic). Rather, by the power of the Holy Spirit, the apostles spoke the languages of the myriad ethnic groups in attendance. This symbolically reverses the language division among human beings.[119]

At the practical level, this event shaped (and should always shape) the mission of the church in the world. It shifts the responsibility of communication/communion toward the apostles and disciples of Christ in at least two ways.[120] The first obvious way is in translating the Gospel's message into the languages of every group who receives a church missionary. One fundamental example of this missionary work is the evangelization of the Slavs in the ninth century. When the Slavonic language at the time was only a spoken language, Sts. Cyril and Methodius invented the Glagolitic alphabet as a step to translate the Gospel for these nations to read. The second—more demanding—way is through striving to find a semantic style which others can understand. In other words, it is incumbent on the church to create avenues of communication/communion with outsiders rather than expecting outsiders to initiate that communion.

The Eucharist: The Ultimate Economy of the Spirit

The church constantly experiences the pneumatological economy in the Eucharistic celebration, the sacrament of thanksgiving. Most recently, theologians rightly argue that the Eucharist is the defining activity of the

---

119. Wehr, "Notes & Comments," 235–44.
120. Trakatellis, "Orthodox Churches in a Pluralistic World," 1–10.

Orthodox Church rather than her dogmatic heritage. Building on the writings of many church fathers, Nicolas Afanasiev (1893–1966) was the pioneer of this Eucharistic Ecclesiology.[121]

A eucharistic ecclesiology highlights two related issues. First, liturgy translates *leitourgeia*, the work of the people, which emphasizes the practical, lively side of communal prayer. Second, regardless of the differences among theologians about the details of this ecclesiology, the mystical experience of God is cardinal to the Orthodox self-awareness. This practical-experiential dimension of the Orthodox self-awareness puts the dogmatic heritage of the church in perspective. Even the Nicaea-Constantinople (NC) Creed, the Orthodox confessional document *par excellence*, is integrated into the liturgy. Although the Creed reads "I believe . . ." in the very beginning, in accordance with the most authentic text, it can only be correctly understood within the prayerful gathering of the entire community of believers.[122]

Ultimately, the Eucharist opens the door to the *eschaton* when "taking communion" in the Body and Blood of Jesus Christ at the end of it; however, it is not the only way the *eschata* are pre-tasted within the limits of time and space.[123] Other elements unveil in-time an array of anticipated eschatological experiences. One element is the weekly celebration of the Divine Liturgy on Sunday as an active re-living of Christ's salvific providence. Many historical reasons compelled early Christian communities to move the celebration of the Lord's Day from Saturday (Sabbath) to Sunday. Primarily, early Christians considered Sunday to be the Eighth day of the week when humanity encounters the Resurrected Christ and the *eschata* present to the temporal reality of the world. Therefore, when the Eucharistic offerings are consecrated, the priest announces "in behalf of all and for all", including the entire humanity for which Christ was crucified and was resurrected.[124] And by the work of the Holy Spirit, the entire created world may be transformed to be in communion *with* and *in* Christ as well.[125]

---

121. Plekon, "Russian Religious Revival," 203–17; Louth, "Patristic Revival," 188–202.

122. Steenberg, "The Church," 121–35; Harakas, "Orthodox Christianity in American Public Life," 377–97.

123. Louth, *Introducing Eastern Orthodox Theology*, 141–59.

124. Steenberg, "The Church," 121–35.

125. Theokritoff, "Creator and Creation," 63–77.

Not only is the timing of liturgy important, the place is also. The liturgy is usually celebrated in a church building full of icons (some buildings have more sophisticated collections of icons than others). The presence of icons in their assigned places (a very detailed issue that goes beyond the scope of this book) opens "windows" toward the divine realities. In the Orthodox theology of icons, icons are not just an artistic depiction of persons or events to invoke passive reminiscence among beholders. Rather, icons present an active personal presence which invites the faithful beholder to grow in communion with their depicted eschatological realities beyond human complexions or time-bound events.[126]

On a general note, the liturgy starts by invoking the presence of the Holy Spirit through praying "O Heavenly King, the Spirit of Truth . . . come and dwell . . ." and situating the entire liturgy as "a time for the Lord to act" (as the deacon—if present—exchanges with the priest right after that). However, at no point at the end of the liturgy do the celebrating clergy or the chanters announce the *conclusion* of the Lord's action. Rather, at the dismissal, the priest announces saying, "Let us go forth in peace"; he leaves it to the faithful to take with them their experience of the Eucharist and to extend it toward the world in their daily lives. This epitomizes what is known in Orthodox circles as "the liturgy after the liturgy."[127] Hence, the Eucharist, as a defining activity of the church community and its mission toward the world, should also shape the way in which every believer engages those around him.

Since the church is not defined in contrast to the world, but rather is defined in terms of her mission toward the world (saving the world in bringing it back to communion with God), it is incumbent on the church to perceive the world from her vantage point, her theology and mystical experience of God.[128] In other words, the world outside the church may seem different from, and hostile toward, the church simply because it is governed by human fallenness and alienation; however, the Holy Spirit has been constantly working in the world to bring the lost humanity back to God. Therefore, the faithful are responsible to communicate God's love to the entire world. For the church, the world is not a foe but the place where the divine love toward humankind (*philanthropy*) should reign.[129]

126. Fortounatto and Cunningham, "Theology of the Icon," 136–49; Chryssavgis, "World of the Icon," 35–43.

127. Harakas, "Orthodox Christianity in American Public Life," 377–97.

128. Harakas, "Church and the Secular World," 167–99.

129. Harakas, "Orthodox Christianity in American Public Life," 377–97.

Counter Eucharistic phronema: The World as a Foe

Contrary to this perspective, many thinkers propagate a sense of enmity toward the world because of the contrast they see between the worldly ethos and that of the church. However, what they miss is the responsibility/mission of the church toward those who are outside. Some of the ethical arguments advanced by Tristram Engelhardt for instance (which will be discussed in further detail in the following chapters) are dressed in Orthodox Christian theology using patristic language. The premise of some of his arguments is a "black box" anthropology which excludes the possibility of moral communication between different humans. Further, he implements "moral strangeness" as a valid boundary between communities; he narrowly emphasizes their moral differences rather than the deeper existential difference among them. In other words, he overlooks the state of alienation among all humans because of their fallenness even when they belong to the same religious community. Furthermore, by adopting a sectarian ecclesiology, Engelhardt condescendingly underlines the difference between Orthodox Christianity and other religious communities in that the former "owns" the true doctrinal heritage. Using such mindset, church doctrines become another ideology vis-à-vis other ideologies in a competitive marketplace of ideas hunting for followers. Engelhardt's perspective is in clear contrast to the missionary ecclesiology that has been illustrated above.[130]

A Eucharistic Mission in a Globalized World

To support a global perspective in bioethics, it is warranted to briefly discuss "the liturgy after the liturgy," i.e., how a eucharistic ecclesiology shapes the Orthodox perspective toward the world. We will explore how the church community should encounter a globalized world with a pluralism of ethos. Yet, the difference between the Christian ethos illustrated so far and a post-Christian post-modern world is not an excuse to absolve the church of her responsibility.

---

130. Khodr, "Church and the World," 33–51; Meyendorff, "Orthodox Theology Today," 77–92; Plekon, "Russian Religious Revival," 203–17.

Unity of the Creation

Central to the advocated *phronema* is the continuous interaction between God and his creation; by creation, it is meant to include all the material, irrational, and rational beings, whether they belong to the Orthodox Church or not. The church fathers believed that the creation of the entire universe from nothingness (*ex nihilo*) (Gen 1) is not meant to offer a scientific theory of the creation of the world. Rather, the narrative in Genesis highlights the creation's fundamental relationship with God and its fragility when separated from the only source of life (even before the fall of Adam and Eve).[131]

This fundamental relationship between the creation and its Creator underscores another aspect that is central to the argument of this book, namely the unity of the created world. Notwithstanding its fragility, the created world is sustained by the divine energies in a tangible harmony. Although disrupted because of the human disobedience, the unity of the created world is fundamentally rooted in its createdness. Regardless of perceivable discordance, the entire creation, unceasingly and concertedly, pursues its life-giving creator. For contemporary Orthodox scholars, this approach toward the universe has been central to develop the study of environmental ethics. It is usually referred to as "ecclesial cosmology", "sacramental cosmology", "Eucharistic cosmology", or "cosmic liturgy."[132]

The mindset of Orthodox environmental ethics is important for bioethics as well. By emphasizing the unity of creation in its createdness, Orthodox bioethics does highlight that pure rationality is not the source of aspired eschatological human unity. Hence, if irrational beings can stand in solidarity/unity as they seek God, human beings can do the same by first recognizing their createdness and its moral implications.

In other words, this book aspires to establish a unity among humans which derives from their createdness rather than from their rational agreement. Thus, the pursued common ground in moral discourse is not founded on a reductionistic anthropology that is fixated on pure rationality. It rather draws on a holistic and inclusive anthropology that is cognizant of the human experience of being created and mortal.[133] Ul-

---

131. Theokritoff, "Creator and Creation," 63–77; Louth, "Patristic Revival," 188–202; Harrison, "Human Person," 78–92; Louth, *Introducing Eastern Orthodox Theology*, 33–49.

132. Theokritoff, "Creator and Creation," 63–77.

133. Louth, *Introducing Eastern Orthodox Theology*, 82–95.

timately, the unifying eschatological reign of God (when God becomes "all in all" (1 Cor 15:28)) should inspire Orthodox Christians to unveil those anthropological elements which genuinely unify all humans who, knowingly or not, pursue God.[134]

A Eucharistic phronema in a Pluralistic World

Taking the eschatological-eucharistic identity of the Orthodox Church seriously is quintessential to illumine her mission in a globalized world where intertwined relations are effacing traditional boundaries. One example of the evolving complexity is the migration of people of different ethnic backgrounds and the formation of pluralistic societies in different parts of the world. Yet, lurking behind this plurality is *globalism*: when every cultural identity melts into a one global identity that is unavoidably dysmorphic and superficial. Globalism contrasts with a globalization that celebrates various identities and pays tribute to rich and enriching diverse cultures.[135]

Therefore, in such a globalized milieu, it is not possible for Orthodox Christians to fixate on the desire to re-build a Christian Empire or achieve the lost harmony (*symphonia*) between church and state under Byzantium;[136] it was arguably a failed experiment.[137] Pluralism is the reality of the post-modern world and Orthodox Christians have to accept it, live within it, and work to transfigure it.[138] Trying to build Byzantium again fundamentally betrays the universal (catholic) mission of the church.

Pastoral, Missionary, and Prophetic

Several Orthodox theologians have reflected on the universal mission of the Orthodox Church in modern times. Alexander Schmemann

---

134. Steenberg, "The Church," 121–35; Scouteris, "Bioethics in the Light."

135. Abou Mrad, "The Witness," 246–60; Trakatellis, "Orthodox Churches in a Pluralistic World," 1–10.

136. Guroian, "Seeing Worship as Ethics," 332–59; Papanikolaou, "Byzantium, Orthodoxy and Democracy," 75–98.

137. Clément, *On Human Being*, 91–107; Meyendorff, "Unity of the Church," 30–46.

138. Trakatellis, "Orthodox Churches in a Pluralistic World," 1–10; Khodr, "Church and the World," 33–51.

(1921–1983), a respected figure in Orthodox renaissance in the West,[139] believes that Orthodox Christian theology has three fundamental tasks in the US, which are also warranted elsewhere. To be relevant, Orthodox theology should be pastoral, missionary, and prophetic in the way it approaches the human condition in post-modernity. Although these are the tasks of theological reflection, they are understood as integral to the daily life of every believer—and thus as the tasks of the entire Christian community at large.[140] Schmemann emphasized that the ultimate goal of the church is to save the entire world through re-establishing the lost communion with God. Thus, theologians cannot elaborate on theology in a cultural vacuum; they should be relevant to every believer wherever and whenever they live.

During his lifetime, Schmemann contended that Orthodox theologians had been disconnected from the daily needs of the faithful because of their unnecessary fixation on academic and dogmatic discourse with peers of other backgrounds. It was important, for Schmemann, to gear theological reflection toward the new global realities of (post)modernism that are affecting Orthodox believers, in Orthodoxy's homeland and in the West. For many reasons including those discussed in the very beginning of this chapter, the (post)modern social milieu is foreign to the Orthodox ethos and worldview and necessitates an active engagement to unfold the uniqueness of Orthodoxy within this new reality. Moreover, Schmemann believed that Orthodox theology has to take the Church's catholicity (universality, as confessed in the NC creed) seriously through a genuine involvement in missionary and ecumenical endeavors (as did many of the pioneers of the modern Orthodox renaissance).[141] For him, and unlike those who criticize ecumenism, ecumenical and missionary involvement does not (and should not narrowly) target those who are outside of Orthodoxy to proselytize. Rather, this involvement broadens the perspective of Orthodox believers themselves to overcome their ethnic and provincial division (especially in the US)—which itself contradicts the catholicity of the Orthodox Church.[142] Furthermore, a missionary work toward those outside of Orthodoxy is authentic inasmuch as it revolves around a sacrificial and self-giving encounter of Christ as

---

139. Plekon, "Russian Religious Revival," 203–17.
140. Schmemann, "Task of Orthodox Theology," 180–88.
141. Plekon, "Russian Religious Revival," 203–17.
142. Cunningham and Theokritoff, "Who Are the Orthodox Christians?," 1–18.

the Truth (John 14:6). An authentic encounter of Christ demands being critically open to all the ideas and values of others as possibly bearing witness to the hidden seed of the Logos in them (as St Irenaeos of Lyons [130–202] advocated and Metropolitan George Khodr did, following his example).[143]

The example of Antiochian Orthodoxy in the Middle East is illumining in this regard. Following the example of Metropolitan George Khodr, many Orthodox Christians engaged in an open and thriving relationship with Muslims. Through a diligent, open-minded, and non-apologetic discourse with Muslim leaders in the area, Met. Khodr was able to garner the respect of Muslims and to open the eyes of Christians to the strong presence of Christ within the Islamic ethos.[144] In Russia, Fr Alexander Men (1935–1990) advocated a similar openness toward the world. He contended that Christ was present in contemporary culture as much as he was two millennia ago in the towns of Palestine.[145]

Lastly, Schmemann believes that the church's voice in (post)modern society should be prophetic in reminding humanity of its authentic mission, which is *theosis*. This can be done through philanthropy, i.e., genuine God-like sacrificial love toward all humanity.

Self-Critical and Inclusive

Similar to Schmemann, other Orthodox theologians reflected on the tasks of Orthodox theology as rooted in the pastoral patristic heritage of the church. It is believed that Orthodox theological reflection should be self-critical and less defensive in encountering the world outside the Church.[146] St Photius the Great, for instance, was able to be critical while not endangering the possibility of an authentic encounter of God.[147]

In the same vein, the post-modern trend to question authorities, religious and non-religious alike, should be a positive opportunity for

---

143. Louth, *Introducing Eastern Orthodox Theology*, 50–65.

144. Abou Mrad, "The Witness," 246–60; Avakian, "Mystery of Divine Love," 39–68; Khodr, *Ways of Childhood*.

145. Plekon, "Russian Religious Revival," 203–17.

146. Ciobotea, "Tasks of Orthodox Theology Today." 117–26; Papanikolaou, "Orthodoxy, Postmodernity, and Ecumenism," 527–47; Khodr, "Church and the World," 33–51.

147. Casiday, "Church Fathers," 167–87; Similar modern example is clear in Clément, "Purification by Atheism," 22–39, and, Yannoulatos, *Facing the World*, 15–48.

Christians to self-search and recognize their share of responsibility for such trend. In other words, Christians, along with other religious communities, should actively engage in *metanoic* self-searching to unveil the reasons pushing people away from theistic/religious faiths.

At a deeper level, Orthodox theologians and communities should emphasize the mystagogical (mystical) encounter with the divine persons rather than fixating on an ideological preaching of Orthodox doctrines.[148] Ultimately, a mystical encounter with the divine persons shall inspire a similar encounter with other human beings regardless of their religious background. By so doing, the ecclesiastical dimension of social life, i.e., "the mystery of the brother [and sister],"[149] is fully revealed. When embracing the world with philanthropy, Orthodox Christians can be true martyrs for (and witnesses of) the unwavering presence of the transcendent within the immanent world and martyrs for a spirituality of active social involvement to serve the most vulnerable. As witnesses of the ever-present God, Christians are not expected to preach in words but also in deeds—even when those may lead to the martyrdom of blood.[150]

Being witnesses of a catholic church, Orthodox Christians should be steadfast non-sectarian proclaimers (evangelicals) of the Orthodox faith in the midst of post-modern uncertainties.[151] Fundamentally, the world needs more philanthropy than ideology.

Conclusion

In short, building on the advocated hermeneutics of the Orthodox theological themes and their anthropological repercussions, it is necessary to adopt an inclusive, yet critical, mindset (*phronema*) that fosters an active witness to the world. This witness is not through preaching the dogmatic truths of Orthodoxy, but through self-sacrificing martyrdom, in deeds and even in blood. These deeds proclaim the personal truth of a philanthropist God and a living Logos louder and more profoundly than any words.

---

148. Ciobotea, "Tasks of Orthodox Theology," 117–26.

149. Plekon, "Russian Religious Revival," 203–17.

150. Ciobotea, "Tasks of Orthodox Theology," 117–26; Payne, "Challenge of Western Globalization," 135–44.

151. Ciobotea, "Tasks of Orthodox Theology," 117–26; Harakas, "Orthodox Christianity in American Public Life," 377–97; Clément, *On Human Being*, 69–90.

Central to this witness are ascetic and mystical practices to help the church reformulate her biblical, patristic, and liturgical heritage to address the pastoral needs of the entire humanity, rather than narrowly caring for her own faithful. This is represented in a church typology that is derived from contemporary sociology but still relevant to Orthodox ethos. The personal (mystical) relationship with God in prayer, Stanley Harakas contends, is necessarily embedded within the communal prayer of the Eucharist. However, the mission of the church should not be limited to those who participate in the Eucharistic Chalice but should rather extend in a non-sectarian openness toward humanity.[152]

To acquire this inclusive and redemptive *phronema*, it is warranted to extend the three-fold vocation of Christ, as the king, the prophet, and the priest of the entire universe, to his body on earth, i.e., his church (Col 1:24).[153] Since the church is defined in terms of its liturgical life, and aspires to the eschatological realities which are pre-tasted now, finding a common ground with other humans is the responsibility of the church.[154] Starting from her genuine understanding of the human condition and rooted in a steadfast hope in divine philanthropy, it is incumbent on the Orthodox Church to stand in solidarity with all humans to confront post-modern uncertainties and injustices.[155]

Building on this responsibility and within the advocated inclusive *phronema*, the argument of this book shall materialize in the following chapters.

---

152. Harakas, "Orthodox Christianity in American Public Life," 377–97; Casiday, "Church Fathers," 167–87; Yannaras, *Freedom of Morality*, 77–88.

153. Bouteneff, "Christ and Salvation," 93–106; Clément, *On Human Being*, 108–25; Wirzba, "Priestly Approach," 354–62; Khodr, "Church and the World," 33–51; Yannaras, *Freedom of Morality*, 89–107; Plekon, "Russian Religious Revival," 203–17.

154. Steenberg, "The Church," 121–35.

155. Similar to the contention by Bulgakov and Men in advocating a "generous ecumenism" in Plekon, "Russian Religious Revival," 203–17; Abou Mrad, "The Witness," 246–60; Clément, "Purification by Atheism," 22–39; Trakatellis, "Orthodox Churches in a Pluralistic World," 1–10; Olivier Clément was brave enough to call this "creative secularism" in Clément, *On Human Being*, 91–107; Khodr, "Church and the World," 33–51; Meyendorff, "Orthodox Theology Today," 77–92.

3

The Interpretive Context of Pluralism in Bioethics

This chapter concentrates on the current status of bioethical discourse within the complex and pluralistic global context. The discussion will highlight the trends that developed over the past few decades in secular and religious approaches to bioethics. It will ultimately advocate a substantive discourse in global bioethics. For the Orthodox Church, the participation in such discourse, it is argued, is justified using an iconic *phronema* which shapes Orthodox bioethics itself.

Procedural Pluralism in Secular Bioethics

As a first step leading to the advocated inclusive *phronema*, it is necessary to understand the prevailing discourse in contemporary bioethics. For several reasons, the pluralistic context of bioethics steered the discourse toward a procedural approach to ethical dilemmas, thus excluding the possibility of a substantive exchange among different value-systems. However, it will be argued that an open and substantive discourse in bioethics is possible, and perhaps necessary, in our contemporary global milieu. The historical factors leading to the development of procedural secular bioethics in the US will be briefly discussed. Then, the evolution of a global discourse in bioethics will be traced and defended as the best approach to handle the demands of new medical technologies in a globalized world.

Pluralism and Dialogue in Bioethics

Globalization as the Context

Globalization is a new phenomenon that has developed over the past few decades. Many reasons have contributed to its emergence including the development of communication technologies, the opening of national borders for free trade, and the flourishing of powerful networks of multinational corporations and financial institutions. All of these developments almost effaced the boundaries among various groups and nations and highlighted the fundamental interdependence among human beings as a basis for them to flourish. However, the promised benefits of the evolving relations plagued many communities with unprecedented injustices and unjustifiable disparities. In a shrinking world, the complex and dialectical processes of globalization are polarized between the universalization of local realities and the particularization of global trends, thus bringing a great deal of ambivalence. Complexity and interdependence are the leitmotifs of the contemporary world at many levels, including economic and financial levels, political relationships, ecological realities, and cultural identities. Collateral to this complexity are the surfacing moral responsibilities due to these relations—however controversial these responsibilities may be.[1] The various levels of globalization will be discussed briefly in what follows, particularly because of their repercussions on rising bioethical dilemmas.

Economic and Financial Globalization

Economic forces have propelled globalization over the past few decades. The demise of the creative tension between capitalism and socialism opened the way for the neo-liberal ideology to take control over financial institutions and economic forces around the world. Through de-regulation, it was thought that the free-market forces of exchange would bring prosperity to everyone on the planet. Although these free exchanges accelerated economic growth and helped accumulate prosperity around the world, the disparities among various social groups in different countries, and inside many countries (developed or developing), have grown ever since. The subsequent unjustifiable inequalities and dehumanizing inequities raise many moral concerns on the legitimacy of free-market

---

1. Clapsis, "Challenge of a Global World," 47–66.

ideology and its claim of trickle-down global prosperity. This situation also raises skepticism as to the moral standing of policies that shape society to serve the market rather than steer the market to serve the common good of society.[2]

Political and National Power

As a result of market-centered economics, emerging powerful multinational corporations and financial institutions strip national governments of their ability to guarantee the well-being of their citizens. The interests of multinational creditors and international financial institutions are being served, in many contexts, at the cost of the well-being of the most vulnerable social groups. The emphasis of these powerful players on cutting down governmental expenses on education, health care, and basic services, has disadvantaged entire populations in developing countries. Privatizing drinking water in Bolivia, for instance, was enough to entice social unrest.[3]

Notwithstanding the downside of weakening political power of certain governments, undeniable advantages have accrued for many in those nations. The emergence of a globalized world put several nation-states under international scrutiny especially regarding their human rights violations. Instant communications and international media coverage reinforce the responsibility of every nation toward its own people and toward its international partners, despite the unfortunate use of double standards sometimes. Moreover, after the fall of communism, religious communities emerged as indispensable players to fill the moral vacuum created by a self-serving free-market mentality.[4] Major religious communities started to actively participate in public discourse and to provide a social safety net to support the most vulnerable. Equally important was the growing ability of minority religious groups to voice their concerns on a global platform and to seek protection against discrimination toward minorities.

---

2. Clapsis, "Challenge of a Global World," 47–66; Falk, "Religion and Globalization," 67–76.

3. ten Have, *Global Bioethics*, 123.

4. Falk, "Religion and Globalization," 67–76.

Ecological Realities and Consumerist Ethos

One of the major results of growing globalization is the exploitation of natural resources at an unprecedented rate for the sake of economic growth. The growing consumerist ethos around the world and the accelerated development of certain markets to meet growing consumption have raised global ecological concerns. Because of pollution, the effects on the ecological system are felt daily in many fast-growing cities, such as Delhi and Shanghai. Similarly, the unsustainable use of fossil fuels and the sluggish development of renewable sources of energy have fueled climate change and have consequently jeopardized the lives of many communities around the world.

Notwithstanding the controversy around the degree of climate change (or even its scientific legitimacy), consumerist trends are not environmentally sustainable. The current level of consumption negates a humane stewardship toward natural resources. It also jeopardizes the health and well-being of the most vulnerable and voiceless of the world, particularly future generations.[5] Moreover, consumerism puts those who produce what others insatiably consume in inhumane circumstances.[6] Several international incidents highlighted the double safety standards in producing clothes and electronics for Western retailers.[7] Similarly, farmers in developing countries are producing fewer varieties of crops in order to meet the demands of a global and season-less market of produce at the expense of their nutritional well-being. While fair trading practices have recently gained momentum (such as with coffee trade), many farmers have been hurt by the global exchange of crops even in developed countries (strikes of French farmers, for instance).[8] Morally troubling as well is the recent invasion of genetically modified crops in Africa under the cover of agricultural development. However beneficial to African farmers this may seem at the first glance, many of these crops

---

5. Dwyer, "How to Connect Bioethics and Environmental Ethics," 497–502.

6. David Barboza, "Electronics maker promises review after suicides," *New York Times*, May 26, 2010; Charles Duhigg and David Barboza, "In China, human costs are built into an iPad," *New York Times*, January 25, 2012.

7. Jim Yardley, "Horrific fire revealed a gap in safety for global brands," *New York Times*, December 6, 2012.

8. "French farmers block Spanish and German borders in foreign food protest," *Guardian*, July 26, 2015.

will be protected under shackling patent laws to the detriment of the farmers who grow them.⁹

Pluralism and the "Clash of Civilizations"?

The dynamics of globalization have brought many people of various cultural backgrounds into direct contact, whether within a specific geographical space or through virtual reality. American society has witnessed the active presence of many communities of different backgrounds in various parts of the country. Similar cohabitation of religious and ethnic groups has been known in different parts of the world and has exponentially grown due to the migration of people in search for better opportunities. The new reality is usually referred to as pluralism with people of different backgrounds interacting with each other. These people bring their diverse religious, ethnic, or cultural identities into conscious or unconscious, intentional or unintentional, exchange of ideas with others through numerous avenues.

There is a great deal of misconception regarding the nature of pluralism. Pluralism is not another word for diversity where various groups of people may coexist in any given space; the interaction among these groups is essential for a fruitful pluralism. Therefore, pluralism is better perceived as a substantiating project rather than as a given reality. Similarly, pluralism is not a passive tolerance of the different other who happens to exist in proximity; the engagement with the other is necessary to know her in her difference. Thus, pluralism is built on a sense of equality and equal dignity regardless of the difference in identity. On the contrary, tolerance is necessarily condescending in that it hinges on a—self-perceived—sense of strength to tolerate those who are different. Finally, pluralism is not simple relativism where one's own commitments are relativized for the sake of universalizing trends. Rather, true pluralism celebrates the encounter of commitments because it shuns a lukewarm adherence to beliefs. In other words, pluralism is a genuine, dynamic engagement of varying serious commitments of equally dignified identities. Religious commitments, more specifically, do not need to be marginalized for the sake of finding their common anthropological ground nor for the sake of building a peaceful coexistence of different identities.¹⁰

---

9. Cahill, *Theological Bioethics*, 211–51.
10. Eck, "Christian Churches," 11–21.

Notwithstanding the advantages of a genuine pluralistic discourse, the reality of the contemporary world allows for sometimes-violent conflict of identities among different communities, even among those who lived together for many centuries. This conflict of identities has been recently generalized as a global "clash of civilizations" in an article by Samuel Huntington.[11] However, the superficial analysis of conflict and the author's ignorance of history ought to be exposed through a better understanding of human culture and various identities.[12] Thus, to advance the argument of this book, it is necessary to explore the nature of the conflict between identities; it is particularly relevant because of the uncritical adoption by Tristram Engelhardt of its root ideology of "culture wars" as advanced by James D. Hunter.[13] Neither the idea of a "clash of civilizations" nor its root ideology of "culture wars" stand the scrutiny of a genuine Orthodox Christian *phronema*.

Cultural Identities and Pluralism

Emmanuel Clapsis adopts an operative understanding of culture that is very helpful to the discussion of identities in a pluralistic world. He maintains that

> a culture provides the system and the framework of meaning which serve both to interpret the world and to provide guidance for living in the world. A culture embodies beliefs, values, attitudes and rules of behavior. It includes the rituals, the artifacts and the symbolization that bind people to communities and enable them collectively to embody and express their histories and values.[14]

Using such dynamic understanding of human culture, a few elements should be highlighted. First, it is not only cultures that are dynamic and constantly evolving, but also associated identities and communities. Identities are not a divine given even for religious communities. Identities are social constructs that develop within the community's internal

---

11. Huntington, "Clash of Civilizations?," 22–49.
12. Said, "Clash of Ignorance," 11–13; Yannaras, "Human Rights," 83–89.
13. Engelhardt, *Foundations of Christian Bioethics*, 49 n. 16.
14. Clapsis, "Challenge of a Global World," 47–66 esp. 49.

and external contexts.[15] This makes drawing nonporous boundaries between different communities an ambitious mission—if at all possible.

Second, community's "values, attitudes and rules of behavior," or its ethos, are also dynamic products of its historical development as a community within a specific context. Therefore, the morality of any community, even a religious one, has some elements that are related to its historical context along with other elements that are divinely (or metaphysically) inspired. All these elements are embedded in a worldview, a mission and/or a *phronema* that are dynamic in nature and open to change. This dynamic understanding of cultural ethos has kept, for instance, Christian communities in a healthy tension between what is authentic to the Christian faith and mission and what is a relative social construct that is adaptable to changing historical, geographical, and cultural contexts. The translation of sacred texts to different languages, for instance, is a sign of this adaptability to different contexts.[16] Contrary to this dynamic understanding of community values and morality, Engelhardt advocates a Christian bioethics that is "non-developmental in the sense of affirming the same moral commitments and insights that directed the Church of the first thousand years: it understands that all that has been essential for the appropriate moral life has been available since the time of the Apostles."[17]

Third, the definition adopted by Clapsis highlights that moral values are not a ready (dictated) ideological core which unites the members of a certain community. Rather, "the rituals, the artifacts and the symbolization" are the source of unity in a community. In other words, what unites a community is the narration which shapes its members and the meanings assigned to various events and symbols, rather than being united because of a dictated set of meanings and beliefs. As a result, strangeness and neighbor-ness are derivatives of the ethos of the community; the community itself decides who is a neighbor or who is a stranger depending on its worldview and mission.[18] In the Good Samaritan parable, the Samaritan decidedly approached the wounded man as a neighbor; he chose to be a neighbor, rather than followed a dictated definition of neighbor-ness. Christians are ordered to do likewise (Luke 10:25–37).

15. Clapsis, "Ethnicity, Nationalism and Identity," 159–73.
16. Clapsis, "Challenge of a Global World," 47–66.
17. Engelhardt, "Orthodox Christian Bioethics," 21–30 esp. 23.
18. Louth, "Church's Mission," 649–57.

For the argument developed here, the category of "moral strangeness" applied by Engelhardt to different communities falls short of sound genealogy of meaning, morality, and community-uniting matrix. For Engelhardt, different communities assign non-concurring different meanings even to the same events or linguistic expressions. He clearly misconceives identity crises and clashes between different identities as being related to a clash between civilizations. However, it is necessary to understand the role of rapid cultural changes in bringing these conflicts to the surface. Because of the processes of globalization and the ensuing cultural change, human identities may develop in three different ways. An identity may become either a "legitimizing" identity when it passively blends into the changing environment. Or, it may become a "resistant" identity which either stays in the past or militantly opposes the changing environment. The third possibility is to develop a "project" identity. When confronted with cultural shifts, a "project" identity critically engages the shifting environment, cooperatively attempts to invoke a positive change, and genuinely derives meanings consistent with its worldview.[19]

Therefore, an Orthodox Christian project identity is not thwarted by a pluralistic milieu; rather, it thrives through pursuing an inclusive universalism (*catholicity, kath-ollos: per everything-everybody*) and engaging in a dialogue which perceives the entire creation as a field of the Lord.

An Orthodox Christian Perspective toward Globalization and Pluralism

The Orthodox Church has been reluctant to engage in the globalization and pluralism discourse for many reasons. Orthodox communities find themselves in an ambivalent position: they equate between secularity and modernity; from this comes the tendency toward withdrawal and isolation among Orthodox Christians.[20] Further, the experience of Orthodox communities varies depending on where they exist. In Western countries dominated by non-Orthodox Christian communities and secular ethos, Orthodox communities have mixed relationship with their context. On the one hand, they have benefitted from an inclusive social ethos which protects different religions. On the other hand, they are immersed in a

---

19. Clapsis, "Challenge of a Global World," 47–66.
20. Prodromou, "Orthodox Christianity and Pluralism" 22–46.

religious environment which has been traditionally occupied with the polemical discourse between Roman Catholics and Protestants.

Moreover, Orthodox communities in the West inherit a deep suspicion toward Western Christianity, especially due to proselytizing in their home countries. The ambivalence lingers even today within the modern states of Orthodoxy's heartland. In a place that traditionally cherished the byzantine church-state symphony, Greece, for instance, faces many difficulties with democratic governance. Even when that symphony was lost under the Ottomans, the millet system preserved the particularity of the Greek people and perhaps uncritically shaped (along with other determinants) their political identity.[21] At the ecclesial level, democratic governance in Greece questions the relation between church unity and formal uniformity, the dynamics between the clergy and the laity, and the separation between religious identity and national-political identity(ies). In a few words, the experience of Orthodox communities in modern countries with Orthodox majority (and their diaspora) have generally conceived modern pluralism and secularity as a threat.[22]

Nevertheless, a more active and creative engagement with a pluralistic world, whether at home or in the West, may be warranted and more fruitful. For instance, and as alluded to in the previous chapter, minority Orthodox communities in the Middle East (especially in Antioch) had a more positive attitude toward secular governance as a way to flourish in their nation-states. They have steadfastly believed that "the church is the heart of the world." Regardless of their denominations, Christians in those communities have been actively open to dialogue across their differences and with their Muslim neighbors. They were among the first advocates for the ecumenical movement as a way to witness to the inclusive loving mission of Christ who was crucified for the humankind. These Christians are at peace having multiple identities and dealing with different ones at the same time. They have been shaped alongside their Muslim neighbors within an Arabic-Islamic culture which, to flourish, was open to the contributions of numerous minorities. They prayed and read their Bible in Arabic, Syriac, and Greek; sharing Arabic with Muslims posed no threat to them. For many centuries, it is the narrative and "creative osmosis" that shaped similar identities among Christians and Muslims of the Levant, despite their different religions. Unintuitive as

---

21. Russell, "One Faith, One Church," 122–30.
22. Prodromou, "Orthodox Christianity and Pluralism," 22–46.

it may sound, Orthodox Christians in Antioch were for many centuries more threatened and harmed by the crusades and colonial mentality of Western Christians than by their Muslim neighbors. Even in the diaspora, Antiochian Orthodox communities were among the first Orthodox churches to welcome converts who embraced Orthodoxy (Engelhardt included)[23] because of their inclusiveness and hospitality.[24]

Therefore, in the face of global pluralism, Orthodox communities should affirm the universality of the divine mission to save humankind while recognizing the uniqueness of every particular human community. Any desire to withdraw from a pluralistic public space to preserve religious purity is a betrayal of the church's mission toward humanity. Ultimately, an authentic Orthodox spirituality should not be dissociated from a global activism that pursues the healing of the world; Orthodox spirituality is an activist spirituality *par excellence*. In a genuine spiritual journey to encounter God in this world, Orthodox Christians should strive to reconcile the way they understand the world and the way they experience God and the different other.[25]

Consequently, Orthodox Christians should be at the forefront of a "spiritual ecumenism" that is shaped by the church's mission. The goal of this ecumenism is not to establish an institutional unity among different Christian denominations; rather the goal is to establish a dialogical platform.[26] It is a spiritual ecumenism that takes seriously the church's eschatological identity and its long-established teachings about silence and detachment to create a space for the voiceless, the marginalized, and the alienated.[27] An ecumenism that is attuned to a globalized world should foster a "globalization of solidarity," as the Ecumenical Patriarch Bartholomew put it, where every one of the faithful strives to countermand the injustices of globalization. A dynamic ecumenism, furthermore, is a movement searching for what it means to be a human being in a globalized world rather than a mere movement to change the structural injustices in today's world.[28]

---

23. Engelhardt, *Foundations of Christian Bioethics*, xvi–xvii.

24. Abou Mrad, "The Witness," 246–60.

25. Chryssavgis, "Orthodox Spirituality," 130–38; Clapsis, "Challenge of a Global World," 47–66.

26. Gennadios, "'God, in Your Grace,'" 285–94.

27. Chryssavgis, "Orthodox Spirituality," 130–38.

28. Clapsis, "Challenge of a Global World," 47–66.

WCC and a Fruitful Dialogue in Bioethics

In the spirit of a "spiritual ecumenism," the ecumenical movement (using the World Council of Churches WCC as its platform) may be the best available avenue for dialogue among various Christian communities. It may also serve as a starting point for inter-religious dialogue between Christians and other religions. The benefit of dialogue is unequivocal for the flourishing of human civilizations throughout the recorded history. Civilizations withered when they lived in isolation from each other; however, enculturation between different civilizations, in times of war and peace, preserved their unique cultural heritage for many generations. Conversely, cultural elitism and imperialism infiltrate our contemporary world and foster a sense of (sometimes-violent) disdain toward different cultural identities. For Orthodox Christians, cultural elitism and imperialism are not justifiable. Therefore, it is arguable that engaging in dialogue within the ecumenical movement, or with any other religious or non-religious tradition, is warranted, if not necessary, to overcome religious violence and hatred. Even if other cultural identities seem challenging to one's own beliefs, there will always be a space to meet the different other in the Orthodox Church.[29]

The experience of the ecumenical movement is informative and formative in this context. Despite the disdain of the ecumenical dialogue by some self-proclaimed Orthodox traditionalists, this dialogue was essential for shaping a Christian theology for modern and postmodern time. The ecumenical dialogue was equally important for the Orthodox inasmuch as it was for other denominations. Many of the leading figures of Orthodox theology in the West were among the pioneers of the ecumenical movement such as George Florovsky. Also, Vladimir Lossky studied in the West and was engaged for many years in a theological discourse with his Western theologian-peers. The dialogue between Orthodox theologians and theologians from other denominations helped shape the Orthodox renaissance of the twentieth century. Because of the dialogue, Orthodox theologians recognize that the Orthodox Church is not a confessional church but an incarnate community of believers. A church that revolves around the incarnation of Christ incarnates people

---

29. Clapsis, "Ethnicity, Nationalism and Identity," 159–73; Clapsis, "Boundaries of the Church," 113–27.

rather than ideas and dogmas. Therefore, even atheism is important for authentic self-searching and repentance among the Orthodox.[30]

Comparatively, the participation of Orthodox Christians in the ecumenical dialogue has also shaped contemporary theological reflection in other Christian communities. Orthodoxy brings to the table challenging and original perspectives about traditionally divisive theological themes—divisive among Westerners. It emphasizes theological concepts ranging from divine *kenosis*, the role of *theosis* and apophatic theology,[31] to martyrdom and icons. It also highlights the organic relation between theology, liturgy, and spirituality as relevant to every believer.[32]

It is arguable therefore that the participation of the Orthodox Church in a global dialogue to address the rising bioethical dilemmas is an extension of her participation in the ecumenical movement.[33] Orthodox theology will learn a great deal from being open to the global discourse on bioethics. Moreover, Orthodox theology has many valuable resources to bring to the dialogue, especially in regard to anthropology and eschatological identity. The most important contributions to this discourse are at two levels at least. First, Orthodox theology recognizes the inability of pure ethical-philosophical and rationalistic discourse to dictate a clear normative path in regard to bioethical dilemmas. Second, the core of the advocated dialogue should be anthropological. Any global discourse to address human suffering, especially related to health and medicine, should be inspired by an authentic understanding of the human condition and its potential. Extracting anthropological foundations for global bioethics may be more accessible and less controversial than philosophically based and dogmatically entrenched moral principles.[34]

However, to unearth these anthropological foundations, the following discussion will briefly explore how the field of bioethics has developed over the past few decades.

---

30. Vassiliadis, "Universal Claims of Orthodoxy," 192–206; Jillions, "Orthodox Christianity in the West," 276–91; Clément, "Purification by Atheism," 22–39.

31. Also in Vlantis, "Apophatic Understanding," 296–301.

32. Vassiliadis, "Universal Claims of Orthodoxy," 192–206.

33. Harakas, "Reflections on Authority in Ethics," 355–73.

34. Turner and Dumas, "Vulnerability, Diversity and Scarcity," 663–70. This idea may be supported in Mantzarides, "Globalization and Universality," 199–207.

Historical Background of Current Trends in Secular Bioethics

Medical Ethics: Concentrating on Physicians' Virtues

Medicine has always been perceived as an art and a science. As an art, medicine is centered on caring for patients; as a science, it uses available medical knowledge to ameliorate patients' suffering. Historically, almost all civilizations and cultures cherished their physicians and guaranteed them social privileges in exchange for their services. Therefore, most of the writings addressing medical practices in various civilizations emphasize three dimensions of the physician's virtues. These dimensions are personal decorum (the outward actions which reflect internal virtues), deontology (the duties and obligations of physicians toward their patients), and politic ethics (especially related to justice and duties toward the entire community). Although the practice of these physicians was not built on scientific principles comparable to contemporary medicine, the care they offered was paramount and much appreciated. In his short survey of the history of medical ethics, Albert Jonsen highlights several similarities among the different civilizations in regard to their perception toward medicine. He notes that these similarities may be indicative of an "inherent and universal moral atmosphere that surrounds the work of caring for the sick and pervades that work, regardless of culturally diverse moral systems."[35]

Professional Ethics: Monopoly, Education, and Social Privilege

By the end of the nineteenth century, the development of scientific medicine facilitated the evolution of medical ethics to a professional ethics.[36] While medical ethics has emphasized the virtues of those practitioners, professional ethics has developed mainly to protect the monopoly of mainstream physicians. The development aimed at the exclusion of hoax practitioners to guarantee a certain level of training in scientific medicine. In his book *Medical Ethics*, Thomas Percival (1740–1804) discussed the main responsibilities of the profession toward society in exchange for privilege. His book was far more influential in the US compared to his home country of England. He inspired the American Medical Association

---

35. Jonsen, *Short History of Medical Ethics*, 13–26, 27–41, specifically 41 for the quoted text.

36. ten Have, *Global Bioethics*, 11–22; Rothman, *Strangers at the Bedside*, 101–26.

(AMA) to develop its own code of ethics and to present to society the physicians guild as a professional entity with high standards of practice. On the other side of the Atlantic, however, the discourse regarding medicine as a profession took another route. There, medical deontology developed around the duties of physicians toward themselves and science, toward their patients, and toward the entire society. Although European societies at the time were far removed from their religious roots, their social discourse on the place and duties of medicine was more substantive compared to that in the US.

Questioning Professional Ethics[37]

After World War II, the monopoly of medical professionals came under scrutiny for many reasons.[38] First, the exploitation of patients by physicians was revealed after the war.[39] In the name of developing scientific knowledge, Nazi physicians, for instance, exploited many captives and sacrificed their lives without respecting their human dignity. Their scandalous research motivated the Nuremberg trials in 1946 and the incrimination of many Nazi physicians.[40] Physicians of other nations committed similar atrocities. More scandalous though were the unethical researches conducted in the US and surfaced around the same time, such as the studies unveiled by Henry Beecher in 1966 and the uncovering of the Tuskegee Syphilis research in 1974, among other scandals.[41]

Second, medical and scientific developments after the war brought a great deal of excitement and fear to society. During this period, many aspects of human life were medicalized, leading to a dramatic change in life and its meaning. Fascination with scientific research drew many physicians away from compassionate clinical care toward research to push the limits of medical knowledge. The development of technologies related to procreation, contraception, and organ transplantation raised many concerns about where to draw the lines when intervening in human life. Other challenges emerged regarding the availability of certain

---

37. ten Have, *Global Bioethics*, 11–22; Callahan, *Roots of Bioethics*, 7–23.
38. ten Have, *Global Bioethics*, 11–22.
39. Rothman, *Strangers at the Bedside*, 30–69.
40. Annas and Grodin, "Nuremberg Code," 136–40.
41. Beecher, "Consent in Clinical Experimentation," 34–35; Rothman, *Strangers at the Bedside*, 70–84, 168–89.

scarce resources and procedures such as dialysis (available since 1960), heart transplantation (first performed in 1967), and life support machines. Underneath these concerns was a mounting suspicion toward the ever-growing physicians' control over life and death.[42]

Third, social and cultural factors enticed serious scrutiny toward authorities in general. Internationally, a cold war was simmering after WWII with a looming nuclear extinction of humankind. Locally, the rise of the civil rights movement in the US brought to the public attention the dehumanizing influence of unchecked traditional social structures. Among these traditional authorities were medical professionals who were brought into public attention demanding for patients an active role in their medical care and health choices.[43]

On the other hand, changes in medical knowledge and practice gave rise to a new understanding of health and the role of physicians. First, changes in medical practice highlighted the role of other team members in caring for patients, such as nurses, and the importance of other specialized caregivers to command the growing body of scientific knowledge. In the same vein, growing specialization in medicine promoted the need for inclusive dialogue among all relevant caregivers, thus weakening the monopoly of one specialty in caring for patients. Further, public health interventions improved the health of communities and attracted attention toward the social determinants of health other than access to medical care, such as nutrition, housing, hygiene, and lifestyle choices. More deeply, invasive medicalization of life brought to the surface a public scrutiny of the role of medicine in shaping the meaning of life, suffering, and death. These themes are traditionally discussed within other reflective disciplines, such as theology and philosophy; however, medicine, in its pure scientific version and on its own, was not capable of depicting a satisfying picture of the human condition.

In a few words, professional ethics was not effective in providing satisfactory self-regulation to prevent exploitation. Also, it was not able to comprehensively address the challenges related to scientific developments, nuanced concerns related to technology and meaning, and the patients' demand for more involvement in their care. These challenges warranted a new approach to moral issues in health care under the label of bioethics.

---

42. Rothman, *Strangers at the Bedside*, 148–67.
43. Rothman, *Strangers at the Bedside*, 190–221, 222–46.

Biomedical Ethics: Mainstream Bioethics in the US[44]

Following the developments during the late 1960s, a new academic venture to address moral concerns in healthcare practice materialized under the label of bioethics. It is thought that the term was coined in the US in 1970 by two advocates of the new discipline, Van Rensselaer Potter and Andre Hallagers.[45] However, an earlier German author, Fritz Jahr, had used "bioethics" in an article that dates back to 1927. These pioneers had several motives to study evolving moral issues under the bioethics umbrella. For Jahr, bioethics was an integrative discipline to emphasize the role of human beings as stewards of the entire creation. From a Christian perspective, he advocated a dignified and comprehensive consideration for the phenomenon of life itself.[46]

On the other hand, Potter's research at the University of Wisconsin on cancer treatment was frustrating; he tangibly recognized the complexity of cancer and the numerous factors possibly linked to its surge. In his 1971 book *Bioethics: Bridge to the Future*, Potter advocated a multidisciplinary approach to science that reunites the art and science in medicine through a biology-informed ethical discourse. The new discourse should use the evolutionary information accumulated in biology to advance a cultural evolution that strives for the betterment of humankind. To face the plights that threaten humanity, a cultural revolution is necessary: humans should acquire new wisdom, i.e., the knowledge of how to use available knowledge. Further, a new culture shall emerge that bridges the gaps between the present and the future, between science and values, between nature and culture, and between man and nature.[47]

Although Hallagers had a global motivation similar to that of Potter, he took part in mainstream bioethics in the US.[48] By mainstream bioethics, it is meant to refer to the discourse held under the auspice of the Kennedy Institute of Ethics at Georgetown University and benefited from governmental and public support (through the work of the *National*

---

44. ten Have, *Global Bioethics*, 23–36.

45. ten Have, "Potter's Notion of Bioethics," 59–82; Reich, "Word 'Bioethics': Its Birth," 319–35; Reich, "Word 'Bioethics': The Struggle," 19–34.

46. Muzur and Sass, *Fritz Jahr and the Foundations of Global Bioethics*, especially the article by Fritz Jahr, "Bio-Ethics," 1–4, and the article by Hrvoje Juric, "Hans Jonas' Integrative Philosophy of Life as a Foothold for Integrative Bioethics," 139–48.

47. Potter, *Bioethics*, esp. 1–29, 183–95.

48. Reich, "Word 'Bioethics': Its Birth," 319–35; Reich, "Word 'Bioethics': The Struggle," 19–34.

Commission for the Protection of Human Subjects of Biomedical and Behavioral Research between 1974 and 1978, for instance, and the promulgation of the *Belmont Report* in 1979).[49] Although the principles adopted within the mainstream discourse were meant to address the ethics of medical research, their popularity brought them to the clinical settings and they became the standard ethical principles for clinical practice. Beauchamp and Childress, two of the engineers of the *Belmont Report*, published an elaborate discussion of these principles in many editions of their *Principles of Biomedical Ethics* since 1979.[50] The popularity of these principles derive from their neutral normative tone which avoided ideological and dogmatic disputes. However, the principles flourished in an individualistic environment, thus shaping mainstream bioethics within the same parochial and individualistic mindset.[51]

The agenda of mainstream bioethics as developed under the auspices of the Kennedy Institute reflected the cultural and political context within which its pioneers discussed rising moral issues. First, when encountering moral dilemmas because of new medical technologies, physicians justifiably invited theologians and philosophers to reflect on best practices. However well-versed these theologians and philosophers were in moral discourse, they used their own old methods to reflect on new issues.[52] This approach may have insinuated that ethics discourse and methodology are not open to development or moral imagination, especially when new knowledge is available. In the work of Beauchamp and Childress, for instance, rather than analyzing the clinical encounter itself to unveil its particularities, they sought to connect ethical theory and clinical practice through four mid-level biomedical principles.[53]

Second, because of an individualistic ethos, minimalist ethics shaped the mainstream bioethics.[54] Within this bioethics discourse, participants clarify various moral concepts, analyze and build coherent arguments, explore alternative approaches, and advise a best possible action (Albert

49. Jonsen, *History of Medical Ethics*, 113–20; Jonsen, *Birth of Bioethics*, 3–33; Beauchamp, "Belmont Report," 149–55.

50. Beauchamp and Childress, *Principles of Biomedical Ethics*.

51. Reich, "Word 'Bioethics': The Struggle," 19–34; Rothman, *Strangers at the Bedside*, 168–89; Jonsen, *Birth of Bioethics*, 90–122.

52. Jonsen, *Birth of Bioethics*, 34–64, 65–89.

53. Welie, *In the Face of Suffering*, 1–15.

54. Callahan, *Roots of Bioethics*, 36–49; Gert, Culver, and Clouser, *Bioethics*, 99–128.

Jonsen, for instance, seems to accept this role for bioethics).[55] Consequently, members of the society cannot value-judge the pursued action as long as it aligns with the cardinal moral principle of respecting the liberty of others and their "free" choices. Therefore, when starting from an individualistic ethos, it is unavoidable to arrive at an anthropology of "black-boxes" and moral strangers. Specifically, two meanings for moral strangeness are accepted by many bioethicists. The first meaning pertains to morality as a private issue that is only decided through a personal "free" choice; thus, morality cannot be objectively judged. The second meaning is more fundamental in that moral convictions cannot be communicated and are not accessible to others; to this meaning, Engelhardt seems to ascribe.[56]

Third, minimally revolving around the individual, bioethics discourse in the US narrowly focuses on moral issues related to the physician-patient relationship. Such focus perceives the clinical encounter as if it happens in an economic, political, cultural, and environmental vacuum; it regrettably overlooks the complexity of factors that affect health and decision making.[57] Furthermore, many of the pioneers of bioethics were employed by medical schools to teach the new discipline. This prevented many from questioning the ultimate goals of medicine, its perception of death as enemy,[58] and the role of healthcare institutions in mending the rife systemic injustices related to health in the US.[59] Along with failing to question the goals of medicine, Daniel Callahan regrets that mainstream bioethics did not engage in searching for the meaning of health and the nature and meaning of human life; the three main issues that bioethics should have addressed.[60] More generally, in a world that is dominated by Western medicine, the Western understanding of health, illness, and morality frames the global discussion of bioethics while overlooking these concepts' numerous and enriching meanings in different cultures.[61]

Fourth, an oligarchy of disciplines controls mainstream bioethics in the US. Philosophy, medicine, and law have a higher voice in bioethics

---

55. Jonsen, *History of Medical Ethics*, 115–20.

56. Welie, *In the Face of Suffering*, 59–85.

57. Also in Jonsen, *Birth of Bioethics*, 377–405; Welie, *In the Face of Suffering*, 159–200.

58. Callahan, *Roots of Bioethics*, 7–23.

59. Jonsen, *History of Medical Ethics*, 115–20; Callahan, *Roots of Bioethics*, 7–23.

60. Callahan, *Roots of Bioethics*, 24–35.

61. Heitman, "Cultural Diversity," 203–23

and leave a limited space for theology and other social sciences. Callahan laments that mainstream bioethics has excluded theology and religion from its discourse since the mid-1970s. He believes that by excluding religion from bioethics, and the self-censoring by theologian-bioethicists, a rigorous source to understand the human condition and values is sacrificed for the sake of a less substantive discourse.[62]

In a few words, Potter and Callahan both regretted the development of bioethics within an individualistic ethos which ignores the complexity of social relations and biological interdependence among various species. Potter was interested in a long-term survival of the human race in the face of various threats. He therefore revised his suggested bioethics in a new book called *Global Bioethics* to account for the multiple dimensions needed to be addressed. Callahan, on the other hand, was more interested in a communitarian discourse where a multi-disciplinary search for the common substantive good of society is possible.[63] This book aligns with Potter's global ambitions for bioethics and responds to Callahan's invitation for a more theological and inter-disciplinary involvement in bioethics discourse.

Bioethics: A Global Bioethics

Because of his disappointment following the individualistic development of bioethics, Potter renamed the discipline he advocated "global bioethics." He understood global in this context as both world-wide or international, and as comprehensive and inclusive. In his work, he argued for a scientifically inspired wisdom for the sake of human survival and for a better future.[64] However, the new discipline had to develop at various levels and in different contexts to achieve its global horizon. The processes of globalization highlighted the need for a new global discipline and helped garner the momentum for it to go through multiple stages. These stages demanded acquiring a broader scope beyond the individualism of mainstream bioethics. (1) The rising of new global issues related to health and its social determinants highlighted, in the next stage, (2) the importance of international cooperation to address these issues, such

---

62. Callahan, *Roots of Bioethics*, 7–23, 24–35; Also: Kass, *Life, Liberty*, 1–26; Kraynak, "Human Dignity," 61–82.

63. ten Have, "Global Bioethics," 315–26.

64. Potter, *Global Bioethics*, esp. 71–94, 151–84.

as organ trade and offshore research. Along with the various processes of globalization, (3) a growing cultural and philosophical discourse seriously engaged multi-culturalism, diversity, and pluralism leading the third stage in developing a global bioethics. (4) The final stage witnessed the agreement on a global ethical framework which, while universal, genuinely respects the particularity of local contexts. The adoption of the UNESCO *Universal Declaration on Bioethics and Human Rights* in 2005 brought these stages into fruition as the first global bioethical framework to address emerging issues.[65]

At the theoretical level, many versions of global bioethics have emerged to reconcile its global scope with its local application; they were thin, thick, or intermediate in regard to their ethical substance.[66] Some of these versions are thin in that they are inclusive of new topics, have a broader scope of discussion, invite more methodologies to address ethical dilemmas, or are built around a dialogical environment without enforcing a specific moral theory. On the other hand, thick versions are more substantive and evolve around suggested global values and responsibilities derived from cosmopolitanism, utilitarianism, human rights theories, or theories of building human capabilities. These versions argue for an established moral framework and claim to heuristically find answers for global issues.

However, unlike thick versions, intermediate versions recognize that finding a substantive ethical theory may not be easily attainable; therefore, intermediate versions accept that such framework is a dynamic project in the making rather than an established one. Intermediate versions of global bioethics, nonetheless, recognize the importance of concepts advocated in thick versions, such as cosmopolitanism, human rights, and the centrality of human capability building. Especially important for intermediate versions is cosmopolitanism: a sense of belonging to a global community across traditional boundaries. However, these versions recognize the need to apply any global ethical framework to diverse cultural contexts. This raises a moral dilemma: where a line should be drawn between acceptable and unacceptable cultural practices. A representative example of such dilemma is female genital mutilation in certain cultures. The ethical dilemma within a global framework is whether such practice should be accepted as a particular cultural element or ought to

---

65. ten Have, *Global Bioethics*, 37–54; Turoldo and Barilan, "Concept of Responsibility," 114–23.

66. ten Have, *Global Bioethics*, 37–54.

be condemned due to its detrimental health consequences (or a myriad of other reasons).

By and large, since global bioethics has evolved to address growing ethical dilemmas related to globalization, it is still a project in the making. In the very beginning, the need for bioethics derived from the development of science and the growing power of medicine. However, global bioethics today recognizes that contemporary moral dilemmas of health are aggravated because of neo-liberal ideology and powerful global financial entities. Thus, ethical problems are not only globalized, but they have a different nature than those traditionally discussed in mainstream bioethics. To address the underlying problems, a concerted global effort is necessary using an inclusive ethical framework that appreciates cultural diversity around the world.[67]

Counter Global Bioethics

Expectedly, global bioethics in its various versions garnered a great deal of criticism.[68] Mainly, it is criticized by those who perceive ethical discourse solely within a market framework; thus, ethical convictions, for them, are conceived as options in a market of ideas fiercely competing for followers. The neo-liberal ideology (which is not a full ethical theory rather a collection of premises) has regrettably invaded bioethical discourse.[69] Neo-liberalism made it difficult to adopt a moral imagination that is open to dialogue within a moral diversity. If the market should control everything, competition becomes the only social "virtue" and there will be no place for dialogue. Engelhardt ascribes to this ideology,[70] and as mentioned before, defends an anthropology of "black boxes" and "moral strangers." It seems that his position derives from the neo-liberal ideology rather than an established moral theory, although he attempts to dress it up in Orthodox theological garment.

Another criticism of global bioethics is related to the fear of moral imperialism especially if the advocated global framework is shaped by a certain cultural makeup. As alluded to previously, this fear may be valid

---

67. ten Have, *Global Bioethics*, 37–54.
68. ten Have, *Global Bioethics*, 76–92.
69. Callahan, *Roots of Bioethics*, 50–61.
70. See a criticism of the use of market ideology by Engelhardt, from a Jewish perspective for instance in Newman, "Talking Ethics with Strangers," 549–67.

when judging certain cultural elements such as female genital mutilation. However, an intermediate version of global bioethics advocates a framework that is in flux; thus, it is unjustifiable to exclude all forms of dialogue for fear of cultural hegemony. Similarly, pioneer bioethicists feared authoritarianism and unjustifiable influence on individual choices. Although such fear may be legitimate, bioethicists should always take into consideration all social factors that may compromise the freedom of choices other than governmental authority.[71]

Therefore, rather than unwarranted emphasis on competing individuals in the ethics marketplace, global bioethics as a project expands the horizon of bioethics through anthropocentric dialogue. The ultimate product of such global discourse in bioethics was the adoption of the UNESCO *Universal Declaration on Bioethics and Human Rights* in 2005. Although this declaration emerges from an international effort rooted in human rights and is mainly a product of political negotiation between nation states, its importance is related to a few elements. First, the Declaration opens the door for effective global dialogue and cooperation to address the root causes of inequality, exploitation, and vulnerability. More importantly, the declaration builds on a different set of principles than the individualistic versions of bioethics. These principles are anthropological in that they derive from the recognition that individuals are not mere consumers competing in the marketplace of ideas to prove the legitimacy of their moral convictions; rather, human persons thrive in communities where cooperation and solidarity are paramount.[72] Perhaps, such anthropological basis can overcome the philosophical impasse in bioethics by highlighting the moral common ground among all humans regardless of their value systems.[73]

Through this brief survey of secular bioethics, the promised (purely) rational consensus among bioethicists is clearly not attainable; humans still belong to conflicting value-systems.[74] Therefore, it seems that other approaches in bioethics, which espouse rationality among other human faculties, are necessary to enrich the moral discourse. Theological anthropology in this context may have a constructive contribution. In general,

71. Callahan, *Roots of Bioethics*, 50–61.

72. ten Have, *Global Bioethics*, 76–92.

73. ten Have and Jean, eds., *UNESCO Universal Declaration*; Andorno, "Global Bioethics at UNESCO," 150–54; Lauritzen, "Listening to the Different Voices," 151–69; Turner and Dumas, "Vulnerability, Diversity and Scarcity," 663–70.

74. MacIntyre, *After Virtue*; Shelp, "Introduction," vii–xiv.

the argument advanced in this book is consistent with an intermediate version of global bioethics: it advocates a bioethical framework that is anthropocentric (in that it is rooted in the respect of human dignity and vulnerability and their relationship with hospitality) rather than a framework that is purely rational-philosophical. Further, this book emphasizes the need for a global framework where ethics is not only about reflection but about activism. And because of current global health affairs, a serious and inclusive dialogue among all communities to reverse rife injustices is necessary.

Ethical Normativity in Religious Bioethics

The discussion will now turn briefly to two different trends in religious bioethics. The goal is to highlight the propelling mindsets behind these trends rather than comprehensively discuss their merits.

Religious Bioethics: Different Ideology, Same Mindset
The Role of Religious Bioethics Today

Among the pioneers of bioethics were several theologians, due to their long experience in addressing ethical issues related to life, suffering, and death. After remarkable contributions by many theologians, Callahan regrets,[75] new generations of theologians were "seemingly" marginalized for a while from public discourse because of the role of "secular" forces in shaping mainstream bioethics. Some of the theologian-bioethicists were forced to adopt a washed-down non-religious language to garner public support of their ideas. This made them look more like moral philosophers than theologians. Nonetheless, many other religious bioethicists, building on their particular dogmatic and spiritual heritage, tried to mend the shortcomings of secular bioethics especially in regard to the teleological ends of medical practice and research.[76] It has been rightly argued that without religion's input, medicine may lose its compass and social service, and perhaps some of its values.[77]

---

75. Callahan, *Roots of Bioethics*, 7–23.

76. Shelp, "Introduction," vii–xiv.

77. Campbell, "Bioethics and the Spirit of Secularism," 3–18; Winslow, "Minding Our Language," 19–30; Lammers, "Medical Futility Discussion," 115–28; Cameron, "Theological Mandate," 35–44; Wheeler, "Broadening Our View," 63–73.

However, the reason behind the marginalization of theologians in bioethics may be related to internal tension in theological thinking between religious identity and the pursuit of general moral consensus.[78] In other words, while theologians were genuinely trying to preserve their religious identity when discussing emerging bioethical dilemmas, they were forced to adapt to a neutral "secular" language to be able to participate in public discourse and commissioned debates over policies and regulations. Three theological models emerged as a result: the autonomous model, the theological continuity model, and the dialectical and interactive model.[79] Advocates of the *autonomous model* emphasize that theological thinking is able to provide a certain and stable moral normativity to the faithful. Theological thinking works independently from scientific developments to secure those norms. Thinkers who advance the *theological continuity model* believe in the similarity between religious and nonreligious views. They are willing to freely derive moral norms from scientific advancements within a natural law mentality. Many theologians, however, adopt a *dialectical and interactive model* to extract theological bioethics that is relevant to modern society. In addressing new bioethical dilemmas, these theologians contend that their theological innovation is authentic to their historical tradition rather than drastically departed from its premises. Although some theologians may fall more along the lines of one of these models, most of them today pursue the dialectical and interactive model.

However, because of post-modern social changes, many theologians reasserted their presence after a period when religious talk in public debates was marginalized. In the very beginning, theologians washed-down their religious phraseology to appeal to the public and to other colleagues. Most recently, theologians engaged in public discourse while clearly expressing their religious identity, not out of an identity crisis but because of their dissatisfaction with the hegemony of absolutist individualistic principlism in bioethics. By and large, theologian-bioethicists engaged in public discourse to influence public policy depending on how they understood their religious identity, on how they conceived the new developments in science and society, and on how they collaborated with non-theologians to formulate public policy.[80]

---

78. Cahill, "Religion and Theology," 73–90.
79. Cahill, "Religion and Theology," 73–90.
80. Cahill, "Religion and Theology," 74.

The post-modern generation of theologians approached bioethical dilemmas with a prophetic voice. They advocated a theological engagement that provides parameters and directions to the faithful while leaving their application to the particular context and dependent upon the developments of scientific knowledge and technology. This role of theology leaves room for humans, being created co-creators, to freely and responsibly make ethical judgments. In regard to the role of theological bioethics in the public sphere, theologians were divided. Some theologians would have preferred to keep the purity of the faith rather than influence public medical ethics and policy. Others were active participants in governmental commissions even when they had to use a neutral language to influence public bioethical policy.[81]

In short, theological bioethics arguably has two-fold mission in society today. First, it unveils specific answers and norms from its particular tradition to direct believers on how to live their faith in contemporary society. Second, theological bioethics has a social role to modulate public policy for the betterment of the faithful of its tradition and of the entire society. A specific religious tradition may prefer to adopt a communal (tribal) morality that is isolationist and separate from the general society; however, such a model was once deemed by Engelhardt to be dangerous in a pluralistic society (thus explains Cahill).[82] On the contrary, more theological bioethicists today emphasize that any community is increasingly international. Therefore, to establish a relevant religious bioethics, social justice and global solidarity must play a major role rather than the morbid emphasis on individualistic liberty and autonomous choices.

It is arguable then that a theological bioethics befitting to the contemporary globalized world needs to advocate a new mindset. Some genuine attempts to provide a thick interpretation for medical ethics fall short of this mission. Two examples will be briefly discussed here to highlight their shortcomings. The goal of this exposition is not to offer a comprehensive study of the thought of the given theologian. Rather, it is to highlight where a genuine pursuit of substantive versions of bioethics may fall short of the ideal, simply by adopting the same mindset as mainstream bioethics.

---

81. Cahill, "Religion and Theology," 73–90.
82. Cahill, "Religion and Theology," 76.

Robin Gill's *Health Care and Christian Ethics*[83]

In his book, Robin Gill provides a Christian contribution to the public discourse on health care ethics within Western pluralistic societies. Christian ethics, he contends, provides a thicker version of bioethics through complementing the four biomedical principles advocated by Beauchamp and Childress with four virtues derived from the healing narratives in the Synoptic Gospels. First, Gill analyzes the current situation of bioethics and adopts a positive stance toward its secular inclinations.[84] While some criticize the principlist account developed by Beauchamp and Childress (the latter being a theologian) for marginalizing the Christian faith, Gill seems to justify their adoption of a secular language in their principles. He disapproves the prevalent polarization between secular and religious ethics, and leans toward accepting a neutral rational discourse in bioethics so that it can be genuinely inclusive. Anyway, he does not think that public bioethics discourse was exclusive to religious input: many theologians continuously played a major role in shaping the decisions of various governmental commissions related to healthcare policies.

To advance his proposal, Gill identifies three gaps in secular bioethics in the West which need to be mended.[85] These gaps are: a gap between theoretical and actual moral communities; a gap between personal resonance and a shared understanding of cosmic order; and a gap between moral demands and human propensity to selfishness. He believes that these gaps are generated because of an individualistic understanding of morality; hence, communities cannot provide a horizon of meaning even to those who belong to them. Further, while individuals desire to pursue moral behavior, secular rational morality may not provide them with a strong motivation to overcome their own selfishness.

To bridge these gaps, Gill contends that public theology in health care ethics has a threefold critical role: to criticize, to deepen, and to widen the ethical debate.[86] When deepening and widening the ethical debate in the public arena, theologians have to be sensitive to the particularity of other beliefs and the risk in improper adoption of explicit theological language in the debate. His contention derives from a realist paradigm of public theology which only perceives relative difference between

---

83. Gill, *Health Care*.
84. Gill, *Health Care*, 1–15.
85. Gill, *Health Care*, 16–33.
86. Gill, *Health Care*, 34–61.

Christian and secular thought. This contrasts with a purist paradigm in which Jerusalem has nothing to do with Athens. Nonetheless, Gill admits that theologians alone cannot bridge these gaps in secular bioethics; they definitely need their secular colleagues to do so.

Ultimately, to offer a thicker account of bioethics, he suggests complementing the four secular rational principles of beneficence, non-maleficence, respect of autonomy, and justice with four virtues. He believes that Jesus' healing stories in the Synoptic Gospels have more to do with the virtues they highlight than the miraculous action itself.[87] These virtues are compassion, care, faith or trust, and reticence or humility. These virtues are equally valuable in other religious traditions including Judaism and Islam. Rather than conflicting with the secular principles, these virtues offer a thicker account for health care ethics that neither the principles nor the virtues will be able to offer on their own.

Although Gill genuinely attempts to offer a more substantive account of bioethics, he fails to liberate his account from the individualistic mindset that shapes secular mainstream bioethics. On the one hand, he indeed offers a deeper discourse in bioethics; he highlights the human experience of health and sickness which requires a virtuous physician to heal the entire person rather than a narrow emphasis on autonomous decision-making. Moreover, Gill's religious identity is not threatened by a non-religious discourse in bioethics. He is content with the religious roots of secular principles even if those roots are not recognized in the public sphere. These roots are well-served so long as the secular principles are given a deeper connotation through complementary personal virtues.

On the other hand, Gill still ascribes to the individualistic mindset which shapes the secular and rational principles of mainstream bioethics. In his criticism of secular bioethics, he does not venture beyond the walls of the clinic. He narrowly concentrates on the individual encounter between physicians and patients rather than on the social and global dimensions of the practice of medicine. Ironically, while he is willing to explore the community's role in shaping the virtues of practitioners, he fails to notice the social forces that shape the entire venture of medical practice as an institution. Furthermore, Gill's theological project seems final rather than ongoing. Theology can offer four virtues to complement the four biomedical principles; it is all that theology can offer at this time.

---

87. Gill, *Health Care*, 62–93.

A spiritual activism and a dynamic, unceasing dialogue are not on his agenda.

Dennis Macaleer and *The New Testament and Bioethics: Theology and Basic Bioethics Principles*[88]

In his dissertation, published later as a book, Macaleer interacts with secular common morality advanced by Beauchamp and Childress within the same mindset that Gill perceives it.[89] Macaleer attempts to enhance the meaning of the three/four biomedical principles using three theological themes derived from the New Testament.[90] He employs an invitation-response hermeneutic to extract the biblical themes of the image of God, the covenant, and the pursuit of healing starting from the twin commandment of loving God and one's neighbor.[91] Macaleer then uses these themes to address three of the pressing issues in medical practice in the US: withholding or withdrawing life-sustaining treatment, access to medical care, and the use of palliative care.[92] He is established in his biblical exegesis which he considers to be one of the unique contributions he brings to the discourse. As a theologian and pastor in the Reformed Church, he justifiably attempts to clarify to his parishioners and co-believers what bioethics is about.

However, what is striking about his approach is that he is entrenched in the same individualistic mindset that brought the biomedical principles to light. He seems to favor the rational common morality behind them. Unfortunate is that his genuine search for a deeper meaning of the principles through biblical exegesis does not lead him to question the mindset behind the principles; his theological contribution enhances the meaning but does not change—or challenge—the mindset.

Macaleer separates himself from other ethicists through a robust exegetical exploration of the New Testament for an enhanced meaning of the taken-for-granted principles.[93] His invitation-response hermeneutic raises valid theological themes and highlights that the invitation extended

88. Macaleer, *New Testament and Bioethics*.
89. Macaleer, *New Testament and Bioethics*, 1–30.
90. Macaleer, *New Testament and Bioethics*, 76–147.
91. Macaleer, *New Testament and Bioethics*, 31–75.
92. Macaleer, *New Testament and Bioethics*, 208–64.
93. Macaleer, *New Testament and Bioethics*, 1–30.

by Christ (to come back to Christ) is toward the entire community of believers and all humanity. However, similar to Gill, his approach does not scrutinize the basis on which the secular principles have emerged, namely the rational individualistic mindset of Western societies.

In short, both Gill and Macaleer do not go far enough in their theological bioethics. They seem to take the individualistic mindset prevalent in mainstream bioethics for granted without challenging the deeper hermeneutical apparatus behind it and without providing a more holistic approach toward the human condition in a globalized world.

Religious Bioethics: Non-ideological Mindset

On the other side of religious discourse in bioethics, theologians have approached rising dilemmas using a different mindset. Rather than ascribing to the prevailing model of bioethics, some theologians used their religious tradition and theological hermeneutics to perceive the evolving reality of medicine in a different light. Two examples will be briefly discussed here. Allen Verhey and Lisa Sowle Cahill belong to different religious traditions but have many things in common in the way they approach bioethics. Verhey is an Evangelical Protestant theologian and Cahill is a Roman Catholic theologian.

Allen Verhey's Reading the Bible in the Strange World of Medicine

In his book, Verhey explores a Christian bioethics for his own Christian community. He contends that theologians may only express a theological voice in bioethics inasmuch as they are able to talk to their particular community and out of its particular experience, although they may not always be able to speak for it. This humble hermeneutical starting point emphasizes that theological perspectives on bioethics are always in flux; ultimately, it is a communal project that is evolving through the narrative experiences of every individual person within the entire community. It is a project for the church and of the church which comes with a "readiness to be formed and reformed" by the Bible and by God. Thus, theological ethics is not final; it is open to revision depending on the shifting experiences of the community.[94]

---

94. Verhey, *Reading the Bible*, 1–31.

Within Verhey's Protestant tradition, the Bible plays a central role in shaping the identity of the individuals and the entire community. Hence, at a practical level, the community of believers should take its inspiration from the Bible to voice an authentic theological contribution to bioethics.[95] Surprisingly, but probably expectedly, he is critical of the individualistic Protestant ethos and its role in shaping Western societies at large, and the bioethical discourse more specifically. While he is rooted in his own religious tradition, he is critical of that tradition when its heritage uncritically elaborated an anthropology foreign to a genuine Christian eschatology.[96]

Although Verhey starts from his particular community and speaks to its members, he does not exclude the entire world outside that community. He is willing to have a talk about God with whomever is interested in this talk, because this is the only talk that he himself is able to have.[97] However, such talk of God does not discount the ability to have a meaningful and critical talk with others when taking human suffering seriously. To acquire the wisdom needed to address bioethical dilemmas today, he advocates compassion, not only as a virtue (as Gill did to supplement the biomedical principles) but as central to a theological critique of mainstream bioethics.[98]

Ultimately, he is critical of the general culture, especially in Western countries. He rightly attempts to expose those cultural elements which contradict an authentic anthropology, an anthropology that takes to heart the inevitable human experience of suffering. For instance, he successfully debunks one of the prevailing cultural elements, namely the meaning of respect of persons. He agrees that respecting human persons is not possible without protecting their freedom; however, moral life cannot be reduced to merely making free choices without considering the content of those choices. Moreover, reducing moral norms to respecting patients' free choices unjustifiably excludes the social context where humans are formed. To genuinely respect persons, Verhey rather rightly contends, one should respect their embodied and communal selves as well.[99]

---

95. Verhey, *Reading the Bible*, 32–67.
96. Verhey, *Reading the Bible*, 68–98.
97. Verhey, *Reading the Bible*, 1–31.
98. Verhey, *Reading the Bible*, 99–144.
99. Verhey, *Reading the Bible*, 68–98.

More generally, Verhey criticizes the medicalized culture which gives technical scientific medicine a broad authority on issues of life and death. He rather emphasizes the role of caring and compassion toward those who are suffering. When those who suffer are treated within the "strange world of medicine," they are alienated from their communal selves as a result. Clearly, he suggests that the strangeness is not in morality itself, but in the world which surrounds those who suffer. Strangeness is in the world of medicine as practiced today, since it deprives the sick of their supporting community, isolates them in medical edifices, but then is not able to effectively relieve their existential suffering.[100]

In short, what Verhey offers to global bioethics is significant although he does not venture into the international meaning of "global". He criticizes both the popular individualistic culture and the narrowly technical approach to medicine especially because of their distorted anthropological bases. He also emphasizes the need to acquire a new mindset to challenge the culture of medicine and to ameliorate the associated suffering. This new mindset can be assimilated through a genuine consideration of compassion in the context of unavoidable human suffering. More critical of his own religious tradition, he challenges this tradition to change when it does not genuinely and adequately address human suffering today.

Lisa Sowle Cahill and Participatory Theological Bioethics

Lisa Sowle Cahill adopts a hermeneutic that revolves around distributive justice and social sin. This hermeneutic shapes the way she perceives the role of theological bioethics and religious communities within a society that is inclined toward a narrow, but still "thick," version of bioethics.

Cahill contends that theological bioethics should be actively present in bioethics using a participatory mode of engagement in the public arena.[101] Theologians should perceive the public arena not only through the lens of their academic engagement in bioethical discourse nor only through a narrow religious influence on official and governmental policy making. Religious participation in public debates, generally and especially

---

100. Verhey, *Reading the Bible*, 32–67. Similar argument is made in Rothman, *Strangers at the Bedside*, 127–47.

101. An example of activism that was inspired by Cahill's participatory theological discourse is discussed in Craig, "Everyone at the Table," 335–58.

in bioethics, is substantiated through a social network of activists who are shaping the culture itself far beyond official avenues. Therefore, through a transformative engagement in their public surrounding, theologians and religious communities can agree with others on moral values and the detrimental effects of social sin.[102] Cahill further contemplates a time when bioethics discussions address all the social, political, and economical determinants of health as essential to a desired common good.[103]

Within her Roman Catholic tradition, Cahill emphasizes that distributive justice is the underlying hermeneutic for an active role of Christian theological bioethics. To further the biblical theme of justice (especially in the healing stories of the New Testament), Cahill builds on the long tradition of Roman Catholic social teachings. For her, theological bioethics cannot only decry injustices through a prophetic stance in contemporary society but should actively participate in various global networks to bring about change. This global engagement does not need to use explicit religious language to communicate across the differences; rather, theologians need to "translate" their work to expressions that emphasize the common good, inclusion, distributive justice, and solidarity.[104]

Therefore, Cahill believes that bioethics in the twenty-first century should be a social ethics, especially because of the effects of globalization on current world affairs. This derives from an obligation to join action to theoretical talk, along with a realistic recognition that individual decision making is always contextual. In a world that is shrinking to an ever-growing complex web of relations, individual health decisions are embedded within a prominent social system and they occupy only a minuscule step within that system.[105]

Ultimately, Cahill's contribution to the public discourse of bioethics is original-prophetic in proposition, activist in practice, and global in scope. In countering a "thick" version of bioethics that is founded on an ideological acceptance of liberal individualism, unlimited scientific progress, and free market economy, theologians should emphasize a similarly

---

102. Cahill, *Theological Bioethics*, 13–42.

103. Cahill, *Theological Bioethics*, 1–12; also in, Lustig, "Reform and Rationing," 31–50; Turner and Dumas, "Vulnerability, Diversity and Scarcity," 663–70; Chryssavgis, "Orthodox Spirituality," 130–38.

104. Cahill, *Theological Bioethics*, 1–12.

105. Cahill, *Theological Bioethics*, 1–12.

thick and inclusive version of bioethics.[106] Theological bioethics should prophetically redefine many taken-for-granted cultural aspects and actively pursue a "preferential option for the poor" [and the vulnerable] locally and globally.[107] For instance, Cahill criticizes a naïve ascription to the rhetoric of pro-life and pro-choice movements; both movements take the worth of the conceived person and the freedom of women's choices out of the social context of health-related decisions.[108]

By embracing pluralism for the sake of human salvation, Cahill's activism resembles the spiritual activism that was earlier highlighted within an Orthodox Christian *phronema*. By the same token, this book assumes that establishing an authentic religious bioethics does not require explicitly religious terminology or literal resources; rather, such bioethics hinges on an authentic religious mindset. The following section will argue that this mindset can be inclusive without glossing over the differences among humans and value systems.

An Orthodox Bioethical *Phronema* in a Pluralistic World

An inclusive Orthodox Christian phronema is arguably possible and can have a unique contribution to the global discourse on bioethics. The discussion here examines the work of a few Orthodox theologians who explored the unique contribution of Orthodox Christianity to bioethics. The list of authors is not inclusive of every theologian who has worked on bioethics; also, even for those whose thought is discussed, a comprehensive study of their work is beyond the limitations of this book. However, the goal is to highlight what these Orthodox theologians have done so far so that this book may extend their work to meet the demands of globalization.

---

106. Cahill, *Theological Bioethics*, 13–42.
107. Cahill, *Theological Bioethics*, 43–69.
108. Cahill, *Theological Bioethics*, 169–210.

An Orthodox Christian *Phronema*: Inclusive Theocentric Cosmo-Anthropology

Creator-Creation Separation

In the previous chapter, the separation between the Creator and creation was shown to have no place within an authentic Orthodox *phronema*. There is no place where God is not present or constantly working to save the entire human race. In a synergic cosmology, St Basil of Caesarea (fourth century) established a framework where the divine and the cosmic creatively interact.[109] Through the continued presence and action of the Holy Spirit, the divine providence is constantly seeking those who are lost.[110] As a result of this mindset, the world reflects God inasmuch as one seeks the divine presence in the created world. Many theologians, therefore, emphasize that a scientific exploration of the world complements theological revelation since both seek the divine truth which was ultimately revealed in the person of Jesus Christ.[111] For many church fathers, ancient and modern, Christ is dormant in the night of world religions awaiting to be sought and unveiled; he is the Logos of every created thing and he is the one who bestows meaning onto the created reality.[112]

Ultimately, Christ's incarnation has revealed him as a person rather than a dogmatic set of tenets. For Orthodox theologians, the authentic personal experience of Christ was preserved in the Orthodox Church; however, they do not exclude the possibility of experiencing Christ outside the church.[113] Even at the time of Christ's earthly mission, he revealed himself to those who did not belong to the chosen people of God, such as the wise men from the East in the Nativity account (Matt 2:1–12), Cornelius the Centurion (Acts 10), the Samaritan woman at the well of

---

109. Costache, "Christian Worldview," 21–56.

110. Basil, "Living in the Future," 23–36.

111. Lemna, "Human Ecology," 133–54; Breck, "Orthodox Bioethics," 119–30; Harakas, *Health and Medicine*, 69–78; Harrison, *God's Many-Splendored Image*, 147–68; Clément, "Science and Faith," 120–27.

112. Lossky, *Mystical Theology*, 91–113; Abou Mrad, "The Witness," 246–60; Munteanu, "Cosmic Liturgy," 332–44; Harakas, "'Rational Medicine,'" 19–44; Martin, "Poetry as Theology," 145–95.

113. Abou Mrad, "The Witness," 246–60; Costache, "Christian Worldview," 21–56; Clapsis, "Boundaries of the Church," 113–27; Haight, "Jesus and the World Religions," 321–44; Tsompanidis, "Church and the Churches," 148–63.

Jacob (John 4:1–42), and the Samaritan leper who was healed along with nine others (Luke 11:19).

The Goal of Orthodox Christian Bioethics

The work of Orthodox theologians on bioethics attempts to answer the concerns of the faithful within the above-mentioned theocentric cosmology. Applauded as it may be, the work of these theologians does not search for a common bioethical ground with other religions and value systems. Rather, starting from an elaborate Orthodox theology, they attempt to shape an Orthodox Christian bioethics that is authentic to the church's tradition. Tristram Engelhardt, to the contrary, starts from philosophical premises and methodology; his account of Orthodox bioethics will be critiqued in what follows as it departs—in certain aspects—from an authentic Orthodox *phronema*.

Orthodox theologians agree on the centrality of the liturgy in shaping Orthodox bioethics.[114] Not only does a liturgical ecclesiology define the identity of the Orthodox Church; it also opens the door of Orthodox bioethics toward the universal divine providence to save the entire world. The goal of Orthodox bioethics is *theosis* (deification) of humanity, similar to the goal of Orthodox theology itself. From the liturgy, John Bekos derives two principles essential to Orthodox bioethics.[115] These principles are not conceived within the prevailing sense of bioethics principlism; instead, they are fundamental concepts highlighting the role of humanity in the divine salvific economy. He contends that memory and justice play a central role in achieving that goal. Through "memory," the faithful are not invited to narrowly remember Christ performing many wonders; rather they are encouraged to remember his suffering and vulnerability exposed on the cross. Remembering Christ's suffering is more important than remembering his wonders, especially because wonders do not heal human vulnerability. For Bekos, it is humanity's thankfulness to God that heals its innate vulnerability. Similarly, "justice" is related to the divine providence. It is not centered on the power of God; rather it humbly highlights the gravity of the divine sacrifice which is asymmetrical to whatever humanity can offer in return. In other words, divine justice is

---

114. Hamalis, "Eastern Orthodox Ethics," 1525–35.
115. Bekos, "Memory and Justice," 100–113.

not about divine power and legalistic rights. Instead, justice emphasizes the incomparable divine sacrifice for the sake of human salvation.

Bishop Nikolaos Hatzinikolaou derives from the liturgical tradition of the Orthodox Church five characteristics that should shape a "spiritual bioethics" for modern times.[116] (1) Orthodox bioethics should protect the sacredness of all human persons. (2) It should discern the will of God through humble recognition of human weakness and the divine desire to save all humans. (3) It should highlight the value of life and foster a respect for death. Despite its enmity, death is the only certain companion to human life. By respecting human mortality, the worth of human life, it is emphasized, does not derive from a wealth of rights that a person enjoys; rather, humans are worthy of respect inasmuch as society is willing to embrace them when they are most vulnerable. More importantly, (4) Orthodox bioethics should avoid being scholastic in searching for perfect and adequate answers for bioethical dilemmas. It should approach the mystery of human life with humility leaving final decisions to the freedom of those who are involved. Therefore, (5) Orthodox bioethics is not conservative, yet it is cautious. It does not fear errors and is willing to confess mistakes with humility. This non-perfectionistic approach parallels an Orthodox anthropology that hinges on a personal experience of God despite human sin, yet within a repentant (*metanoic*) way of life.

All these characteristics highlight that an Orthodox bioethics, according to Hatzinikolaou, is a project which does not offer final answers to all bioethical dilemmas.[117] Instead, within the entire mission of the church, Orthodox bioethics is meant to nurture a conscience (a mindset) which, while nurturing human freedom, fosters a discourse that reveals the personal and divine truth of Christ. Thus, for Hatzinikolaou, the dogmatic heritage of the Orthodox Church is not enough to reveal normative ethical principles that are legally binding. Bioethics is rather embedded in an ascetic and liberating spirituality which is sensitive to the vulnerable and marginalized in any given circumstances.

In a similar vein, Father John Breck contends that an Orthodox bioethics should be *theonomous* rather than autonomous.[118] God's authority shapes a *phronema* within which no boundaries persist in the constant

---

116. Hatzinikolaou, "Ethics of Dilemmas," 165–88.

117. Similar to Harakas, "Orthodox Christianity in American Public Life," 377–97; Breck, *Sacred Gift of Life*, especially in his preface to the book, 1–4; Harakas, *Health and Medicine*, esp. 138–44; Clément, "Witness in a Secular Society," 4–16.

118. Breck, "Orthodox Bioethics," 119–30; Breck has more detailed theological foundations for Orthodox Christian ethics in his book, Breck, *Sacred Gift of Life*, 19–53.

interaction between God, human persons, and the natural world. Under the divine authority, all the created world is the field of God and is invited to his kingdom. Orthodox bioethics, for Breck, has one mission, which is to "commend ourselves and each other and all our lives unto Christ our God" (a frequent petition in Orthodox liturgical prayers). He alludes to the responsibility of the Christian community to bring back to God what belongs to him.

Unfortunately, Breck, somewhat similar to Macaleer, accepts the four biomedical principles and the principle of double effect as useful to guide practical decisions in health care. He grounds them in the divine authority and the sacredness of human life in its pursuit of true communion with God and others. However, while he recognizes that they are foreign to an Orthodox ethos, he explores a deeper theological meaning of these principles. Yet, he does not critique the narrow scope of topics explored in mainstream bioethics. Other theologians have done the same. When Harakas wrote his entry in the *Encyclopedia of Bioethics* on Orthodox bioethics, he explores only the topics discussed in mainstream bioethics and highlights what is special about an Orthodox perspective. Understandably, when Harakas wrote that entry in 1995 (reprinted in the 2004 edition), global bioethics as advocated in this book was still in its nascence.[119]

Notwithstanding the nuanced differences among these theologians in regard to the mission of Orthodox bioethics today, they all criticize the ethos behind mainstream bioethics.[120] They contend that God is not the point of reference for mainstream bioethics; there is a great deal of emphasis on individual autonomy as if the individual is eternal or her health is of ultimate value. Also, they all point to the common distorted perception of scientific medicine. On the one hand, contemporary medicine operates within a consumerist mentality; it claims to aim at improving the health of everyone but actually very few can afford its expensive technology and patented medications. On the other hand, there is a great deal of financial interest in modern medicine which Hatzinikolaou perceives as the "financial captivity and corporate totalitarianism" of human scientific venture.[121]

---

119. Harakas, "Eastern Orthodox Christianity, Bioethics," 691–97.

120. Breck, "Orthodox Bioethics in the Encounter," 119–30; Hatzinikolaou, "Ethics of Dilemmas," 165–88; Bekos, "Memory and Justice," 101–7; Engelhardt, *Foundations of Christian Bioethics*, xi–xxii.

121. Hatzinikolaou, "Ethics of Dilemmas," 181; Mantzarides, "Globalization and Universality," 199–207.

Applauded as it may be, the work of these pioneer Orthodox bioethicists does not go as far as the mission of the church should go. None of these bioethicists discuss the global dimension of bioethics, whether international or comprehensive; rather, they focus more on mainstream bioethics questions and how Orthodox bioethics should address them. While they explain to their target audience, the faithful Orthodox, what is special about Orthodox bioethics, they understandably refrain from searching for a global common ground in bioethics. In other words, their main interest is to elaborate on what is unique to Orthodox bioethics rather than on where it meets with other bioethics (save for Breck who uses the secular principles within a different mindset). Their perspectives, nonetheless, do not exclude the possibility of finding this common ground. They all embed their bioethics within the liturgical identity of the Orthodox Church which is necessarily "catholic/universal" in its seeking to save the entire world.[122]

Engelhardt's Version of Orthodox Christian Bioethics

To the contrary of this unexplored global mission, Engelhardt's version of Christian bioethics intentionally excludes the possibility of finding any "rational" common ground between different religions and value systems. Engelhardt "[In] sometimes whimsical way (though quite seriously) . . . made his case for Orthodox Christianity as an alternative response to the chaos of an essentially irrational world."[123] He builds his bioethics on dubious, allegedly Orthodox, cosmological and anthropological foundations. Not least among these foundations is Engelhardt's ascription to a narrowly rational discourse, even when he argues from a particular religious perspective; such narrowly rational discourse is necessarily reductionistic when discussing issues of life and death and human flourishing.

Before converting to Orthodox Christianity, Engelhardt ascribed to the Enlightenment project pursuing, in ethics, a rational common ground among all human beings. He defended rational foundations for bioethics to which every reasonable human being may ascribe.[124] However, by the dawn of post-modernity and consequent uncertainties, Engelhardt

---

122. Breck, *Sacred Gift of Life*, 11–14, 258.

123. Harakas, Review of *At the Roots of Christian Bioethics*, 376–79; Harakas, "Reflections on Authority in Ethics," 355–73.

124. Engelhardt, *Foundations of Bioethics*.

revised his foundations and dropped the Enlightenment project and defended the necessity of numerous versions of particular bioethics. He moved to explore the Christian foundations of bioethics through the lens of a traditional (Orthodox) Christian bioethics. He consults a wealth of church fathers' writings and the long-standing liturgical heritage of the Orthodox Church. Although he agrees in some details of his Orthodox bioethics with the above theologians, he constructs a fundamentalist-conservative version,[125] which is unjustifiably dressed in Orthodox garments and which seriously contradicts—at least—Orthodox cosmology and anthropology. He heavily quotes early church fathers and some later ones without comprehensively engaging their mindset (*phronema*) and premises. Comparatively, he scarcely discusses the works of contemporary Orthodox theologians/ethicists as if they do not exist. An anecdotal search for the names of some influential Orthodox theologians and bioethicists reveals this trend. Even when he does mention them, in his *Foundation of Christian Bioethics* for instance, he only includes them in the footnotes.

In a book that should critically discuss the thought of Engelhardt—*At the Roots of Christian Bioethics*—his theological premises are taken for granted. Father Stanley Harakas, a proliferative Orthodox ethicist, regrets that such a book does not invite Orthodox Christian ethicists, nor Jewish Orthodox ethicists (whose tradition Engelhardt consults frequently in his articles). Harakas, rather sarcastically, describes Engelhardt's version of the Orthodox faith and commitments as being "whimsical (though serious) Texan traditional(ist) Orthodox Christian commitments." On a general note, Harakas emphasizes in his review of that book, as he does in many of his articles and books, the importance of an ecumenical dialogical spirit to counter-balance Engelhardt's "sharp sectarianism."[126]

Along with Engelhardt's cosmological and anthropological premises, there are many other reservations on the theological components of his Orthodox bioethics, for which there is not enough space here to discuss in detail. However, to uncover his cosmological and anthropological elements, a reference to one of his recent articles will be made below, unless otherwise mentioned.[127] This article suffices to demonstrate these

125. Engelhardt, *Foundations of Christian Bioethics*, xv.

126. Harakas, Review of *At the Roots of Christian Bioethics*, 376–79. Similar criticism of Engelhardt's Orthodox bioethics is established in Harakas, "Reflections on Authority in Ethics," 355–73.

127. Reference in what follows is made to the following article unless otherwise mentioned: Engelhardt, "Christian Bioethics in a Post-Christian World," 93–114.

elements, although a future, more comprehensive study of his thought is warranted in the light of the mindset advocated in this book.

Abysmal Separation between God and Creation

In his version of Orthodox bioethics, Engelhardt accepts a drastic difference between the uncreated and the created realities. Although Orthodox theology acknowledges this difference, the gap between the created and uncreated has finally been bridged in the person of Christ. Engelhardt maintains, for instance, that "the truth is a Who" and that "this truth is hidden by immanence."[128] However, too much emphasis on the hiddenness of Christ sounds contrary to what has been maintained in Orthodoxy, i.e., that there is no place to which God does not have access, no place where God is not already present, and no place where God is not actively pursuing the fallen world to save and bring back to His kingdom. A separation between the secular and the sacred is artificial in Orthodox *phronema*.[129] Moreover, while God may have fully revealed the divine providence through the person of Jesus Christ in the Orthodox Church, the Holy Spirit continues to work in the world despite the world's fallenness.[130] Paul Evdokimov expressed this succinctly saying: "Secular humanism denies God, exaggerated asceticism denies the world, pietism overstresses the transcendence of God, but Orthodox ethics balances the earthly and the heavenly."[131]

Furthermore, Engelhardt is decidedly against any ecumenical encounter, depending on marginal Orthodox authors who, despite their sainthood, do not represent the mind of the entire Church. He intentionally uses authors, such as Justin Popovich,[132] while ignoring the scores of authors who participated in the ecumenical movement, were nourished within its spirit, and as a result enlivened an Orthodox renaissance around the world.[133]

---

128. Engelhardt, *Foundations of Christian Bioethics*, xiii.

129. Crow, "Orthodox Vision," 7–22; Martin, "Poetry as Theology," 145–95; Theokritoff, "Creator and Creation," 63–77; Harakas, "Integrity of Creation and Ethics," 27–42.

130. Basil, "Living in the Future," 23–36.

131. As quoted in Harakas, "Church and the Secular World," 167–99.

132. Such as in Engelhardt, "Why Ecumenism Fails," 25–51, esp. note 2, 46.

133. Meyendorff, "Unity of the Church," 30–46.

In a pluralistic world, Engelhardt advocates a procedural approach to bioethics. Since rational consensus on moral values is not possible because of his anthropological premises (more to come in the next section), the only way to live in a pluralistic society is to respect value differences so long as differences do not affect the well-being of others.[134] Such an ideological captivity to liberal individualism prevents Engelhardt from being open to a social discourse about possible common good and common values.[135] Ironically, while ascribing to liberal individualism, he criticizes modern Western (post-Christian) states for being fundamentally secularist and laicist;[136] both of these attributes result from the same liberal individualistic ideology that he adopts. His opinion divulges two troubling premises.

First, he defends liberal individualism as long as it advantages his particular community (in this case Christian community). However, he claims that a secular state becomes fundamentalist when it systematically tunes down its Christian components. In other words, when a secular state equally treats all different groups in a pluralistic society, it is not clear why it becomes fundamentalist, according to Engelhardt, although its governance is built on the same liberal individualistic ideology to which he ascribes.

Second, when he derogatively describes modern states to be laicist, he alludes to (and sometimes clearly expresses) his nostalgia for a Byzantine model of state-church symphony.[137] Many theologians have discussed the perils of such symphony and explained its detrimental consequences on the Orthodox Church, some of which are still felt to this day.[138] Similarly, through using the term "laicist," he is probably attracted to an outdated (and dangerous) clericalist theocracy. In contemporary globalized and pluralistic society, it is not clear how Engelhardt's theocracy would be less fundamentalist than a secular state. Establishing a purely Christian West after Christendom (with the expansion of "the Empire of Holy Texas"[139]) is as fundamentalist as the secular ideology which excludes the role of religion in shaping the human person.

---

134. Engelhardt, *Foundations of Bioethics*.
135. Potter, *Global Bioethics*, 119–21.
136. Engelhardt, "Christian Bioethics in a Post-Christian World," 93–114.
137. Harakas, "Reflections on Authority in Ethics," 355–73.
138. Russell, "One Faith, One Church," 122–30.
139. Engelhardt, *Foundations of Christian Bioethics*, 393.

In his ideological ascription to a Byzantine (theocratic) political system, Engelhardt departs from the above-mentioned theologians advocacy for a theocentric bioethics. A theocentric bioethics aims at continuing the divine providence to save the entire world; a theocratic bioethics is interested in political power and enforcing Christian values on pluralistic societies. John Meyendorff contends that the authority of Christ cannot be identified with the political power of the state and the universality of the Gospel cannot be defined in political terms.[140] The difference between theocentric and theocratic bioethics is drastic.

Distorted Anthropology

Similarly, Engelhardt's anthropology departs from an authentic Orthodox Christian anthropology. The three components of his anthropology are: "black-box" anthropology, moral strangeness, and culture wars. These three components are co-centered around the individual person and her relation, in matters of morality, to herself, to her surrounding community, and the entire world (the latter component also includes how any particular community interacts with other communities at large). Engelhardt's model parallels and contradicts the inclusive church typology within which Harakas perceives the mission of the Orthodox Church in the world. In congruence with other Orthodox theologians, Harakas believes that the personal (mystical) relationship with God in prayer is necessarily embedded within the communal prayer of the Eucharist. However, he emphasizes that the church's mission is not limited to those who participate in the Eucharistic Chalice but is extended to the entire world in a non-sectarian openness toward humanity.[141]

Engelhardt believes that only the individual person, as a "black-box", is responsible for her own moral choices, whose reasons are not communicable with the outside world. Further, he believes that people are moral strangers across their communities. If a person who belongs to a certain religious community wants to communicate her moral convictions to outsiders, she will not be able to do so. The reason, Engelhardt contends, is that different communities speak different moral languages

---

140. Meyendorff, "Unity of the Church," 30–46.

141. Harakas, "Church and the Secular World," 167–99; Harakas, "Orthodox Christianity in American Public Life," 377–97; Casiday, "Church Fathers," 167–87; Yannaras, *Freedom of Morality*, 77–88.

because of their different worldviews. However, empirical evidence shows that religious communities in the US, for instance, may not be as monolithic in regard to many morally relevant social and economic issues as Engelhardt would wish.[142] Even among Orthodox Christians, there is no unison around bioethical issues such as organ transplantation,[143] and feeding the terminally ill.[144]

Theologically speaking, it is not clear why strangeness should only be perceived in terms of morality. Engelhardt uses expressions such as "[r]eason without grace, ..., cannot restore the *moral unity* shattered by sin"; "united in Christ... can one unite the *fragmented elements of morality*"; and "[o]nly in a relationship through worship... can *fragmented moral practices* be made whole" (emphasis added).[145] In the larger scheme of things, the deepest anthropological dilemma is not moral strangeness; rather, it is the utter alienation of humans from God and from each other. Since the fall of Adam and Eve, humans became strangers and they needed the reconciliation achieved through Christ to bridge broken relationships. Hence, it is not theologically justifiable to single moral strangeness out of the entire human condition, nor is it warranted to perceive unity only in terms of "moral unity."

Moreover, Engelhardt fails to justify the ability to communicate moral values within any given community despite human "black-boxness." It is not clear how individuals can be morally shaped within their communities if moral reasoning is not communicable. Nor is it clear why individuals can communicate within their moral communities but are not able to do the same outside of it (regardless of Engelhardt's claim of different moral languages).

An extension of Engelhardt's abysmal separation between creator and creation is his defense of unbridgeable separation between the religious and secular. Such separation is deemed among many Orthodox theologians to be the first seed of nihilism in modern society.[146] Further,

142. Davis and Robinson, "Religious Orthodoxy," 229–45.

143. Breck, "Bioethical Dilemmas and Orthodoxy," 171–88; Breck, *Sacred Gift of Life*, 258.

144. Harakas, "Orthodox Christianity in American Public Life," 377–97.

145. Engelhardt, "Orthodox Approach to Bioethics," 108–30, esp. 120–21.

146. Loudovikos, "Nations in the Church," 131–47; Chryssavgis, "World of the Icon," 35–43; Papanikolaou, "Orthodoxy, Postmodernity," 527–47; Martin, "Poetry as Theology," 145–95; Andreopoulos, "Modern Orthodox," 10–23; Valliere, "Russian Religious Thought," 227–41; Munteanu, "Cosmic Liturgy," 332–44.

Engelhardt's attack on any secular mindset suggests that secularism is monolithic or has one established and achievable agenda. However, rational-philosophical discourse, in morality at least, has produced several secular (or non-religious) varieties that are contradictory in some respects. Engelhardt claims that any secular discourse has "thin" morality and that anything that is done within a secular mindset is meaningless. However, Lisa Sowle Cahill has rightly highlighted that contemporary secular discourse is as "thick" as its religious counterpart because it builds on a specific anthropology and cosmology especially when some thinkers decidedly exclude the role of religion in shaping human identity.[147] Yet, a secularism that is respectful to religious identities is not as detrimental as Engelhardt would argue.[148]

This brings to the front a general question about what makes a discourse in the public arena a religious or a secular discourse. It seems that Engelhardt prefers a public discourse which clearly mentions God or explicitly emphasizes the Judeo-Christian heritage of American society. However, several times in history, heresies explicitly spoke in the name of Christ, however distorted his image and their experience of him were. At these times, the church established in dogmatic formulae what was her genuine experience of the true Christ. In other words, it is not the phraseology (the use of words like "God," "Christ," or "Christian") that makes a discourse genuinely religious rather than secular; it is rather the mindset, the *phronema*.[149]

More importantly, in a pluralistic and post-Christian world, Orthodox theologians should face non-religious discourse with humble repentance. Olivier Clément advocates a creative secularism and an inclusive anthropology which embraces the entire human experience of life to minister to those who thirst for meaning today.[150] Similarly, religious communities, including Christian ones, he admits, have committed mistakes throughout history which have probably led to the death of God in contemporary culture. Prevailing atheism and secularism should elicit

---

147. Cahill, *Theological Bioethics*, 13–42.

148. Guroian, *Ethics after Christendom*, 175–99.

149. Harakas, *Living the Faith*, 344–92; Hatzinikolaou, "Ethics of Dilemmas," 165–88.

150. Clément, *On Human Being*, 91–107. Also in: Valliere, "Russian Religious Thought," 227–41; Hierotheos, "Christian Bioethics," 29–41.

self-criticism and repentance among Christians rather than acrimonious polemical rhetoric.[151]

At a larger scale, Engelhardt uncritically adopts the politically charged rhetoric of "culture wars" advanced by James D. Hunter.[152] However, there is enough sociological evidence to doubt the premises of Hunter's worldview and to explain the perceived lack of consensus among the general public.[153] Further, "[B]y arming ourselves for [a cultural] war we make war more likely."[154] It is hence arguable that the roots of culture wars can be found in liberal individualism and neo-liberal ideology rather than in the prevailing differences in moral perspectives.[155]

Although "culture wars" has not attracted enough comments by Orthodox theologians, its offspring by Samuel Huntington, the "Clash of Civilization," has,[156] perhaps because of the embedded attack on Orthodoxy-related civilizational heritage. By dividing different peoples according to their religious-civilizational heritage, Huntington does not leave a place for diversity within any given culture, civilization, or religion and he crafts blanket judgements using inaccurate reading of history.[157] So does Engelhardt. Engelhardt does not explore the long-standing experience of the Orthodox Church in the face of cultural diversity and does not evaluate the consequences of a culture-wars mentality in the light of the universal (catholic) mission of the church. An inflamed culture-wars rhetoric diametrically contrasts with an eschatological reality that is pretasted in the Orthodox Church; in Christ, and because of Him, there is no difference between Jew and Greek, slave and free, male and female (Rom 10:12; 1 Cor 12:13; Gal 3:28; Col 3:11).[158]

---

151. Clément, "Purification by Atheism," 22–39; Clément, "Witness in a Secular Society," 4–16. Also in: Tsompanidis, "Church and the Churches," 148–63; Jillions, "Orthodox Christianity in the West," 276–91; Harakas, *Living the Faith*, 344–92.

152. Engelhardt, *Foundations of Christian Bioethics*, 49 n. 16; Engelhardt, "Conflicting Moralities and Theologies," 3–8.

153. Imber, "Doubting Culture Wars," 31–37; Davis and Robinson, "Are the Rumors of War Exaggerated?," 756–87.

154. Olson, "Dimensions of Cultural Tension," 237–58.

155. Callahan, *Roots of Bioethics*, 50–61.

156. Huntington, "Clash of Civilizations?," 22–49.

157. Said, "Clash of Ignorance," 11–13.

158. Louth, "Church's Mission," 649–57; Papanikolaou, "Byzantium, Orthodoxy," 75–98.

An Orthodox Phronema for Modern Dilemmas

An Iconic Phronema

To advance an Orthodox approach to global bioethical dilemmas, I weave the above theological and anthropological tenets into an iconic *phronema*.[159] This *phronema*, as will shortly be explained, does not only shape the community's perceptions toward innovative medical technologies and attempt to clarify a roadmap for believers to follow when encountering ethical dilemmas; this iconic *phronema* also shapes the engagement of the Orthodox Christian community in the global discourse of bioethics and moves believers to advocate for the most disadvantaged within the human community worldwide. The advocated *phronema* is inspired by the special status of the icon in Orthodox theology and in the liturgical (and supposedly daily) lives of the believers. Icons are not mere pieces of art that depict certain religious realities. They rather stand as windows between two different worlds, extending an invitation from the one to the other.[160] Icons open the created reality of this world toward the eschatological reality that is depicted on them. That eschatological reality stands in front of the beholder not as a space to be objectively explored (which is still possible) but as an inviting reality which targets the mindful beholder. Orthodox icons do not follow conventional geometrical rules for that reason. The lines in icons do not meet in the infinity; they rather inversely meet in the beholder in an inviting gesture to become involved in the presented divine reality. To explore this *phronema* in regard to bioethics, the following dimensions of icons are most relevant: the eschatological, the realist, and the hospitable dimensions.

The Eschatological Dimension of Icons

It is because of the incarnation of Jesus Christ that the Orthodox Church draws icons as an integral part of her liturgical practice.[161] Icons, therefore, depict the divine reality that is beyond the human ability to comprehend, especially as a means to help those who are illiterate and cannot read the gospel (traditionally, drawing icons is perceived as an act of writing icons to unveil the Good News). However, since icons do not only

---

159. Similar to Guroian, *Ethics after Christendom*, 29–52.
160. Athanasios, "*Eschata* in Our Daily Life," 37–49.
161. Chryssavgis, "World of the Icon," 35–43.

depict the person of Jesus Christ who was incarnate but also the saints, they highlight the divine destiny of every believer. Icons emphasize that the created reality is not the only reality; rather, every human person is invited to be transfigured (trans-form as Christ did on Mount Tabor).

Therefore, an Orthodox bioethics built on an iconic *phronema* is first incarnational in that it recognizes ethical dilemmas as affecting embodied human beings rather than as riddles for intellectual (rational-dogmatic) minds. Humans who seek medical attention struggle with diseases as embodied beings. As humans, they deserve that their dignity be respected with love and compassion rather than through mere honoring of their choices.

Moreover, an Orthodox bioethics is hopeful because icons depict an eschatological reality beyond human comprehension. It witnesses to that which was once described: "Eye has not seen, nor ear heard, nor have entered into the heart of man the things which God has prepared for those who love Him" (1 Cor 2:9). Thus, an authentic Orthodox bioethics recognizes that the ultimate goal of humanity is beyond this created world, it is *theosis*, the deification of humankind, the becoming of humans like God as Christ himself became like humans through incarnation. Ultimately, this goal is what gives meaning to the human experience rather than any imminent and ephemeral set of beliefs or rational convictions.

Furthermore, the eschatological dimension of icons penetrates and permeates the created world to transfigure it, to change the reality of the beholder. Therefore, it is the responsibility of the mind(*nous*)-ful beholder to bring this eschatological reality into the life of the world and for the life of the world (John 6:51). The mindful beholder is the one whose noetic eye is illumined to recognize the invitation depicted on the icon. In the liturgy, the faithful pre-taste the eschatological reality and are asked to forcefully bring it into their daily lives in the "liturgy after the liturgy." Ultimately, as the body of Christ, it is the responsibility of the church "to create unity where there is division, to bring forth reconciliation where there is alienation, to heal and restore a sick and deprived human nature, and to free persons from the spiritual and physical violence of evil."[162]

---

162. Guroian, "Seeing Worship as Ethics," 347.

The Realist Dimension of Icons

On the other side of the icon stands the beholder and the entire created world. To extend a meaningful invitation to the created world, the theology of icons recognizes the reality of the invited world. On the one hand, icons extend their invitation to the entire world. When Christ himself took a human body, he did not only take on human flesh; rather he took the entire created reality as his body which brings salvation to the whole universe, not only the humankind. On the other hand, iconographers use the materials of this world to depict the ineffable divine reality. Thus, icons are made of the corrupt materials of the world to transfigure the world. Some Orthodox theologians have gone even further to contend that the created world (despite its corruption) is an icon of the divine reality;[163] however, it is the responsibility of the faithful beholder to unveil the iconic dimension of the world.[164] In the same vein, every human being is an icon because she is created in the image of God. It is the liturgical practice of the Orthodox Church to cense those who are attending any liturgical service (whether they are Orthodox or not) along with censing the icons mounted inside the church building; censing venerates the eschatological reality of the icons and the eschatological aspirations of those who are attending.

Therefore, using an iconic *phronema* in bioethical discourse would necessarily expand the mission of bioethics beyond its current narrow agenda. Bioethics was meant to connect the biological sciences (bio-) to the moral heritage of the humankind (ethics). The ultimate way to bridge these two dimensions is the icon, because only the icon unfolds the ultimate meaning (*logos*) of creation while deeply understanding its current—fallen—status. In perceiving the current world through the lens of icons, the Orthodox Church cannot ignore the prevailing iniquities.[165] Clearly, the world is plagued by corruption and death. Suffering and injustices are everywhere. Pluralistic perspectives are the norm, while interdependence among various groups is unavoidable. Strangeness in the world is the result of human fallenness rather than the result of purely rationalistic disagreement. In a globalized world, human vulnerability is frequently exploited, and environmental degradation is threatening

---

163. Chryssavgis, "World of the Icon," 35–43.

164. Clément, "Science and Faith," 120–27; Chryssavgis, "World of the Icon," 35–43.

165. Chryssavgis, "Orthodox Spirituality," 130–38.

the survival of humans and other species. An iconic *phronema* takes on the responsibility to extend a divine invitation to save the entire created reality. Similarly, an authentic Orthodox bioethics cannot overlook the plight of the human race and the environment and dwell upon the narrow agenda of mainstream bioethics. An iconic *phronema* has to be hospitable/inclusive.

The Hospitable Dimension of Icons

As a window open to the uncreated divine reality, icons are hospitable; icons are constantly open toward and inviting to the entire world through a converted, microcosmic beholder. A converted beholder is a beholder who is willing to change her mindset through repentance to acquire a new *phronema* toward the world.

Because of the liturgical place of the icon in Orthodox worship, icons are invitations extended to a community of believers rather than to isolated individuals.[166] An iconic *phronema* is dynamic since it is shaped within the community's lively experience of the Lord. Thus, it does not seek dogmatic certainty; it breaks away from rigid conservative demands and seeks to have a meaningful and dynamic experience of the Lord. An iconic *phronema* is not a dogmatically correct endeavor but a constantly repentant human experience of the *eschata*. Hence, an authentic Orthodox bioethics does not search for normative directions with dogmatic certainty; rather it is a constantly repentant project aspiring to participate in the divine realm.

At a practical level, starting from an iconic *phronema*, Orthodox bioethics can only work on one variant, namely the converted beholder of the icon. Orthodox bioethics shapes the *phronema*, the perspective, and the actions of the faithful person to espouse an iconic agenda, namely saving the entire world. Only the converted and mindful beholder of icons can extend a hospitable invitation toward the entire world. As a microcosm, a human person can bridge the gap between the created world and the Creator.[167] Therefore, a deep anthropological understanding of the human experience of disease and dying is necessary for bioethics to overcome the current reductionistic rational impasse and to address rising global dilemmas.

166. Guroian, "Seeing Worship as Ethics," 332–59.
167. Harakas, "Integrity of Creation and Ethics," 27–42.

Starting from a theocentric anthropology, Orthodox bioethics is *theonoumic* in that the invitation to save the world is freely extended by God. The invitation is not theocratic; it cannot enforce a certain universal morality. It rather leaves a space for humans to be free as created co-creators. Moreover, the iconic invitation to save the world extends the responsibility of the faithful beholders to reveal the eschatological reality to those who do not know it. Such revelation is not judgmental but occurs through genuine Christ-like love and mercy. A genuine iconic *phronema* is aware of the deepest needs of the human being so it bears the responsibility to unfold the common anthropological ground to address ethical dilemmas. St Gregory of Nyssa (fourth century), for instance, emphasizes the anthropological commonalities between slave-owners and their slaves; an idea that can be extended to our time when differences among humans should not overshadow their commonalities. Gregory contends: "… you who are lord and the one subjected to lordship are to an equal extent dominated by the passions of soul and body: pain and good cheer, joy and sadness, grief and pleasure, anger and fear, sickness and death. Is there any difference in these matters between the slave and the lord?"[168]

As a result, an authentic Orthodox bioethics should be at the forefront of global bioethics discourse to highlight the common anthropological ground of the experience of life and death.[169] An Orthodox bioethics should also be activist in that it aspires the hospitable iconic *phronema* to tend to the needs of the most vulnerable human beings. It is missiologically prophetic in that it brings the Good News to the entire world by clarifying the misunderstood concepts in mainstream bioethics. On the one hand, this mission is propelled by a vulnerable love that is open to dialogue with the different other.[170] On the other hand, it is the responsibility of the royal priests of the community to show the face of Christ in the midst of a politicized bioethical discourse.

For instance, rather than perceiving freedom as the freedom of the market, an Orthodox bioethics emphasizes the ascetic freedom of those who perceive the world as an icon.[171] Similarly, rather than pursuing a bioethics that is a legalistically binding enterprise, an authentic Orthodox

---

168. As quoted in Harrison, "Gregory of Nyssa," 338.
169. Hamalis, "Eastern Orthodox Ethics," 1525–35.
170. Duraisingh, "Christian Mission in a Pluralistic World," 207–18.
171. Chryssavgis, "Orthodox Spirituality," 130–38.

bioethics brings Christ to the world through mercy and compassion.[172] Ultimately, Orthodox bioethics condemns extreme positions because they imbed distorted premises, such as the idolization of biological life or individual autonomy in the clinical setting. Both cases negate the divine providence to save all humans and eliminates the Orthodox genuine hope in resurrection at the deathbed.[173]

Conclusion

In short, it is the responsibility of the Orthodox Church to take the three callings of Christ, as the king, the prophet, and the priest to develop a working plan to effectively engage in the global bioethics discourse. The rest of this book will argue that Orthodox theology offers a constructive understanding of three moral concepts which resonate with other value systems and religious traditions. Derived from the three-fold vocation of Christ, these concepts are so organically connected that any one of them cannot stand alone. Parallel to Christ's kinghood, prophethood and priesthood, the relation between human dignity, human vulnerability, and hospitality (*philoxenia*: the love of the stranger) underscores the dynamism of global bioethics as a project and opens the door for constructive and substantive dialogue in health and medicine. Yet, these moral concepts do not offer final answers to all bioethical dilemmas at a global level; they are a starting point for further meaningful discourse at that level.

---

172. Clément, "Orthodoxy and Politics," 1–6.
173. Guroian, *Life's Living*, xiii–xxvii; Soelle, *Suffering*, 151–78.

4

The Meaning of Human Dignity
A Systematic Interpretation

In this chapter, the discussion focuses on the first concept advocated for an inclusive Orthodox Christian bioethics and as a basis for a common ground in global bioethics, namely, human dignity. The foundations of human dignity in Orthodox theology and in secular bioethics will be demonstrated. The goal is to promote a substantive and globally sensitive bioethics which nourishes gratitude in health care. Ultimately, gratitude should play a major role in shaping both the clinical encounter and medicine as an enterprise.

The Theology of Human Dignity in Orthodox Bioethics

I will briefly reiterate in this section the theological themes, explored in chapter 2, to establish an Orthodox Christian understanding of human dignity. As a result, several principles will emerge to constructively engage in the global discourse of bioethics.

A Christocentric Hermeneutics for Human Dignity

Respecting human dignity occupies a prominent place in Orthodox Christian theology. The creation of humans in the image and according to the likeness of God is the basis of respecting human dignity. As the prototype for all humanity (a prominent idea among various Christian denominations),[1] Christ executes a threefold vocation which should shape the mission of humanity, especially an Orthodox bioethics in a globalized world.[2] Respecting human dignity should hinge on the embodied and communal experience of sickness and suffering rather than on a misplaced emphasis on autonomous decision making.

Christ the King

Christ's kinghood derives from his being consubstantially united with God the Father and his involvement in the creation of the entire universe before all ages.[3] Adam and Eve were both created in the image of Christ (Genesis) who will later incarnate of the Virgin Mary, taking on the entire human nature, save the sin, to save humanity. Christ re-establishes the possibility of communion with God which was lost because of the ancestral disobedience. Through his salvific providence, including crucifixion and resurrection, Christ reiterates the original dignity with which God has created humanity.[4]

The Creation Narrative

In chapter 2, three lessons emerged from the Orthodox reading of the creation narrative in Genesis 1–3. First, the narrative emphasizes the special place of humanity in God's economy. Although Adam was made out of the dust of the ground (*adama*), God formed Adam by an active action—rather than by a simple order—and "breathed into his nostrils the breath of life" (Gen 2:7) giving him dominion over all other creatures. God intended for Adam to be a steward of his land, rather than to selfishly exploit it. Further, whereas in ancient religions only kings were divine, divine royalty was bestowed upon all humans in the Old Testament by the virtue of being created in the divine image.[5]

---

1. Koterski, "Human Nature," 809–39.

2. Louth, "Orthodox Dogmatic Theology," 253–67; Bouteneff, "Christ and Salvation," 93–106

3. Yannaras, *Freedom of Morality*, 89–107.

4. Bouteneff, "Christ and Salvation," 93–106; Lossky, *Mystical Theology*, 114–34; Lossky, *In the Image*, 111–23, 125–39, especially 211–27.

5. Harrison, *God's Many-Splendored Image*, 89–106; Barilan, "From Imago Dei," 231–59.

Second, because of the common origin of the entire humanity in the anonymous man, Adam, human unity in his person precedes human diversity.[6] Even the creation of Eve out of the side of Adam demonstrates the inseparable origin of both genders and their equal dignity in the divine perception.[7] A Triune God inspires a trinitarian communion among human beings who are created in the divine image; it is ultimately the entire humanity that bears the image of God rather than an isolated individual.[8] Hence, to achieve the sought God-likeness, humans need to engage in authentic communal relationships to conform their identities to that ideal.[9]

Third, because of the ancestral disobedience, human communion with God was severed leading to alienation from God and from each other. This alienation epitomizes the root of the current human condition of estrangement and enmity.

In the Divine Image and According to the Divine Likeness

It was noted earlier that the divine image is, innately and inalienably, ingrained in human beings and manifests at several dimensions.[10] Contrary to the narrow modernist emphasis on rational human faculties, church fathers discuss many attributes that are analogically similar to divine attributes. However, clearly in their writings, none of these attributes exhaustively recapitulate the divine image in all human beings.[11] These qualities include freedom and responsibility, spiritual perception and communion with other humans and God, and virtues and royal dignity, along with cultural creativity in the arts and sciences. Whereas modernity emphasizes rationality and freedom of choice as the highest human characteristics worthy of respect, church fathers and contemporary Orthodox theologians warn against their misuse. For instance, by trying to become gods without God, Adam and Eve misused their freedom and

---

6. Pentiuc, *Jesus the Messiah*, 5–24.

7. Harrison, "Gregory of Nyssa," 333–44; Behr, *Becoming Human*, 72–83; Lossky, *In the Image*, 169–81, 183–94; Lossky, *Mystical Theology*, 114–34.

8. Harrison, *God's Many-Splendored Image*, 169–84.

9. Bobrinskoy, "God in Trinity," 49–62; Lossky, *In the Image*, 97–110.

10. Harrison, "Human Person," 78–92.

11. Lossky, *In the Image*, 125–39; Kraynak, "Human Dignity," 61–82.

chose to disobey the divine command (Gen 3:5).[12] Likewise, contemporary misunderstanding of freedom to mean "market freedom" departs from the ascetical dimension of freedom which hinges on liberation from selfishness, greed, and consumerism. Indeed, without a full understanding of the universal divine providence and the human condition, many of the divine-like attributes are open to abuse, to the detriment of the entire human race.

Eventually, many church fathers contend that the *nous*, the spiritual perception (according to the Holy Spirit) or the higher appreciation of the *logoi* of the created world, is the "focal point of the divine image."[13] Without such noetic perception, one cannot appreciate the divine realities depicted on icons, neither can she perceive the imprinted divine image in every other human being. Therefore, those whose noetic perception is illumined bear a grave responsibility; they must perceive in others the inalienable image of God regardless of how alienated from God those others may seem. Those who are closer to the likeness of God because of their illumined *nous*, ought to perceive God as present in the created world, rather than condemn the world for being estranged from God.

Only through an illumined perception can one see the human condition as a common ground to respect the dignity of other humans. St Gregory of Nyssa (fourth century) demonstrates, in forceful words, the equality of lords and slaves by saying: "… you who are lord and the one subjected to lordship are to an equal extent dominated by the passions of soul and body: pain and good cheer, joy and sadness, grief and pleasure, anger and fear, sickness and death. Is there any difference in these matters between the slave and the lord?"[14] This equality expands beyond lords and slaves to apply to all human beings regardless of their differences and religious backgrounds. Therefore, religious communities bear the responsibility to nourish an ethos that instills the respect of human dignity through genuine personal rapport with those who are different.[15]

Notwithstanding the fallen human condition, the potential to grow in God's likeness brings hope to humanity. While the inalienable divine image is the basis for respecting dignity, the potential of divine likeness

---

12. Harrison, "Human Person," 78–92. Lossky, *In the Image*, 211–27.
13. Harrison, "Human Person," 78–92.
14. As quoted in Harrison, "Gregory of Nyssa," 338.
15. Jonker, "Learning the Spirit," 224–40.

leaves room for dynamic improvement of the human condition.[16] It is through ascetical practices, though, that humans are able to achieve *theosis*, becoming Christ-like. With this in mind, *theosis* inspires the mission of the Orthodox Church in the contemporary globalized world,[17] certainly in regard to bioethical discourse. Being a microcosm, humanity in general, and the Orthodox Church in particular, strives to bridge the existential gap between the created and divine realities; it is through the merciful and loving reign of God that this is possible (as it is succinctly captured in the Lord's prayer: "Our Father . . . Thy kingdom come . . .").

Human Dignity and Humanity's Mission

Pursuing Unity as Microcosm

The patristic heritage of the Orthodox Church emphasizes that humans are microcosms in that they stand between the divine and created realities, trying to bring them together. Although our human ancestors failed to do so because of their disobedience, Christ became man, so that he might bridge the existential gap between the two realities. Recent theologians extend the microcosmic mission of humanity. Whereas some theologians emphasize that humanity is a "macrocosm," a world writ large, others contend that the world is a "macro-*anthropos*," to highlight the human responsibility of bringing the entire universe back to God.[18]

Starting from this ultimate and unique human mission toward the universe, Orthodox theologians maintain that the unity of the created world is rooted in its createdness. Because of the human disobedience, as the book of Genesis narrates, the "goodness" and harmony of the created reality were disrupted; yet, the entire world stands in solidarity seeking God, the only source of life. It is the createdness of the world, including humans and all irrational creatures, that unites them in the presence of God rather than any rational human ability. If the unity of irrational created things is possible while seeking God—despite their lack of rationality—then it is unjustifiable to exclude the possibility of agreement among humans. Perhaps, the unrealistic emphasis on rational common ground hinders the effort at finding commonality across moral differences.

---

16. Harrison, "Human Person," 78–92.
17. Bouteneff, "Christ and Salvation," 93–106; Lossky, *In the Image*, 97–110.
18. Louth, "Orthodox Dogmatic Theology," 253–67.

Therefore, from an Orthodox theological perspective, it is warranted to pursue a common ground with other value systems building on realistic anthropological principles, including the inalienable worth of humans (for being created in the image of God), and the human potential of achieving *theosis* (God-likeness) despite their innate (but not divinely intended) fallenness. Starting from her genuine understanding of the human condition and rooted in a steadfast hope in divine philanthropy, it is incumbent on the Orthodox Church to stand in solidarity with all humans to confront post-modern uncertainties and injustices.

Orthodox Bioethics, Principles for a Global Discourse

Many important theological and anthropological principles have surfaced so far to shape the way in which the Orthodox Church should engage in global bioethical discourse. First, the human embodied experience is fundamental to any genuine discussion of bioethical dilemmas. The human body is essential to the divine image imprinted in all humans as emphasized in many church fathers,[19] and in Jewish exegesis of the creation narrative.[20] In the Orthodox understanding of *theosis*, asceticism does not aim at releasing the human soul from its bodily captivity. Rather, asceticism transforms the embodied experience and sublimates human natural (related to human nature) needs toward their original God-intended purpose.[21] Above all, following Christ does not imply "becoming other-worldly" or bodiless.[22]

Second, authority and dominion are not the only human values which derive from the divine image. Rather, human freedom and dominion over the natural world interweave into a synergic cosmology wherein humans are invited to be co-creators with God. Hence, human dominion comes with a responsibility that hinges on a different understanding of God's authority and justice. Within the Eucharistic experience of the Orthodox Church, divine authority and justice come with an immeasurable divine sacrifice; a sacrifice that is incomparable to any human sacrifice. Humans should emulate this sacrifice rather than only

---

19. Harrison, "Human Person," 78–92; Ciulinaru, "Anthropology of the Holy Fathers," 182–89.
20. Barilan, "From Imago Dei," 231–59.
21. Wirzba, "Priestly Approach," 354–62.
22. Behr, *Becoming Human*, 102–9.

claim an unhindered freedom over their lives.[23] In the face of transhumanist aspirations, for instance, an Orthodox perception emanates from authentic anthropological realism. Although a pursuit of God-likeness may aspire medical interventions to improve human technical abilities, these interventions would become available only to a few due to their cost, for instance. This raises a serious concern for social justice, specifically when affordability could deprive some humans of the hope of becoming "God-like" (or trans-human in its narrow meaning). Similarly, medical transhumanist interventions promise to technically perfect an already mortal human existence rather than attempt to transcend the human nature beyond its limitations.[24]

Furthermore, Hatzinikolaou advocates a spiritual bioethics which respects the dignity of every human life while being mindful of the inevitable limitation because of death.[25] He argues that human worth is not rooted in a wealth of rights to protect individualistic desires and needs. Rather, he unmistakably emphasizes that respecting human worth hinges on the willingness of society to embrace its most vulnerable members when their dignity is attacked. Therefore, the previous chapter emphasized that an authentic bioethical *phronema* should humbly seek the amelioration of human suffering through active solidarity rather than through pursuing perfectionistic rational bioethical principles.

Generally speaking, the human experience of life takes precedence over rationalistic formulations of bioethical principles. On the one hand, according to Orthodox spirituality, the humble acceptance of nofinal answers to all bioethical dilemmas does not disqualify tentative answers from being authentic to the Orthodox tradition. It is enough to remember that *theosis*, the ultimate goal of Christian life, necessitates persistent, humble, and repentant strife to achieve God-likeness, rather than a flawless pursuit of perfectionist sainthood. Saints, in the Orthodox Church, are those who are humbly repenting everyday rather than those who are flawless. On the other hand, the core of Orthodox spirituality is the personal encounter of Christ in the liturgy. Thus, as explained in the previous chapter, dogmatic formulations cannot recapitulate, on their own, all the possible unique encounters with Christ. Dogmas, important as they are, cannot reveal static normative principles for bioethical dilemmas.

23. Bouteneff, "Christ and Salvation," 93–106.
24. Jackelen, "Image of God," 289–302; Körtner, "Human Dignity."
25. Hatzinikolaou, "Ethics of Dilemmas," 165–88.

Therefore, to explore meaningful and redeeming bioethical answers in a globalized world, only an ascetic and liberating spirituality which seeks the face of Christ can help. This dynamic/project mentality in bioethics is not unique to Orthodox theological deliberation; rather, authors from other religious traditions recognize the importance of a continued deliberation on ethical issues across religious and non-religious traditions.[26] Building on dynamic anthropological experience and the Orthodox understanding of human dignity, Orthodox bioethics cannot be a procedural and autonomic venture, whether at the internal ecclesial level or when addressing a broader audience.

In a critique of Engelhardt's version of Orthodox bioethics in the previous chapter, autonomous decision-making is shown to not be the only value in bioethics. Comparatively, John Breck clearly emphasized that an authentic Orthodox bioethics is *theonomic* in that it centers on God's authority and eagerness to redeem the entire universe. In a sect-like mentality, the inevitable alternative to a *theonomic* bioethics is a theocratic one in which God is assumed to give clear normative directions in bioethics. In such a community of presumably like-minded believers, there is no place for the "glorious liberty of the children of God" (Rom 8:21). Further, Engelhardt's emphasis on autonomous decision-making misses the point, from a *theonomic* perspective, in that it subtly presumes an eternal human life or an absolute value for health. In general, Engelhardt's version of Orthodox bioethics builds on two dubious anthropological categories, "moral strangeness" and "culture wars." Both categories are not compatible with an authentic understanding of the human condition and the church's mission in a globalized world.

Eschatological Dimension of Iconic Phronema

At the end of the previous chapter, it was argued that an authentic Orthodox *phronema* for global bioethics today should be iconic, in that it is inspired by the place and meaning of icons in Orthodox theology. In such *phronema*, the eschatological dimension of icons is relevant to the discussion of human dignity.

By taking human dignity seriously, the eschatological dimension of Orthodox iconography highlights the hopeful message of the Christian faith; the potential of becoming like God is what keeps humans striving

---

26. Barilan, "From Imago Dei," 231–59.

with hope and trust. Hence, what gives meaning to the bioethical discourse is the human strife to achieve *theosis*, rather than an exclusive set of assumed meanings to moral concepts.[27]

On the one hand, the unifying principle of all humans, in a *theosis*-centered life, is the person of Christ, regardless of the prevailing religious diversity. The createdness of the universe unites all in their innate attraction toward God, the only giver of life. In the person of Christ, further, the created world is drawn toward unity, a unity that preserves the uniqueness of every person but transforms her into a Christ-like status.[28]

On the other hand, an eschatological dimension of icons permeates the world and shapes the faithful's mission toward those who bear the same divine image. While an Orthodox *phronema* recognizes the eschatological potential of every human being, it heeds the current human (and universal) condition of corruption, suffering, and death. Thus, an Orthodox bioethics ought not limit its mission to those who belong to the Orthodox Church but should be open to the anthropological reality of a globalized world.[29] The church's mission is "to create unity where there is division, to bring forth reconciliation where there is alienation, to heal and restore a sick and deprivated human nature, and to free persons from the spiritual and physical violence of evil."[30]

The Anthropological Implications of Human Dignity for Secular Bioethics

To further explore the concept of human dignity, I will briefly discuss its meaning and use within the prevalent philosophical framework and contemporary secular bioethics. This discussion will establish a non-religious support for its use in bioethical discourse as fundamental to the advocated common ground.

---

27. Boingeanu, "Personhood in Its Protological and Eschatological Patterns," 3–19.
28. Harrison, "Gregory of Nyssa," 333–44.
29. Bobrinskoy, "God in Trinity," 49–62.
30. Guroian, "Seeing Worship as Ethics," 347; Bouteneff, "Christ and Salvation," 93–106.

Human Dignity in a Secular Mindset

To understand the role that human dignity may play in global bioethics, I will start by briefly exploring its philosophical relevancy and historical development and its most recent use in advocating human rights.

Difficulties of Human Dignity Discourse

The use of the concept of human dignity in moral discussion encounters many difficulties. Regardless of the various meanings connected to dignity, the idea of a special value/worth for human beings, collectively or individually, is problematic. Starting with these difficulties will help sort through the various meanings of dignity and their use in global bioethics.

One of the fundamental problems with human dignity is that humans cannot realistically judge their own worth. It is a delicate issue for humans to objectively decide their worth vis-à-vis other species, especially when human limitations and ephemeral existence are to be considered. Comparatively, exaggerated self-appreciation on the side of humans may lead to arrogance and unhindered exploitation of others (of less worth) and natural resources. Therefore, contenders of the use of human dignity in moral discourse maintain that humankind is not different from other animal species and uphold that human atrocities throughout history disqualify them from having any special worth. For instance, in case of abuse, attributing an equal worth to victims and their victimizers is disheartening.[31] Moreover, if humans were to have a special worth because of their abilities, attributes, or achievements, social inequalities and varying innate talents unavoidably intensify a sense of unequal dignity. If different individuals unequally contribute to human flourishing, it may be tempting to treat them unequally due to their merit. Hence rises the challenge to balance between a universal and equal worth for all humans and the unique value of every individual.[32]

As a moral value, human dignity encounters other kinds of criticism.[33] On the one hand, some assert that human dignity is not a universal value as its advocates claim. Different cultures adopt different codes of honor and self-worth. Some cultures may attribute honor to certain

---

31. Kateb, *Human Dignity*, ix–xiii, 1–27.
32. Kateb, *Human Dignity*, 174–217.
33. Rosen, *Dignity*, 1–62.

behaviors that are abhorred in others. This highlights the difference in the cultural understanding of what matters most for a dignified human life. On the other hand, some authors are skeptical of its contribution to moral discourse. Critics of dignity contend that it does not add anything new to moral discussions; dignity is only a reiteration of other moral arguments. Some uphold that respecting human dignity is not any different from respecting the autonomy of the pertinent individuals.[34] For other critics, dignity is a laden concept that is influenced by various external political, economic, social, and religious factors; this excludes the possibility of a meaningful use for universal moral discourse. Since dignity grows out of a religious ethos (especially a Judeo-Christian one), some critics avoid its use in a pluralistic and global society.[35]

Preliminary Considerations of Difficulties

Although several of these difficulties may seem legitimate, further consideration of them is warranted before a detailed exploration of the meaning of human dignity and its role in ethical discussions.

On the one hand, one should acknowledge the religious roots of the concept of human dignity. Those roots in Christian theology were discussed in the previous section. Besides, contemporary Western understanding of dignity derives from the concept of the "sanctity of human life" as understood in Judeo-Christian tradition. Hence, re-integrating those religious dimensions into mainstream ethical discourse would arguably enrich the discussion of human dignity and its application in a pluralistic society.[36] However, since all established religious traditions attribute special worth to human beings for various metaphysical reasons, it is not justifiable to limit a religious input into dignity to the Judeo-Christian heritage.

On the other hand, the value of human dignity is universal despite any possible controversies regarding its meanings and applications.[37] Dignity is an umbrella concept similar to freedom, love, justice, and

---

34. Macklin, "Dignity," 1419–20.

35. Barilan, *Human Dignity*, 1–22; Pinker, "Stupidity of Dignity," 28–31.

36. Gelernter, "Irreducibly Religious Character," 387–405; Barilan, *Human Dignity*, 1–22; Kraynak, "Human Dignity," 61–82.

37. Johnson, Jung, and Schweiker, "Introduction," 1–16; Schulman, "Bioethics and the Question," 513–39.

integrity in that it is intuitively understood but may not be clearly defined.[38] Because of that, many communities are emotionally invested in, and morally committed to, preserving human dignity.[39] Notwithstanding human atrocities, humanity is ultimately different from all other natural species. Humanity's stature makes humans stewards of the entire natural universe since they are "only partly natural."[40] Humans break with the natural world because of their innate ability to care for it over many generations. Human language and rational abilities are the tools which make this possible through recording, understanding, and appreciating the natural world with a sense of gratitude for existence.[41] Such partly natural status of humanity resonates with the previously discussed microcosmic mission of humanity as understood in Orthodox theology. Human stature is not only connected to humanity's relation to nature but is also tangible through human self- and other-awareness. Humans are unique in their ability to process ideas (ideational uniqueness), in their ability to shape their individual identity (idiographic uniqueness; unlike animals), in their being existentially unique as persons (existential uniqueness; they are immeasurably different from animals), and in their moral abilities as social creatures (ethical uniqueness). Even if humans may have evolved from other mammals, the genetic difference between them and their closest relatives in the animal kingdom is so drastic that the difference in abilities is immeasurable.[42]

Furthermore, the uniqueness of humanity as a species is equally applicable to every human being. It is arguable that no one individual can stand for the entire humankind whether she is an average person or an exceptional one. Although humanity in general is endowed with exceptional abilities and individuals do not equally contribute to human achievements, every human being has an innate and irrevocable worth.[43] George Kateb advocates this differentiation between humanity's stature and human status within a secular mindset; however, this differentiation

---

38. Rolston, "Human Uniqueness," 129–53. Barilan, *Human Dignity*, 1–22.
39. Barilan, *Human Dignity*, 93–147.
40. Kateb, *Human Dignity*, 1–27.
41. Kateb, *Human Dignity*, 113–73.
42. Rolston, "Human Uniqueness," 129–53; Kateb, *Human Dignity*, 1–27; Lee and George, "Nature and Basis of Human Dignity," 409–33.
43. Kateb, *Human Dignity*, 1–27.

resonates with the ideas of the early Christian anthropologist Nemesius of Emesa (fourth century).[44]

In general, the present-day idea of equal and universal human dignity has developed over a long period of time.[45] In the West, input from multiple traditions dating back to the Stoics shaped the place and meaning of dignity.[46] From the Stoics comes the universality of ethics regardless of religion, which puts all humans on equal footing in regard to their moral responsibility. In Judeo-Christian tradition, the creation of humans in the image and likeness of God highlights the universal and unique mission of humans and their metaphysical equality. Whereas Immanuel Kant was very influential in shaping modernity's moral discourse using human dignity, post-modern phenomenology along with universal threats to humanity (because of nuclear and mass destruction weapons, environmental degradation, and genetic manipulation) established human dignity as a basis for identity, solidarity, and compassion.

Notably, Kant was very influential in shaping the discussion of human dignity for modern ethical and philosophical discourse. In moral discussions, Kant is usually used to advocate respecting the autonomy of individuals as a sign of respecting their dignity. However, a deeper exploration of Kant's philosophical contribution unveils the frequent but unjustifiable abuse of his thought. For one thing, Kant restricted the meaning of dignity to refer only to human dignity, which prompted a general abandonment of other meanings of dignity. Kant also connected dignity to morality, making the two words interchangeable in certain contexts.[47] Further, by connecting dignity and morality to autonomy, he opened the door to a secular discourse on morality and dignity.[48]

Unfortunately, the consideration of autonomy as the sole criterion for morality and dignity betrays Kant's system of thinking and narrowly applies his categorical imperative, i.e., not treating humans as means to other ends. Kant's position on suicide highlights this disparity. While defenders of suicide (especially in the context of unbearable suffering) deploy Kantian autonomy as justification, Kant abhors suicide for being dishonorable. Kant does not exclude suicide for existential reasons, i.e.,

---

44. Ciulinaru, "Anthropology of the Holy Fathers," 182–89.
45. Rosen, *Dignity*, 1–62.
46. Barilan, *Human Dignity*, 23–92; Andorno and Pele, "Human Dignity."
47. Kateb, *Human Dignity*, 1–27.
48. Rosen, *Dignity*, 1–62; Andorno and Pele, "Human Dignity."

in that suicide annihilates the very person whose autonomy is being respected. Rather, permitting suicide betrays the duty to respect dignity, not only the dignity of those who are committing suicide, but also the dignity of those who permit it. Suicide is dishonorable to humanity; by disrespecting the humanity of others, we undermine the humanity in ourselves.[49] In short, Kant's account of respecting human dignity goes beyond the narrow respect of individual autonomy; there is more to human dignity than autonomous decision-making and free choices.

This brings the discussion to the meaning of freedom as a sign of human dignity.[50] Respecting the individual's freedom as a sign of respecting her dignity bears several meanings. (1) Being free evokes a sense of freedom from interference (negative freedom: to be left alone). (2) Similarly, being free demands a freedom from surveillance by authorities or others. More fundamentally, freedom demands (3) independence from a need for others to sustain one's life and (4) access to basic necessities while being able to act freely. (5) At the existential level, freedom demands an inalienable ability to shape one's own life without a reference to outside criteria. In this case, dignity is owed to people regardless of their fulfilling certain outside moral criteria or beneficially contributing to their communities.

For instance, if a person enhanced certain abilities he has, he will not become a better human being inasmuch as a winning athlete is not a better human being than all the rest.[51] In general, when discussing human dignity and autonomy, the above overlapping meanings of freedom should always be taken seriously. An autonomous and free choice is not only about the ability to choose from among numerous options; rather, a free choice presupposes an existential freedom to shape one's own life which necessarily requires the capability (material and aptitudinal) to do so. This capability can only be available within a caring community.

Meaning of Human Dignity

Building on the existential meaning of freedom, it is justifiable to think of human dignity as an existential value rather than as a moral value. This is because the personal identity of the involved individuals (and at large,

---

49. Rosen, *Dignity*, 63–128, 129–60.
50. Barilan, *Human Dignity*, 93–147.
51. Barilan, *Human Dignity*, 93–147.

every human being) is at stake. When an individual is treated with disrespect, her uniqueness is compromised, and she is considered, symbolically and actually, only as one more human being.[52] Here lies the root of many atrocities committed against humanity. This again brings to the front the balance between human stature as a species and the individual achievements of every human being. Whereas personal achievements are central to a sense of dignity (or pride), there is more to being treated with dignity than having a high self-esteem.

To strike this balance between the commonness of dignity and the importance of individual uniqueness, further unfolding of dignity is necessary. Through a meticulous study of the history of the concept, Michael Rosen explains that dignity has been used in different contexts to refer to more than a transcendental and worthy human kernel. He adopts four strands of meaning; his model is different from a classical model of expanding dignity to include more individuals.[53] Similarly, Daniel Sulmasy studies the different meanings of human dignity and how they apply to bioethical discourse.[54] Their two models correspond in the following manner. (1) The inherent value of human beings is the most-used meaning of dignity. This meaning corresponds to Sulmasy's category of intrinsic dignity; it refers to the innate value of every individual that is inalienable and irrevocable. (2) Dignity as status for Rosen corresponds with Sulmasy's category of attributed dignity; it refers to the value conferred on humans by their community for any given cultural reason. (3) Dignity as behavior, character, and bearing corresponds with Sulmasy's category of inflorescent dignity; it refers to the excellence achieved through behaviors, attributes, and attitudes which put the person in a respected position compared to others (without making him a better human being).

Sulmasy, furthermore, rightly highlights that, logically and linguistically, the intrinsic meaning of dignity is prior to the attributed and inflorescent meanings. Unless humans recognize and appreciate the intrinsic value of every human being, it would not be possible to recognize an attributed or inflorescent value in certain individuals.[55] Other scholars

---

52. Kateb, *Human Dignity*, 1–27.

53. Rosen, *Dignity*, 1–62.

54. Sulmasy, "Varieties of Human Dignity," 937–44; Sulmasy, "Dignity and Bioethics," 469–501.

55. Sulmasy, "Varieties of Human Dignity," 937–44; Sulmasy, "Dignity and Bioethics," 469–501.

recognize the difference between two values: the innate (basic) human value and the flourishing value; the latter is dependent on cultural and social contexts, is achievable, and may be withheld or distinguished.[56]

Whereas Sulmasy only includes these three categories of meaning, Rosen unfolds another strand that is usually taken for granted in any given human society. According to Rosen, one human practice across all cultures illumines the understanding of dignity: that is respecting human cadavers. Because it does not benefit anyone, respecting human cadavers through rituals stirs a moral dilemma (whether these rituals include cremation or interment). He argues that even the last living human being has a moral duty to respectfully bury the person who has just died. This radical and universal idea underscores that every person should be treated respectfully.[57] Rather than respecting human dignity by respecting certain "attributed" rights, Rosen contends that humans have a right to be treated respectfully; dignity requires respectfulness.[58] In his analysis, Rosen meets Y. Michael Barilan's emphasis on the universal taboo of homicide. Although Barilan starts from a biblical (Old Testament) perspective on human dignity, he highlights the universal prohibition of homicide and the general respect for human cadavers regardless of cultural differences.[59]

Barilan goes even further in discussing what the respect of human dignity means in a pluralistic global community where the language of human rights prevails. Barilan highlights four formal elements of human dignity: (1) universality, (2) equality, (3) primacy (dignity does not need to be condoned by an outside entity), and (4) inalienability and irrevocability.[60] He acknowledges the shift of moral discourse from being agent-centered (where emphasis was more on the agent's virtues and duties) to being recipient-centered (where emphasis is more on utility and rights).[61] However, Barilan defends a consideration of human rights as a tool within an ethos that is respectful to human dignity. The advocated ethos is sensitive to expanding circles of needs; meeting these needs is a sign of respecting human dignity. To show respect to any agent's dignity,

56. Rolston, "Human Uniqueness," 129–53.
57. Rosen, *Dignity*, 129–60.
58. Rosen, *Dignity*, 1–62.
59. Barilan, *Human Dignity*, 23–92, 93–147; Rosen, *Dignity*, 129–60.
60. Barilan, *Human Dignity*, 93–147.
61. Barilan, *Human Dignity*, 1–22. Similar to, Gelernter, "Irreducibly Religious Character," 387–405.

meeting (1) vital human needs and providing favorable circumstances (2) to pursue rational human goals and values and (3) to assert one's own freedom is quintessential. However, beyond the provision of these needs as a sign of respecting human dignity, Barilan discusses what he calls "residual dignity." He contends that residual dignity is respected in all cultures and is attributed to all humans and only humans. Respecting "residual dignity" is intuitive in many instances and is usually taken for granted, such as by giving names to infants at birth, by ritually burying human bodies (regardless of the ritual), and by covering the genitalia and keeping sexual activities private. The intuitive importance of residual dignity in shaping human communities underscores that morality goes beyond a narrow respect of individual choices.[62]

Disrespecting Human Dignity

Notwithstanding the possibility of a positive definition of dignity, it is much easier to discuss what degrades the dignity of a human being.[63] Although humiliating practices may be delineated differently in various cultures, they all violate human dignity. The most dangerous type of humiliation is the one that is practiced in the name of God or any metaphysical authority.[64] In these cases, and because of a self-referring certain acquisition of truth, humiliating others becomes subjectively justifiable.

It seems problematic to discuss the possibility of degrading human dignity (through certain actions) while at the same time emphasizing its innate and inalienable nature.[65] However, it is suggested that a dynamic understanding of dignity as necessarily embedded in a social context is warranted. A dynamic relation exists between dignity as a duty toward people, on the one hand, and dignity as an expectation of people, on the other. In the same vein, a sense of honor and self-worth is socially determined through relational and comparative valuation of traits and achievements. Such sense of honor and self-worth bridges the gap between the respect humans owe to others and the respect they expect from them.[66]

---

62. Barilan, *Human Dignity*, 93–147.
63. Rosen, *Dignity*, 63–128; Pellegrino, "Lived Experience," 513–39.
64. Churchland, "Human Dignity," 99–121.
65. Rosen, *Dignity*, 63–128.
66. Barilan, *Human Dignity*, 1–22.

Therefore, any self-awareness of pride, honor, shame, embarrassment, or humiliation is agent-centered; it may be provoked by different culture- or society-specific practices and norms. On the contrary, respecting human dignity is recipient-centered in that it is the responsibility of the beholder and the entire society to treat every member of that society with respect.[67] In other words, to respect human dignity, it is necessary to seriously take its relational dimensions within a caring social context rather than exaggerate the role of autonomous choices. To treat every member with dignity, it is arguable, is fundamental for any society, *qua society*, rather than promulgating a utilitarian and choice-centered understanding of dignity. Whereas every society sensitizes its members, as they grow up and integrate its values, to certain norms and practices, the social environment shapes an agent-centered sense of self-worth.[68] Hence, the former necessarily precedes the latter; society's respect to individuals precedes their sense of self-worth. This is the case even when some individuals, because of mental disability for instance, are not able to register any meaningful sense of self-worth.

Torture offers an edifying example of disrespect to human dignity. Regardless of the tools and methods used to execute torture, all practices humiliate and violate the dignity of the victim. Therefore, torture is abhorred not only for the associated and unnecessary pain but also for not recognizing the shared humanity between the persecutor and her victim.[69] Christianity, for instance, underscores the shared dignity between the torturer and her victim. With enthusiasm, early Christians faced death at the hands of their persecutors without betraying their faith in equal human dignity.[70]

Unfortunately, denying the humanity of victims has justified numerous human atrocities throughout recorded history. Genocidal propagandas everywhere focus on the less-than-human nature of their victims. Torturers necessarily dehumanize their victims to be able to execute them.[71] Practically, victims are dehumanized when, for instance, they are prevented from behaving in a dignified way, such as by forcing them to

67. Barilan, *Human Dignity*, 93–147.
68. Barilan, *Human Dignity*, 1–22.
69. Kateb, *Human Dignity*, 1–27; Soelle, *Suffering*, 61–86; Marcel, *Existential Background*, 136–53.
70. Kolbet, "Torture and Origen's," 545–72; Similar to Barilan, *Human Dignity*, 93–147.
71. Kolbet, "Torture and Origen's," 545–72.

defecate and urinate in their cells or by exposing their private parts (war prisoners frequently fall victims to dehumanizing treatment).[72] By the same token, torturers tell cold jokes to distract themselves from the brutality of their actions. While innocent humor and acrimonious satire frequently bear dehumanizing aspects, humor in the context of torture has a distracting effect away from brutality.[73] Humor is closely related to the experience of medical students in the anatomy lab, as will be discussed in chapter 6; for medical students, dehumanizing cadavers through humor is necessary to ameliorate the trying experience.

Furthermore, to the global bioethical discourse, two aspects related to torture and human suffering are paramount. First, because of degrading conditions, those who constantly suffer may stop registering the dehumanizing treatment they receive. They may stop perceiving themselves as respectable humans because of their persistent state of humiliation.[74] Second, witnesses of constant human suffering may stop being moved by dehumanizing and brutal treatment of other humans. In both cases, it is the collective responsibility of society to resist all humiliating practices and to mend all circumstances that strain dignity. In this vein, different societies and international entities have adopted the language of human rights as a safeguard to protect the dignity of every human being.

Human Dignity and Human Rights

By and large, the discourse of human dignity is ubiquitous and supported in various religious and nonreligious value systems. To ensure the validity of rights claims in a pluralistic world, United Nations' 1948 *Universal Declaration of Human Rights* adapted human dignity as its basis.[75] The use of dignity in this and similar international legal documents, it has been argued, play a heuristic role; the concept fosters a dynamic search for rights rather than introduces a clear-cut set of enforceable rights.[76]

In a legal context, human dignity may seem merely axiomatic in the sense that to specify a set of fundamental rights and enforce it is what

---

72. Rosen, *Dignity*, 63–128; Barilan, *Human Dignity*, 93–147.
73. Rosen, *Dignity*, 63–128, 129–60.
74. Kateb, *Human Dignity*, 1–27.
75. Andorno and Pele, "Human Dignity."
76. Hughes, "Concept of Dignity," 1–24.

matters in the end.⁷⁷ However, confusion in regard to the meaning and role of human dignity and rights may be attributed to their adoption into many national and international legal documents. Similar to many legal terms, dignity and rights are not clearly defined, are open to interpretation, and may solicit disagreement and confusion.⁷⁸ Notwithstanding the importance of dignity and rights in legal discourse, their legalization may be related, as referred earlier, to the shift from an agent-centered (virtue) to a recipient-centered (rights) discourse of ethics. However, reversing this trend and re-orienting the global moral discourse may not be attainable now.

Nonetheless, it is warranted to perceive the status of dignity discourse and its relation to human rights through a positive lens so that improving the human condition globally may be attainable. As previously discussed, Barilan defends an ethos respectful of human dignity which deploys human rights as an instrument to show respect. Yet, he admits, an ethos respectful of human dignity does not address all moral problems, and human rights discourse does not cover all dignity-related issues. At a general level, although the language of human rights is perceived as individual-centered, Barilan rightly emphasizes that rights derive their meaning and authority from the community within which they are applied.⁷⁹ Furthermore, human rights have a limited mission; they do not aim at achieving justice. Rather, rights should be limited to the provision of basic goods and to the respectful and equal treatment of every human being. In the final analysis, human rights discourse is not a moral doctrine; rather it is a tool within an ethos which safeguards the dignity of everyone.⁸⁰

An Orthodox Perspective on Human Rights

Here, I do not intend to offer a comprehensive discussion of the Orthodox Christian perspective toward human rights discourse. There are many authors who have discussed this issue within the national, political, and practical contexts where Orthodox Christians live.⁸¹ However,

77. Kateb, *Human Dignity*, 1–27.
78. Rosen, *Dignity*, 63–128.
79. Similar to Andorno and Pele, "Human Dignity."
80. Barilan, *Human Dignity*, 295–302.
81. Brüning and van der Zweerde ed., *Orthodox Christianity and Human Rights*.

for the sake of the argument of this book, it is warranted to highlight a positive Orthodox perspective toward human rights that is built on a robust theological basis.

A contemporary Orthodox theologian, Aristotle Papanikolaou, thoroughly examines the different trends among recent Orthodox theologians and church entities.[82] He ultimately opposes a suggested mutually exclusive relation between modern liberal notion of human rights and an Orthodox theological anthropology. His argument hinges on developing an Orthodox notion of personhood within the realism of divine-human communion.

Papanikolaou admits that contenders of the language of human rights are ambivalent due to its connection to atheistic humanism, its marginalization of Orthodoxy in its heartland, and its grounding in individual, a-relational, and solipsistic anthropology. He rightly debunks some of these presuppositions and emphasizes that the language of rights predates the Enlightenment and modernist humanism. He also gives theologically based arguments to explain that freedom, even to reject God, should be protected within a traditionally Orthodox country. Fundamentally, human rights are not individualistic *per se*, but are social in that they need a social context to be protected.[83]

At a general level, political communities, Papanikolaou believes, are necessary because humans have failed to relate to each other as God relates to each one of them. Political structures are hence inevitable because of the sinful and fallen human condition and out of fear of exploitation and abuse. Therefore, so long as the language of human rights defends the uniqueness and irreducibility of every human being, all Orthodox (and Christians in general) should support it. Although this language falls short from expressing all that humans are meant to become—from a theological perspective—it is still a good start for a pluralistic global community.

In short, the qualified compatibility between the language of human rights and Orthodox anthropology makes it possible, in global bioethical discourse, to find a common ground with other value-systems. By the same token, other Christians find themselves attracted to this language despite its shortcomings. Even if the language of human rights seems secular and is frequently abused, it is no excuse to abandon it; there is always

---

82. Papanikolaou, *Mystical as Political*, 87–130.
83. Similar to Barilan, *Human Dignity*, 295–302.

a possibility to find a Christian—or generally speaking, a religious—basis to profoundly respect every human being.[84]

Human Dignity for Secular Bioethics

The Politicization of Human Dignity in Global Health

The integration of human dignity in many national and international legal documents is used to defend various human rights. Because of the universal experience of illness and clear disparities in health around the world, human dignity was also deployed to defend certain universal rights in regard to health care. In the UNESCO's 2005 *Universal Declaration on Bioethics and Human Rights*, the interplay between human dignity (and vulnerability) and human rights language is very clear. Not only does human dignity shapes the global discourse related to health and illness, it also fashions the daily clinical encounter between patients and providers.[85]

Difficulties in Using Dignity in Health

Similar to the discussed difficulties with its general use, the concept of human dignity encounters several difficulties in the context of health care.[86] Contenders of its use in health care and bioethics emphasize that dignity does not bring anything new to the discourse; it only reiterates the principle of respecting the autonomy of patients.[87] However, dignity has an important moral meaning that is enriching to the bioethical discussion.[88] Even for the critics of the use of dignity in bioethics, a minimal and cautious respect of dignity is warranted. Dignity is critical to avoid mistreating vulnerable patients; lest a beholder be hardened by witnessing excruciating suffering, emphasizing patients' dignity is unavoidable.[89] Moreover, for contenders, dignity is rooted in the religious concept of sanctity of life which makes it unsuitable for the pluralistic practice of

---

84. Jeffreys, "Influence of Kant," 507–16.
85. Andorno and Pele, "Human Dignity."
86. Pinker, "Stupidity of Dignity," 28–31.
87. Macklin, "Dignity," 1419–20.
88. Sulmasy, "Varieties of Human Dignity," 937–44.
89. Pinker, "Stupidity of Dignity," 28–31.

medicine.[90] Similarly, because political, social, economic, and religious factors influence its meaning, the concept of dignity may be confusing to health care practitioners; there is no clear way to pinpoint what it demands of them.

A Unique Role for Dignity in Medicine

Notwithstanding these difficulties, it is still arguably necessary to pragmatically discuss the concept of dignity to unravel prevailing bioethical controversies,[91] especially when it is used to justify diametrically different positions, such as for and against euthanasia and physician-assisted suicide. Undoubtedly, respecting human dignity occupies an important place in the unique context of medical care.[92]

In the clinical context, patients do not choose to be sick and to seek medical attention. Although patients freely choose their provider or hospital (even if their choices are initially restricted depending on their insurance plan), they would prefer not to be ill in the first place. Further, by seeking medical attention to treat their ailment, they implicitly succumb to the power gradient embedded in medical provision. When a patient meets her doctor, she indirectly acknowledges that he knows more about her body than she does. More generally, this physician-patient encounter takes place within an institution (or at the fringes of an institution) which is governed by faceless administration and industry. These unknowable (to the patient) institutions make many decisions that may affect the "choices" and health of the patient, such as: what medication is covered by the insurance, which diseases are targeted in pharmaceutical development research, and the incentives offered to physicians to use a certain intervention . . . etc. Within this complicated—and hidden—web of relations and interests, the patient seems to be the most disenfranchised player, especially in that she did not "freely" choose to enter that web.

More important, different players are embedded within a cultural context that shapes their interactions. When the overarching culture highly values self-independence, control, and autonomy, medicine and health care conform in a way to serve those idols rather than their

---

90. Gelernter, "Irreducibly Religious Character," 387–405.

91. Churchland, "Human Dignity," 99–121; Sulmasy, "Dignity and Bioethics," 469–501; Pellegrino, "Lived Experience," 513–39.

92. Pellegrino, "Lived Experience," 513–39.

patients.[93] On the side of patients (and every human being), a culture that idolizes health accordingly shapes patients' self-esteem and their own sense of dignity.

Within the dire context of medicine, human dignity may be compromised for different reasons, or feel to be so. Whereas the internal worth of the person cannot be compromised regardless of the circumstances or the disease, in the context of illness, the ontological vulnerability of the patient and her sense of self-worth are exposed.[94] Being a "patient" is etymologically connected to vulnerability.[95] Besides, a dynamic relationship between what the patient demands to feel dignified and what the team offers in respect to her dignity is constantly at play. A patient will feel undignified when the medical team treats her as one more patient, as another case of heart failure, or as a room number.[96] Although these expressions may sound benign in the hectic environment of a hospital unit, they deprive a patient of her sense of uniqueness as a dignified human being.

Aside from the clinical context, patients bring along their cultural beliefs which mold their sense of self-worth. When a patient values her independence and autonomous decision making, she may feel worthless when she is not in control of simple things like bowel movement or when medications sap her clarity of mind. A patient's dependence on others may not be blamed for her sense of worthlessness; rather, one should blame the wide-spread cultural perception that autonomy is what makes humans dignified. Caring and compassionate relationships, by family members, medical teams, and the entire society, are what preserve a patient's dignity.[97]

These examples and many others show the fundamental relationship between dignity and vulnerability, especially in the context of health care provision.[98] As previously discussed, dignity is usually linked to the intellectual abilities and free will of humans. However, human dignity goes

---

93. Hilfiker, "Unconscious on a Corner," 3155.

94. Sulmasy, "Dignity and Bioethics," 469–501; Solbakk, "Vulnerability," 228–39; Marcel, *Existential Background*, 114–35, 136–53; Pellegrino, "Lived Experience," 513–39.

95. Andorno and Pele, "Human Dignity."

96. Dresser, "Human Dignity," 505–12; Marmot, "Dignity and Inequality," 1019–21.

97. Eibach, "Protection of Life," 58–77; Pellegrino, "Lived Experience," 513–39.

98. Andorno and Pele, "Human Dignity"; Marcel, *Existential Background*, 114–35, 136–53; Pellegrino, "Lived Experience," 513–39.

beyond autonomous decision making, especially when patients are most vulnerable due to the nature of their illness and the institutional context where they seek medical attention.[99] The experience of vulnerability underscores the universality of the human condition as ailing and fragile contrary to the mainstream moral relativism in bioethics.[100] As dignified but vulnerable beings, humans have more in common because of their affliction than when they rationally agree on particular moralities.

Human Dignity and Transhumanist Medical Interventions

As previously discussed, the transhumanist aspirations of some thinkers may be related to a certain understanding of religious thought concerned with improving the human condition. However, even within a secular mindset, transhumanist aspirations challenge medicine when it is used as a tool to fulfill these aspirations, especially because of their possible impact on human dignity. It is hoped that accumulated medical and scientific knowledge will help improve the human body, its longevity, its immunity against certain diseases (and probably death), and physical and intellectual abilities (such as sport performance and unaided computing abilities). To advance their agenda, transhumanists usually refer to the ubiquitous methods currently in use to improve human abilities such as vaccines, coffee, and education . . . etc. However, when transhumanist interventions meddle with genetic makeup, some of these improvements may become "innate" to evolving human (or trans-human) beings.

Regardless of the success prospect of these interventions and the arguments used for and against them, one aspect is still relevant: the dignity of the human species in its current condition and the dignity of the evolving trans-human species.[101] In academic discussion of transhumanism, scholars are divided between three camps in this regard. Some believe that enhancement threatens human dignity, while others believe that it may contribute to dignity. Others, however, prefer to frame the

---

99. Barilan, *Human Dignity*, 23–92; Benner, "When Health Care," 119–35; Soelle, *Suffering*, 151–78; Kass, *Life, Liberty*, 231–56.

100. Turner and Dumas, "Vulnerability, Diversity," 663–70; Andorno and Pele, "Human Dignity."

101. Rubin, "Human Dignity," 155–72.

discussion about transhumanism away from those two possibilities and advocate a cautious acceptance of some enhancement.[102]

As previously discussed, nothing that humans do will affect their innate and inalienable worth. The intrinsic value is equal for a rising athlete, a brilliant scholar, and a mentally challenged newborn. They all deserve to be treated respectfully as unique human beings regardless of their achievements or the lack thereof. Thus, any projected improvement of the human species through genetic intervention or enhanced interaction with machines (implanted memory chips, for instance) would not yield better-than-human species; the evolving humans have enhanced abilities but not more dignity or worth.

However, because of the social nature of human dignity, as has been highlighted several times, further challenges arise because of the projected transhumanist changes. When transhumanist improvements become available, one challenge to the dignity of many humans will be related to the just distribution of enhancing technologies and the public perception toward those who are not "enhanced." Such challenge is similar to when an athlete, for being an athlete, is treated with special care compared to another patient who is ignored for not being a celebrity. The underlying discrimination contradicts the duty of health care professionals to treat every patient with dignity. If a trans-human with super-powers is admitted to the hospital, it is questionable if he will be treated with equal respect compared to other "human" patients. If a culture evolves that idolizes super-powers (its roots are already growing in contemporary culture), it would be expected that such a culture would perceive more worth in those who have such powers. In the same vein, if enhancements become available, it is uncertain who will be able to afford them. The already wide gap in access to basic health care between different nations and within the same nation threatens to become even wider.[103] This will add another dilemma to the persistent question of justice in health.[104] Notwithstanding the importance of these questions, one concern remains in regard to the dynamics between medical practice and human dignity to answer the following questions: what is the role of the

---

102. Lebacqz, "Dignity and Enhancement," 51–62.
103. Turner et al., "Vulnerability, Diversity," 663–70.
104. Daniels, *Just Health*, especially 333–55.

concept of dignity in shaping medicine? And what is the role of medicine in defending human dignity?[105]

In the next section, a connection between human dignity and gratitude will be established. It will also defend a practical role for gratitude in shaping medicine in a global world.

A Systematic Interpretation of Human Dignity for Global Bioethics: The Role of Gratitude

To further the discussion on the practical dimensions of respecting human dignity, I will embrace gratitude as a proper virtue for dignified humanity. Gratitude should shape medicine as an enterprise and during the clinical encounter. In a globalized world where human beings of various backgrounds come into contact as never before, national and cultural boundaries are far less significant, especially in medical practice. When facing human vulnerability and inevitable death, human dignity highlights the role of gratitude in shaping the ethical discourse.

Gratitude for Entangled Human Lives

Social Construct for Gratitude

Human dignity is necessarily socially constructed. Many social factors and entities, near and far, play a role in respecting the dignity of individuals and in fostering a healthy sense of self-worth. Hence, dignity can be thought of as a social gift. While dignity is innate to every human, it can only flourish and be recognized within a social context.[106] Recognition here does not mean that dignity needs to be approved by others or that a person needs to have certain qualifications to be considered worthy of respect. Rather, a nourishing social context is paramount for a person to grow a healthy sense of self-worth. Conversely, in isolation, dignity and its respect are meaningless since human linguistic ability to construct meaning is necessarily embedded within a community. If a person is born into a community that enslaves her since birth (or treats her with disrespect), she will grow with a limited understanding of self-worth (yet without being deprived of dignity).

---

105. Andorno and Pele, "Human Dignity"; Hilfiker, "Unconscious," 3155.
106. Pellegrino, "Lived Experience," 513–39.

In this manner, every society bestows on (ideally) every member a gift of understanding and respecting dignity. In other words, when a given society respects the dignity of its members, those members are expected to show gratitude toward society and to pay it forward through respecting the dignity of others. Through a sense of gratitude, every member of the society recognizes her existential dependence on other members; even a true understanding of personal freedom and autonomy entails a recognition of one's dependence on others.[107] Being on the recipient side of a gift, especially if the gift is the ability to recognize one's own worth as a dignified human being, brings along several obligations. These obligations are toward God (who bestowed this innate dignity, if a theistic understanding of dignity is adopted), toward one's neighbors (in the form of paying forward the generosity of others), and toward one's own self (in the sense that one has an obligation toward one's own self to show respect to others).[108]

In the same vein, if gratitude (or any of its derivative virtues: humility, compassion, and forgiveness)[109] does not play a role in one's way of life, one would "lack a quality or capacity of humanly definitive spiritual and moral significance."[110] Having gratitude toward the surrounding social matrix, one recognizes the importance of gratitude at two levels at least: first, gratitude is essential to know one's self and limitations; second, without gratitude, one is inclined toward "personal alienation and social isolation."[111]

Preliminary Definition of Gratitude and Its Role

To advance the role of gratitude in shaping bioethical discourse, it is warranted to start with a working definition of gratitude. This definition will be revised and expanded to support the general argument of this book. However, initially, a basic definition will show the fundamental need for gratitude in a deeply entangled human life, especially when it pertains to medicine and health.

---

107. Lawler, "Modern and American Dignity," 229–52; Martinsen, *Care and Vulnerability*, 71–121.

108. Dolff, "Obligation to Give," 119–39.

109. Bono and Odudu, "Promoting the Development of Gratitude," 185–98.

110. Carr, "Counting Blessings," 179.

111. Emmons, "Is Gratitude Queen," 141–53.

Gratitude is defined as a "positive emotional response of a beneficiary directed to a benefactor for benefits provided intentionally to the beneficiary." This definition is usually broadened to include those cases when a benefactor attempts (or intends) to provide a benefit, whether he was successful or not.[112] Three conditions are usually adopted: "That gratitude ought to be a response to a benefit (. . . or an attempt to . . .), a benefit given from an appropriate motivation (usually benevolence), and a benefit that was either wanted or accepted by the beneficiary." These conditions are rightly challenged by Patrick Fitzgerald (see next section).[113]

Building on this narrow definition only, any community member clearly thrives because of the generosity and kindness of others. One is born into a family whose members provide all material and emotional needs for a healthy and productive citizen to grow.[114] Without the generosity of a family, one may not have existed in the first place. Further, each member of this family depended while growing up, and continues to depend at any given time, on her interaction with her surroundings to receive her basic needs (such as food, shelter, and other essentials to sustain life). Without these cooperative, interdependent relationships, no community would thrive. Thus, while many social interactions may seem contractual at the surface, they are actually embedded in a fundamentally generous ethos; benefits or goods are more existential gifts than contractual exchanges. Within such an ethos, a good recipient of social generosity is a generous benefactor to others, who adopts gratitude as a way of life. At a deeper level, the dynamic between social generosity and gratitude is vital to society; gratitude helps shape a collective moral memory without which society would fall apart.[115]

Medicine without Borders

Similar to how human life itself is dependent on the generosity of many others near and far, the practice of medicine cannot be contained within the boundaries of certain institutions or countries. Thus, gratitude is

---

112. Fagley, "Construct of Appreciation," 70.

113. Fitzgerald, "Gratitude and Justice," 121.

114. Harrison, *God's Many-Splendored Image*, 169–84; Kass, *Life, Liberty*, 231–56; Cassell, *Nature of Suffering*, 158–75.

115. Camenisch, "Gift and Gratitude," 1–34.

advocated to shape the practice of medicine, research agenda, and the training of new practitioners. At three levels, health and medical practice are entangled for humans regardless of their geographical location; in many examples, some people are disempowered and undignified under the auspices of medicine.[116] These levels are as follows: at the level of establishing medical knowledge and research; at the level of medical and health-related practices; and at the level of medicine's role within the social and environmental contexts.

At the Level of Establishing Medical Knowledge and Research

This level includes all of the practices to acquire new medical information to advance medicine and preserve health. Numerous examples illustrate a medicine without borders at this level.

Searching for new drugs overlooks national boundaries.[117] Western pharmaceutical companies extract new drugs from plants that are indigenous to faraway countries. People of these countries are usually aware of their therapeutic benefits and have been using them for centuries. However, pharmaceutical companies usually patent the derivative medication and market it to their own nationals, sometimes without meaningful acknowledgement of the original users. Similarly, researchers sometimes use the genetic material from isolated human communities to gain priceless medical knowledge. Then, pharmaceutical companies patent pieces of these genes or develop interventions building on the acquired knowledge. However far the link between the genes and the developed intervention is, it would be morally dubious to not be grateful toward those who shared their genetic material.[118]

In the same vein, developing new vaccines that benefit only a few people without acknowledging the contribution of others is problematic. In 2007 for instance, Indonesia raised a valid point by holding off avian flu samples from the World Health Organization because of unequal distribution of the disease burden among various nations. While Indonesia,

---

116. Lebacqz, "Empowerment," 133–47. Personal experiences of this disempowering force of medicine is discussed in many books especially those written by doctors when they become patients, such as: Rosenbaum, *Taste of My Own Medicine*.

117. Many examples of Western companies developing medications from plants indigenous to different parts of the world are mentioned in Salim et al., "Drug Discovery from Plants," 1–25, and in, Veeresham, "Natural Products."

118. Hoffmann, "Benefit-Sharing," 246–56.

by gratuitously providing these samples, would help develop an effective flu vaccine, the vaccine might be only affordable to Western countries where it is developed.[119]

After new medications are discovered and developed, pharmaceutical investigation of their safety and effectiveness is sent offshore to developing countries. Although many international and local entities attempt to safeguard the autonomy and well-being of human participants, a great deal of exploitation takes place away from the eyes of international laws and moral principles. Such research benefits from lax regulations in these countries and from prevailing misconceptions about the nature of research in communities with minimal—if any—access to health care.[120]

Therefore, gratitude toward those who participated in research, whether autonomously or sometimes coercively, is the responsibility of those who benefit from these drugs daily. Without those faceless human subjects, the safety of many drugs could not have been established.

At the Level of Medical and Health-Related Practices

When practicing medicine in a globalized world, national borders are effaced, and the movement of knowledge, practitioners, and services brings unprecedented realities and challenges. For instance, organ transplantation to needy patients overlooks traditional boundaries between countries and creates a global—illegal—market for organ trade.[121] In 2007 for instance, it was estimated that 5 to 10 percent of annual kidneys transplanted around the world were provided by commercial living donors through trafficking. By the same token, transplant centers in destination countries attract clients from around the world while fueling the market of medical tourism in their communities.[122] Similarly, a market for surrogate mothers is tapping into the meager provision of health care in developing countries while—dubiously—promising marginalized women a way out of their misery.[123]

---

119. "Indonesia's Avian Flu Holdout," *New York Times*, February 16, 2007.
120. Petryna, *When Experiments Travel.*
121. Goodwin, *Black Markets.*
122. Budiani-Saberi and Delmonico, "Organ Trafficking," 925–29.
123. Lasker, "Surrogacy," 2760–67; Mukherjee, "Why altruistic surrogacy is impossible in India," *Asia Times*, November 3, 2016; Geeta Pandey, "India Surrogate Mothers Talk of Pain of Giving up Baby," *BBC News*, August 15, 2016.

Whereas medical knowledge and technologies are developed in Western countries, their application travels the world and shapes the lives of many in developing countries. In many places, medical knowledge has even contributed to the exploitation of vulnerable populations. In a similar manner, the migration of health care professionals from developing to developed countries, and within these countries from rural to urban areas, is detrimental to the health of many communities. Many factors play into the movement of health care workers along these routes, especially better compensation and opportunities. However, the detrimental effects of this trend go beyond any compensatory "pay back." By recruiting physicians from developing countries, for instance, developed countries can meet the needs of their own populations; yet, their migration is detrimental to the health systems in resource countries in a way that money alone cannot amend.[124]

Clearly from these examples, the practice of medicine in a globalized world is intertwined across national boundaries. They highlight the interconnectedness of human lives around the world, particularly pertinent to health care and medical practice.

At the Level of Medicine's Role within the Social and Environmental Contexts

Similar to the previous levels of medical practice, at this universal level, numerous factors related to the environment and social dynamics affect human health.[125] The existential interdependence among humans is embedded within a broader dependence of humans on the environment at large.

A basic need for food, for instance, underscores the reliance of every human not only on the generosity of those who produce food (through their labor) but also on the environment as a source for this food (including fertile soil, appropriate weather, and timely seasons). Thus, in face of this generosity, humanity is invited to sacrifice, asceticism, and gratitude. Although these requirements are usually discussed within a religious mindset, they are not foreign to what modern science has shown to be necessary. To protect the environment, self-denial and taming consumerist and controlling desires are warranted. In gratefulness for life itself,

---

124. Dwyer, "What Is Wrong" 36–43.
125. Farmer, *Pathologies of Power*, especially 51–90, 115–33.

humans would embrace each other with hospitality and become united in political solidarity as a species and with the entire creation.[126] Consequently, when environmental hazards are detrimental to the health of many, medical practitioners and institutions cannot, conscientiously, stand on the side. Regardless of how much medicine can cure sicknesses, it is more responsible and cost-effective to prevent these sicknesses through better public health measures such as through providing clean water, sanitary systems, and sufficient nutrition.[127]

At a more focused level, an ethical practice of medicine cannot exclude the social factors that affect health. As has been previously noted, mainstream bioethics in the US has ostracized those who criticized social injustices detrimental to health. It is arguable that bioethical discourse cannot be sufficiently pursued if restricted to the clinical encounter between physicians and patients. The social and cultural backgrounds of both parties should be seriously considered in order to fully understand the processes of disease and healing. Hence, an anthropological basis for modern medicine and bioethics is warranted to prevent possible atrocities committed in the name of advancing science.[128] Within a broader anthropological consideration of human illnesses as embedded in social and cultural contexts, medical practice will be more sensitive to the many dimensions of suffering. Furthermore, medical education will take a different route in shaping new practitioners (more to come in chapter 6).

For instance, notwithstanding the successful integration of narrative medicine into training, its presence in medical textbooks is still minimal, at least when presenting pathological cases. In general, patients are presented as puzzles to be solve, with their intriguing clinical presentation, rather than as full-fledged human beings with established histories. If pictures are included, they usually show the relevant lesion without the patient's face (or while covering her eyes) so that she becomes faceless. While these measures are propagated to protect patients' privacy, the parallel sacrifice in medical education is significant. By the same token, Eric Cassell highlights recent changes in preparing human anatomy books. He illustrates how contemporary anatomical illustrations de-humanize the cadaver; they depict a cadaver as only a tool to teach anatomy rather than as the body of a "real" human being.[129] Although these aspects of

---

126. Wirzba, "Priestly Approach," 354–62.
127. Dos Anjos, "Medical Ethics," 629–37.
128. Dos Anjos, "Medical Ethics," 629–37.
129. Cassell, *Nature of Suffering*, 176–213.

medical education may seem marginal to the nuts and bolts of treating diseases, they are indeed very important in shaping the ethos of new practitioners. They, along with other factors, are elemental in drafting a hidden curriculum that influences the quality of care future practitioners will provide to their patients (chapter 6 will further discuss these issues).

By and large, because of how entangled human life is, especially under the umbrella of medicine, it is arguable that gratitude should shape medicine as a profession (and the system that is built around it), and should influence the way medicine is practiced at the clinical level. Medicine as a profession should acknowledge and show gratitude toward the many generations of patients and research subjects who helped advance merdical knowledge, regardless of how far removed, physically and chronologically, these people may seem. In the next section, a broader understanding of gratitude will be adopted to argue that physicians have many moral reasons to show gratitude toward the patients they serve on daily basis.

Gratitude as a Sign of Dignified Humanity

Gratitude and Morality

Now that the entanglement of human life, especially in medical practice, is established, it is time to discuss gratitude itself and extend its applicability in medicine (to be discussed in chapter 6). The discussion of gratitude started in the previous section from a narrow working definition. Gratitude was defined as a "positive emotional response of a beneficiary directed to a benefactor for benefits provided intentionally to the beneficiary (or for the intention of providing a benefit)."[130] Beyond this definition, gratitude has three functions that are relevant to moral discussion. (1) Gratitude is a moral barometer in that it is a response to a perception of a benefit. (2) Gratitude is morally motivating in that it encourages the beneficiary to act pro-socially toward the benefactor and others. (3) Gratitude is therefore a moral re-enforcer in that it encourages the benefactor to behave morally in the future. In general, gratitude has a pro-social effect since it encourages those who enter a relationship of gratitude to act benevolently toward others.[131]

---

130. Fagley, "Construct of Appreciation," 70.
131. McCullough et al., "Is Gratitude a Moral Affect?," 249–66.

Gratitude has a prominent place in discussing morality and moral formation in various disciplines. It is appreciated in several religions, in philosophical discourse, and in positive psychology. One reason for this broad appreciation is that gratitude correlates with other positive values (virtues) and human qualities, such as humility, compassion, and altruism. These values and qualities are nourished more because of gratitude than because of a sense of social indebtedness or reciprocity.[132] In other words, gratitude has far reaching implications in morality and moral formation compared to mere indebtedness or reciprocity.

Gratitude in Religion

Gratitude is central to any religious mindset.[133] Regardless of the metaphysical system behind the religious tradition, gratitude grows out of the idea that humans are not the source of their existence and that they are indebted to some form of benevolent deity.[134] In Orthodox theology, humanity's kinghood derives from its being created in the image of God (as previously discussed); hence, out of gratitude, humans are expected to be stewards of the world as a divine gift. This manifests most clearly in the Eucharistic identity of the church. As a community of Eucharistic beings, the church constantly practices the sacrament of thanksgiving (eucharist) bringing back to God, with gratitude, the entire world as a "sacrifice of praise" (from the Anaphora).[135] It is not only in the Orthodox Church that gratitude occupies this central role in shaping the community, but also in other religious communities. Sufism, for instance, also adopts gratitude as central to its Islamic religious ethos.[136] In empirical research, a clear connection was found between gratitude and religiousness/spirituality.[137]

Religious communities are not the only ones to foster gratitude in society; psychologists and philosophers have also discussed the important

---

132. Camenisch, "Gift and Gratitude," 1–34.

133. Emmons, "Is Gratitude Queen," 141–53.

134. Emmons and Kneezel, "Giving Thanks," 140–48; Wirtz, Gordon, and Stalls, "Gratitude and Spirituality," 287–301; Schweiker, "Distinctive Love," 91–117.

135. Steenberg, "The Church," 121–35; Cyprian, "Christian Gratitude," 13–25.

136. Khalil, "On Cultivating Gratitude," 1–26; and Khalil, "Embodiment of Gratitude," 159–78.

137. Tsang and Martin, "Psychological Perspective," 154–68; Emmons and Kneezel, "Giving Thanks," 140–48; Wirtz, Gordon, and Stalls, "Gratitude and Spirituality," 287–301.

role of gratitude, irrespective of religious frameworks. Notwithstanding these independent disciplinary interests, a more interdisciplinary work on gratitude is still lacking.[138]

Gratitude in Psychology

Gratitude has a pro-social function. In the field of positive psychology, ingraining and nourishing gratitude are thought to be possible and desirable since gratitude is associated with more personal agreeableness and less narcissism. Gratitude, moreover, is one of the best predictors of individual well-being and thriving in any given society.[139] At the cultural level, gratitude helps balance the materialism and objectification that are rife in a consumerist society.[140] It goes as far as being essential for the flourishing of democracy.[141]

When gratitude motivates individuals to improve the well-being of other community members, these individuals indirectly contribute to their own well-being. Hence, for some scholars, the gift is not separable from the opportunity to give; this eliminates the need for the language of rights. While a beneficiary receives her due need because of an act of kindness on the side of a benefactor, the latter also benefits from the opportunity to give. As such, there should not be a need to use the demanding language of rights, because those who can give have an equal interest in giving compared to those who receive.[142]

Gratitude in Philosophy

In philosophical discussion, the mutual benefit to the benefactor and beneficiary is taken a step further. Historically, gratitude has a prominent place in philosophy because of its connection to the discussion of gifts.[143]

---

138. Davidson and Wood, "State of Psychological Research," 215–28.

139. McConnell, "Gratitude's Value," 13–26; McCullough et al., "Is Gratitude a Moral Affect?," 249–66; Emmons and Kneezel, "Giving Thanks," 140–48; Emmons, "Is Gratitude Queen," 141–53.

140. Bono and Odudu, "Promoting the Development of Gratitude," 185–98.

141. White, "Gratitude," 43–52; Jonas, "Gratitude," 29–46.

142. Dolff, "Obligation to Give," 119–39.

143. Camenisch, "Gift and Gratitude," 1–34; Konstan, "Freedom to Feel Grateful," 41–53.

Philosophers contend that gratitude goes beyond the reciprocal exchange of benefits; gratitude is the "truest approach to life,"[144] and a proclamation of a certain attitude toward the world.[145]

However, because of the mutual benefit associated with gifts, challenges to the narrow definition of gratitude emerge. One challenge arises because of the dissociation of a narrow understanding of gratitude from the historical discussion of other important moral concepts, such as duty, obligation, and reciprocal indebtedness. Another challenge when gratitude is narrowly understood as a reaction to a specific benefit arises because its connection to morality is severed; gratitude is then appreciated for its instrumental value rather than for its own value.[146]

One reason for the dissociation between gratitude and moral discourse is attributed, according to Fitzgerald, to posing the wrong philosophical question. Usually, the discussion seeks to answer the question of when gratitude is owed so that those who were treated with ingratitude may complain. However, Fitzgerald contends that the discussion should rather seek the moral reasons for showing gratitude; and because of the importance of gratitude for the flourishing of individuals and communities, there is a plethora of moral reasons to express gratitude.[147]

Here lies a seed for change in the ethos of medicine.

Extending the Narrow Definition

Fitzgerald's argument evolves out of the Buddhist tradition, although his perspective resonates in other religious and secular mindsets. He contends that gratitude is warranted in at least two cases which usually fall below the radar of contemporary philosophical discussion: gratitude is warranted toward those who harm us and toward those whom one benefits.[148]

In the first case, having gratitude toward those who harm us may not be directly related to the discussion of this book. Yet, gratitude in this case is philosophically justifiable and has significant ramifications,

---

144. Emmons, "Is Gratitude Queen," 151.

145. Boleyn-Fitzgerald, "Gratitude toward Things," 112–25; Camenisch, "Gift and Gratitude," 1–34; Dolff, "Obligation to Give," 119–39.

146. Emmons, "Is Gratitude Queen," 141–53.

147. Fitzgerald, "Gratitude and Justice," 119–53.

148. Fitzgerald, "Gratitude and Justice," 119–53.

especially when considering the "nonidentity problem." This problem highlights that without certain persons, states of affairs, and unintended sequences and consequences of historical events, a certain individual may not have existed. Therefore, this person has moral reasons to be grateful toward those persons and events, although harm may have been intended in some cases.[149]

Comparatively, having gratitude toward those whom one benefits is paramount to this discussion, especially regarding the role of gratitude in shaping medical practice and systems. Gratitude in this case goes a bit further than the case of mutual benefit in gift-giving as discussed previously. Within a narrow understanding, beneficence toward those in need is encouraged since it benefits both the benefactor and the beneficiary; hence, beneficence is established mainly on utilitarian grounds. However, the philosophical argument advanced by Fitzgerald hinges on finding moral reasons for showing gratitude toward those whom one benefits. He argues that such gratitude is common in various social contexts and is felt by volunteers, those who do community service, and is warranted even in medical practice.[150]

Fitzgerald garners three moral reasons. (1) In the Buddhist tradition specifically, compassion is central to the spiritual growth of followers. Thus, when compassion motivates an individual to be beneficent toward others, she should be grateful to them since they offer her the opportunity to feel compassion. (2) The beneficiary is unintentionally benefiting the benefactor; if it was not for the need of the beneficiary, the benefactor would be absorbed in her self-centered interests. (3) Gratitude is warranted to prevent harm. In any one-directional exchange, the beneficiary occupies a disadvantaged position because of her need. Benefactors stand on stronger grounds because of their charitable work. However, when benefactors give with gratitude toward their beneficiaries, they prevent the psychological harm that is usually associated with receiving charity.[151] Fitzgerald most recently extended his argument even further to defend a sense of gratitude toward things, body parts, and other non-rational beings. He rightly insists that gratitude toward (being grateful to), rather than mere gratefulness (being grateful for), is the right attitude.[152] Grati-

---

149. Smilansky, "Gratitude," 126–37.
150. Hilfiker, "Unconscious," 3155.
151. Fitzgerald, "Gratitude and Justice," 119–53.
152. Boleyn-Fitzgerald, "Gratitude Toward Things," 112–25.

tude opens the door to meet the other in her otherness and to see her (or even things) in different lens. On the contrary, gratefulness to the state of affairs or sequence of events remains self-centered in some sense: gratefulness here is about being grateful for how things worked out for my own benefit, rather than being grateful toward persons or things.

Gratitude in Medicine

These moral reasons are fundamentally relevant to medicine. On the one hand, patients will, expectedly, have gratitude toward their physicians, nurses, and other healthcare workers and institutions. In their case, the narrow understanding of gratitude applies; patients receive a well-intended benefit from their providers, regardless of the financial exchange taking place in the background.

On the other hand, because of the looming existential threat of death (as concealed in every sickness), patients may approach their benefactors/physicians with a sense of inferiority where their dignity may be at stake. To mend this imbalance, physicians (and other healthcare workers) have many moral reasons to approach their patients with gratitude. (1) Physicians should approach their patients with compassion (as will be discussed in the next chapter) to safeguard their vulnerability. (2) Physicians' gratitude is necessary to remind them of the goal of their profession—which is serving those who are most vulnerable—rather than mindlessly occupying themselves in advancing science for its own sake (or for any material gain). (3) Without a sense of gratitude, medical practitioners may fall prey to cynicism and become numb to human suffering.[153] (4) Most importantly, when physicians approach their patients with gratitude, the dignity of these patients is served and safeguarded. In a similar vein, when gratitude is warranted toward things and body parts, physicians and medical researchers would have moral reasons to show gratitude toward genetic material because of the benefit they may derive from it.[154] Gratitude may then shape how medicine handles human material, body parts, cells, genes, and embryos.

In general, gratitude plays a central role in cultivating moral communities. The interplay between gratitude and history in Buddhism, for instance, orients the emotional lives of believers toward the past to shape

---

153. Hilfiker, "Unconscious," 3155.
154. Boleyn-Fitzgerald, "Gratitude Toward Things," 112–25.

a moral community in the present. It is maintained in these communities that without the efforts of previous faithful members, contemporary communities would not have a path forward.[155] This idea is not foreign to Orthodox Christianity; the living memory of the divine redemptive work engenders a synergic relationship between humans and God and shapes the church's mission in/toward the world. It is by the gratitude nourished in the Eucharistic celebration that the brokenness of humanity may be healed.[156]

This applies to the medical community in a similar manner. Without the historical contribution of many generations of practitioners (at some point most of whom were quacks per our contemporary criteria) and patients (some of whom were indeed hurt rather than benefited), medicine as known today would not have existed. Therefore, medical practitioners need gratitude to model a moral community centered on serving other dignified human beings. And, at the personal level, clinical practitioners need to approach their patients with gratitude, so that the dignity of those patients is safeguarded.

The Dark Side of Gratitude

Despite the positive impression it may leave, gratitude has a darker side that cannot be ignored. Although some negative aspects of gratitude may not be related to gratitude *per se*, and some are not directly related to the present book, it is warranted to briefly mention some of them. Objections to the adopted broad definition of gratitude, that which demands gratitude toward one's beneficiaries, are expected. Only beneficiaries receive a tangible benefit and they are to be grateful rather than their benefactors. However, as Fitzgerald argues, benefactors have moral reasons to show gratitude rather than have an obligation to gratitude. Furthermore, starting from the narrow definition, some philosophers warn against the possibility of offensive gratitude (when the benefactor is doing what a decent human being is expected to do), misplaced gratitude (when the alleged benefactor, for instance, did not intend any benefit toward the beneficiary), and foolish gratitude (when the beneficiary has gratitude toward an abusive or oppressive "benefactor" because of her low self-esteem and expectations).[157]

155. Berkwitz, "History and Gratitude," 579–604.
156. Steenberg, "The Church," 121–35.
157. Card, "Gratitude," 99–111; McConnell, "Gratitude's Value," 13–26; Fitzgerald, "Gratitude and Justice," 119–53.

Moreover, gratitude, regardless of its definition, may encounter opposition that is not directly related to it. Gratitude is usually opposed in an individualistic culture that idolizes autonomy and self-sufficiency and that categorizes gratitude as a humiliating emotion. In such a society, a sense of entitlement and a fear of dependency may thwart moral motivation toward gratitude.[158] By the same token, when the language of rights is understood as setting a moral agenda (contrary to the argument of this chapter), one may not feel obliged to have gratitude because of her belief that what she receives is owed to her as a right.[159] Hence, it is arguable that further empirical studies on general attitudes toward gratitude are necessary to better understand its social role and how to nourish its presence.[160]

Conclusion

Building on an Orthodox bioethical *phronema*, this chapter discussed the first concept for a common ground in global bioethics. Respecting human dignity hinges on the creation of humans in the image and likeness of Christ whose kinghood is transferred to every human being. Respecting human dignity, it was shown, is also supported in a secular discourse of bioethics. In this context, it opens the door to shape an ethos in which the language of human rights is a tool to show respect to every person. At the practical level, a social understanding of human dignity was advocated to highlight the nature of dignity as a gift and to unveil the many moral reasons to foster gratitude in society. In medicine, as an enterprise and as a clinical encounter, gratitude proves relevant because of how human life and medicine seem entangled in a globalized world. Therefore, gratitude is argued as cardinal to illumine the various aspects of medicine (along with compassion and solidarity), such as its research agenda, public policies, and educating new generations of practitioners. These practical aspects will be further discussed in chapter 6.

---

158. Roberts, "Gratitude and Humility," 57–69; Emmons and Kneezel, "Giving Thanks," 140–48; Camenisch, "Gift and Gratitude," 1–34; Emmons, "Is Gratitude Queen," 141–53.

159. Dolff, "Obligation to Give," 119–39.

160. Gulliford and Morgan, "Empirical Exploration," 199–214.

5

The Meaning of Human Vulnerability
A Systematic Interpretation

This chapter will elaborate on the second of the three concepts central to the advocated Orthodox Christian bioethics and the common ground for an inclusive global bioethics. The understanding of human vulnerability will be discussed within Orthodox Christian theology and secular bioethical discourse as it hinges on the universal embodied experience of all human beings.[1] The goal is to promote a substantive bioethics that nourishes compassion in health care. Ultimately, compassion can play a significant role in shaping medical practice at the clinical level. In combination with gratitude and solidarity, compassion shall model medical education and systems as healing enterprises.

The Theology of Vulnerability in Orthodox Bioethics

This section explores a theological understanding of human vulnerability within Orthodox Christian hermeneutics and its practical ramifications to ameliorate human suffering.

A Christocentric Hermeneutics for Human Vulnerability
Christ the Prophet

In the previous chapter, the kinghood of Christ was explored in Orthodox theological *phronema* to connect it to respecting human dignity and

---

1. Barilan, *Human Dignity*, 93–147.

its relation to gratitude. In this chapter, the prophethood of Christ is explored as it relates to human vulnerability and compassion. Christ the prophet has revealed himself in two stages, within the Old Testament and then following his incarnation. His prophethood reveals a personal God to the created world and his providence to save it.[2]

In the time of the Old Testament, God assigned numerous prophets to announce the divine word to the chosen people. In their prophecies, those prophets did not fore-tell the future; they rather situated the daily experience of the people of God, favorable or not, within the entire providential economy.[3] One theme runs through the prophecies of the Old Testament: the people of God were frequently reminded of how God called and saved them through philanthropy (love toward humankind). Without the life-giving divine philanthropy, the chosen people would have perished.

When the Son of God took a human body, himself being the Word of God (John 1), the divine revelation was fully proclaimed in the person of Jesus Christ. Throughout his salvific indwelling among humans, Jesus Christ reiterated the prophetic message of the Old Testament, i.e., the mortality of humankind due to its disconnection from the living God. However, it took a divine savior to change the *status quo* and to re-establish that relationship. Therefore, Jesus Christ acquired the entire human nature (except sin) and submitted himself to the universal human experience of death so that he may redeem all those who were bound to death for ages. In his philanthropic death on the cross, Christ has revealed the Almighty God to be also vulnerable; God has loved the world to the extent that Christ died for the entire world to have everlasting life (John 3:16). Christ's submission to vulnerable death saves humanity of its ultimate enemy, death, and strips it of its thorn. In short, what appears as vulnerable submission to death out of true love and solidarity leads to resurrection and ever-lasting life. Only true love defeats death.[4]

---

2. Bouteneff, "Christ and Salvation," 93–106; Yannaras, *Freedom of Morality*, 89–107.

3. Schmemann, "Task of Orthodox Theology," 180–88.

4. Bouteneff, "Christ and Salvation," 93–106; Clément, *On Human Being*, 25–58; Louth, *Introducing Eastern Orthodox Theology*, 50–65; Behr, *Becoming Human*, 20–25.

Human Fallenness

Although humans were originally created in the divine image and aspire to become like God, the disobedience of human ancestors has changed the human condition since then. As previously discussed, church fathers perceived this change within a communal mindset rather than a legalistic one. The ancestral sin was more about breaking communion with God through disobedience rather than breaking a legal rule which deserved a proportionate penalty.[5] In freely choosing to disobey God, Adam and Eve separated themselves from the only source of life, thus giving way for corruption and death to occur.

Therefore, illness and death are not understood in the Orthodox Church as legal punishment proportionate to the sin. Rather, corruption, illness, and death are a "natural" (though originally unintended by God) consequence to the free disobedience of the human ancestors.[6] God did not intend that illness and death should afflict humanity. It is understandable from the creation narratives and many church fathers that humans were originally created incorruptible and immortal as long as they were in communion with God. However, due to their sin, Adam and Eve would exchange their ingrained yearning toward God for a distorted desire to become gods apart from God (Gen 3:5) and to enshrine themselves as idols.[7] What the offspring of Adam and Eve inherit is not their sin, but is rather the result of that sin, namely corruption and death. Humans since then are under the bondage of death, and because of their existential fear of death, they continue to sin and perpetuate corruption and death. In the words of St Paul: "The sting of death *is* sin, and the strength of sin *is* the law "(1 Corinthians 15:56).

Along with human mortality as a source of vulnerability, sinfulness puts humans in vulnerable situations due to their distorted desires leading to greed, anger, hatred, and exploitation. Because humans fear the existential threat of death, they compensate by asserting their might (when they can) through using others for their own benefit. Hence, political systems are necessary in any society to protect humans from each other, because humans frequently fail to treat each other with the same

---

5. Yannaras, *Freedom of Morality*, 29–48.

6. Hierotheos, "Christian Bioethics," 29–41; Pentiuc, *Jesus the Messiah*, 25–39.

7. Louth, *Introducing Eastern Orthodox Theology*, 82–95; Avakian, "Mystery of Divine Love," 39–68; Khodr, "Church and the World," 33–51; Larchet, *Theology of Illness*, 17–53.

dignity with which God treats them.[8] In the same vein, the weakness of the human will manifests in the universal human inclination to develop a strong identity and to emphasize individual autonomy.[9] St Paul shows the human fallen status in saying: "For what I am doing, I do not understand. For what I will to do, that I do not practice; but what I hate, that I do" (Romans 7:15).

In Orthodox Christian monasticism, human fallenness and death are experienced within a disciplined context in search for healing. Authentic spiritual living in a monastery reveals that humans are not only vulnerable because of their mortality, but they are also vulnerable in facing their sinful spiritual passions. While passions (from Greek *pathos*) are originally meant to serve the lofty goal of fueling a "passion-ate" love toward God and "com-passion" toward the entire creation, human fallenness distorted their compass. Therefore, rather than cultivating virtues, passions have nourished vices. To mend this universal vulnerability and grow spiritually, the monastic tradition emphasizes the importance of knowing one's own vulnerability and assuming the vulnerability of others by bearing with them their burdens (Gal 6:2).[10] In other words, to grow spiritually closer to God-likeness, one should stand in solidarity with others while recognizing the universality of human vulnerability.

Illness, Suffering and Death

As a result of the new human condition, health is only precarious. In a comprehensive study of the theology of illness and suffering, Jean-Claude Larchet, a contemporary Orthodox theologian, contends that "'health' is always in some sense 'illness' that has simply not appeared as such and/or is not significant enough to be identified as such."[11] This understanding leaves room for a positive perception of illness. On the one hand, illness cannot separate humans from God: it is actually a result of the separation caused by the fall.[12] On the other hand, health is only good in

---

8. Papanikolaou, *Mystical as Political*, 87–130; Turner and Dumas, "Vulnerability, Diversity and Scarcity," 663–70.

9. Barilan, "From Imago Dei," 231–59; Barilan, *Human Dignity*, 93–147.

10. Chryssavgis, "Spiritual Way," 150–63; Hamalis and Papanikolaou, "Toward a Godly Mode," 271–80.

11. Larchet, *Theology of Illness*, 53.

12. Khushf, "Illness," 102–20; For a more comprehensive study of the book of Genesis and the meaning of the fall see, Bouteneff, *Beginnings*.

appearance. Health may give a false sense of self-sufficiency which would perpetuate the human separation from God.[13]

Therefore, in line with many church fathers, Larchet advocates a positive perception toward illnesses; human illnesses may be "cathartic" in that they foster humility, patience, and hope through debunking illusory self-sufficiency and independence.[14] Moreover, the patristic consensus, Larchet explains, emphasizes that illnesses are not directly related to the personal sins of the afflicted. Yet, a few church fathers contend that personal sins and lifestyle may still directly cause someone to fall prey to certain diseases.[15] In general, church authors highlight that sickness is a reminder of human mortality where death itself is an "educational experience."[16] Sicknesses remind everyone of the vulnerability of the human body and its susceptibility to the corruptible forces of nature. It is because of looming death and its existential threat that suffering may occur.

In general, suffering is an existential experience with holistic spiritual repercussions.[17] It is an experience which afflicts the entire person, not only her body. In Christian theology, the person exists in a unity of soul and body contrary to the Cartesian dualism which shapes contemporary culture. Hence, when afflicted with a serious illness, one suffers because of the disruption in life conditions and personal relationships especially because of the growing isolation from self, others, and God.[18]

Perhaps, some of our perceived contemporary suffering is rooted in a frustrated hope in idolized medicine. Modern scientific medicine focuses on diseases as phenomena isolated from the person who is afflicted, which makes it difficult for practitioners to address the concurrent existential anguish. By the same token, when contemporary culture idolizes medicine and enthrones physicians as the new saviors of humanity, it fuels false hopes in those who are suffering.[19] It is ironic that whenever humans claim, in "self-aggrandizing" hopes, their dominion over the

---

13. Larchet, *Theology of Illness*, 55–77.
14. Larchet, *Theology of Illness*, 55–77.
15. Larchet, *Theology of Illness*, 17–53.
16. Behr, *Becoming Human*, 58–71.
17. Khushf, "Illness," 102–20.
18. Larchet, *Theology of Illness*, 17–53.
19. Khushf, "Illness," 102–20; Larchet, *Theology of Illness*, 17–53, 79–131; Callahan, "Death, Mourning," 103–15; Callahan, *Troubled Dream of Life*, 23–56.

human body and diseases, they betray the lurking vulnerability of their existence.[20]

Nonetheless, when suffering is perceived against the background of human fallenness and divine providence, those who suffer may have a way to extract a positive outcome. It is through patience, prayer, and thankfulness that the afflicted faithful may get closer to God. By the same token, those who witness the suffering of others are invited to get closer to God through respect and openness toward the afflicted; among those afflicted faithful may be another Job in the making. By so doing, witnesses will learn a great deal from the afflicted one's perseverance so that they may grow in their own spiritual life.[21] Moreover, when vulnerability, illness, and suffering are embedded within the divine providence to save humanity, death itself acquires a positive meaning. Death for Orthodox theology is a "defining moment, not end but beginning" which should shape the human perception toward life and what ultimately matters in life.

Similar to Orthodox Christianity, all other religious traditions perceive vulnerability as ontological to the human condition, especially because of human mortality.[22] However, religious communities recognize that some people are more vulnerable than others because of their social standing, especially children, women, the disabled, and the elderly. This understanding of vulnerability encourages religious communities to pay special attention to the needs of the most vulnerable among them, regardless of how different their responses may seem. Religious communities recognize that human vulnerabilities are not solely related to medical or health issues but are embedded within the social circumstances of each community.[23] Similarly, non-religious perspectives on vulnerability are rooted in the universal and unifying embodied experience of life regardless of cultural particularities.[24]

Notwithstanding the care afforded to the vulnerable within their communities, religious, social, and cultural practices may themselves expose the vulnerable to further exploitation because of the fallen nature

20. Barilan, "From Imago Dei," 231–59; Barilan, *Human Dignity*, 23–92.

21. As illustrated in Larchet, *Theology of Illness*, 55–77; see also Behr, *Becoming Human*, 58–71.

22. Heyd, "Jewish Perspective," 203–14.

23. Tham, Garcia, and Miranda, eds., *Religious Perspectives*, especially, Tham, "Lessons Learned," 215–24.

24. Turner and Dumas, "Vulnerability, Diversity and Scarcity," 663–70.

of humans; natural vulnerabilities may be ameliorated on the one side, but interpersonal vulnerabilities may be further exposed on the other.[25]

Mending Human Vulnerability

Mending Alienation

As it has been discussed previously, human vulnerability and mortality derive from breaking communion with God. Therefore, to genuinely address the human condition, the existential gap between God, the only giver of life, and humans should be bridged.

After the human ancestors freely followed the Devil's advice (*ho diabolos*: the divider), their alienation from God, other humans, and within the self, took hold.[26] Human alienation from each other first manifested itself in the exchange of accusations which took place after breaking the divine command. Adam accused Eve of leading him into sin. Eve, who was until then "bone of my bones and flesh of my flesh" for Adam (Gen 2:23), became "the woman whom you [God] gave me to be with me" (Gen 3:12). Similarly, Eve accused the serpent of tempting her into eating of the tree while evading any responsibility for her actions saying: "The serpent deceived me, and I ate" (Gen 3:13). This alienation continues to this day among humans through greed and selfish exploitation of others for one's own pleasures and benefits. Therefore, enmity and conflict among humans are much more existentially rooted in the human condition than in mere moral strangeness: moral strangeness is the outer layer of a much deeper alienation among humans.

At the personal level, estrangement similarly afflicts the human will and embodied identity. On the one hand, humans have a weak will because of their fallenness. Thus, contemporary attempts, in medical context or elsewhere, to emphasize the power of human autonomy or decisiveness overlook the existential weakness of decision-making and internal conflicting desires. On the other hand, personal embodied unity is severed when humans are exposed to the nihilistic threat of diseases and death. Although humans do not recognize this threat until they bluntly face their existential frailty, alienation lurks inside the self and threatens its soul-body unity.[27]

---

25. Barilan, "From Imago Dei," 231–59; Barilan, *Human Dignity*, 93–147.
26. Bouteneff, "Christ and Salvation," 93–106.
27. Khushf, "Illness," 102–20; van Hooft, "Suffering," 125–31.

To mend this ingrained alienation, the Son of God took on the human nature in its entirety (save sin), in a "self-risking" initiative,[28] in order to bridge the existential gap between the divine and created realities. Through genuine divine and compassionate love that defeats death, he opened the door for humans to re-establish their lost relationship with God.[29] Through *suffering with* humans (compassion), Christ was able to heal human mortality. Thus, humans have a new way to perceive death: death as a beginning of a renewed itinerary toward God rather than as an end to life and its meaning.[30] In the same vein, any attempt by humans to heal their condition aspires to the reconciliatory mission of Christ. Christ opens the door to defeat death without eliminating mortality and corruption. He leaves intact human freedom and gives a different meaning to human attempts to encounter death.[31] In short, Christ's mission to heal vulnerability and mortality reminds humans that the problem is not health or illness; rather it is sin and the consequent alienation from God, others, and the self.[32]

Principles to Face Death

When sickness and mortality became ingrained into the human condition after the fall, humans used all available resources to heal their affliction and fend off death. Traditional medicine and its most recent scientific iteration were among the promising havens, though with limited success.

Similar to many religious communities, the Orthodox Church coexisted with medicine for the majority of its history, from the time when practitioners used herbal and primitive unscientific methods to the time when the art of medical care was interweaved into science. While contemporary Orthodox theologians do not propagate any specific medical diagnostics or prognostications, they express favorable perception toward medicine and its practitioners.[33] In general, this has been the case with Christianity since its very beginning. Christianity was known to many

---

28. Davies, *Theology of Compassion*, 212–24.
29. Pentiuc, *Jesus the Messiah*, 139–85; Davies, *Theology of Compassion*, 212–24.
30. Behr, *Becoming Human*, 40–48.
31. Larchet, *Theology of Illness*, 17–53; Tzitzis, "Ethical and the Legal Aspects," 53–60.
32. Khushf, "Illness," 102–20.
33. Larchet, *Theology of Illness*, 79–131; Hierotheos, "Christian Bioethics," 29–41.

outsiders as the "religion for the sick" because of many believers who took care of outcast and absolute strangers in times of plagues.[34] Similarly, Christian communities in Byzantium modelled the first known hospitals and shaped hospitable and caring systems for the sick and suffering.[35] Many Christian saints are still celebrated for their inspiring practice of medicine and the healings they accrued for their patients through spiritual advice and genuine care. These saints are known to be "unmercenary" in that they received no monetary compensation for their care. They modelled genuine care that was the ultimate expression of the virtue of charity.[36]

In general, Orthodox theology emphasized, in action and in theory, that the true healing comes from God since Christ is the true physician of the human body and soul. Even the availability of herbal medicines, the art of extracting them, and their beneficial use are intended and inspired by God to bring healing to humanity.[37]

Therefore, to face human illnesses and death, the Orthodox Church does not reprimand those who seek medical attention for their ailments. Contrary to this general rule, some extreme opinions, though not representative of the entire tradition, understandably prefer not to seek medical treatment. These authors, especially within the monastic tradition (but still not representative of all monastics), encourage a positive welcoming of sickness as a source of healing to the soul rather than seeking medical treatment. The underpinning idea of these opinions is rather understandable and shared among church fathers, which is that life should be lived only toward God. Therefore, it would be better not to restore health, if restoring health would boost a sense of self-sufficiency (thus leading to being alienated from God again). In other words, a healthy life not lived toward God is not an absolute good which should be pursued at any cost.[38] Within such mindset, medical treatment—whether successful or not—should inspire humans to seek the true healing of the human condition, rather than a temporary (however long it may be) cure of

---

34. Larchet, *Theology of Illness*, 79–131.
35. Larchet, *Theology of Illness*, 79–131; Harakas, *Health and Medicine*, 69–78.
36. Khushf, "Illness," 102–20; Larchet, *Theology of Illness*, 79–131.
37. Larchet, *Theology of Illness*, 79–131.
38. Larchet, *Theology of Illness*, 55–77.

certain diseases.³⁹ This is a reminder to be wary of enshrining medicine or its practitioners as the new saviors of humanity.⁴⁰

At a more general level, Orthodox spirituality perceives mending human alienation from God as a two-directional effort.⁴¹ While Christ did his part through his incarnation, death, and resurrection, Christians have to live their lives spiritually (in accordance with the Holy Spirit, not according to an elusive pietism) so that they may truly heal.⁴² In Orthodox monasticism, where spiritual living is constantly sought, asceticism respects the embodied experience of humans and does not deny material needs. The human body is central to the *imago dei* and is the dwelling place of the Holy Spirit, the focal point of transfiguration and sanctification. Hence, asceticism sublimates the meaning of human needs and redirects them toward God.⁴³

One principle is paramount to Orthodox asceticism, for monastics and lay people alike: namely constant and silent (*hesychastic*) remembrance of death.⁴⁴ Through silence (*hesychasm*), a Christian may be able to know herself, especially her fundamental need for others. A need for others is not only related to the provision of material necessities; rather, more importantly, others are necessary to know one's own self.⁴⁵ Furthermore, through remembering death, a Christian is training to recognize the vulnerability of her life and its inevitable mortality. It is through embracing one's own vulnerability and inevitable mortality that she is able to recognize the fragility of every human life and to embrace those who are suffering with sincere compassion and solidarity.⁴⁶ In other words, it is only through embracing one's own vulnerability that she is

---

39. Hierotheos, "Christian Bioethics," 29–41; Khushf, "Illness," 102–20.

40. Khushf, "Illness," 102–20; Larchet, *Theology of Illness*, 79–131; Callahan, "Death, Mourning," 103–15; Callahan, *Troubled Dream of Life*, 23–56.

41. Steenberg, "The Church," 121–135.

42. Chryssavgis, "Spiritual Way," 150–63; Yannaras, *Freedom of Morality*, 119–36; Andreopoulos, "Modern Orthodox," 10–23.

43. Chryssavgis, "Spiritual Way," 150–63; Theokritoff, "Creator and Creation," 63–77; Harakas, *Health and Medicine*, 25–34; Yannaras, *Freedom of Morality*, 109–17; Wirzba, "Priestly Approach," 354–62.

44. Chryssavgis, "Spiritual Way," 150–63; Silence and stillness are important for Wirzba so that one is able to feel and listen to the presence and voices of others.

45. A similar idea is discussed in, Pellegrino, "Lived Experience," 513–39; Davies, *Theology of Compassion*, 3–23.

46. Clément, *On Human Being*, 9–24; Chryssavgis, "Spiritual Way," 150–63; Harakas, *Health and Medicine*, 45–55.

able to recognize what unites her with every other human being, namely their mortal existence. It is the recognition of the frailty of their mortal existence that brings human beings together rather than an impeccable rational consensus.

As a result of acknowledging one's mortal life, one can assume the vulnerabilities of others and strive to relieve their burdens (Gal 6:2) as a stipulation to grow spiritually in God-likeness.[47] In Dostoevsky's *The Brothers Karamazov*, this collective responsibility to mend human vulnerability in particular persons surfaces in the words of Starets (Elder) Zossima when he says: "Each of us is responsible before all, for everyone and for everything."[48] Therefore, when they have to handle rising bioethical dilemmas, Christians should remember that Christ did not heal human mortality through his miracles but through exposing his loving vulnerability, suffering, death, and resurrection.[49] Moreover, in facing death, Orthodox theology values human life inasmuch as it fosters a respect for death, the only certain companion to human life. Within such *phronema*, theologians and ethicists emphasize that human worth is not derived from an enjoyable wealth of rights but rather from universally embracing humans when they are most vulnerable.[50]

In short, to address bioethical dilemmas, Orthodox communities start from an ascetic and liberating spiritual *phronema* that is sensitive to the most vulnerable and marginalized wherever they are. More importantly, out of this *phronema*, Orthodox communities should assume the responsibility to change their circumstances.[51] Especially near death, the responsibility shifts from those who are dying (to autonomously protect their own interests) to those who accompany and care for them. Similar to Christ's mission, with compassionate care, i.e., suffering with those who suffer, humans are able to ameliorate the vulnerability of those who suffer especially before their looming death.[52] Ultimately, "compassion is the potentiation of the *imago dei*" in all humans.[53]

---

47. Harakas, *Health and Medicine*, 59–60; Clapsis, "Challenge of a Global World," 47–66; Jones, "Opening the Doors," 4–20.

48. Larchet, *Theology of Illness*, 17–53.

49. Bekos, "Memory and Justice," 100–13.

50. Hatzinikolaou, "Ethics of Dilemmas," 165–88.

51. Labi, "Injustice," 189–91.

52. Jones, "Church as Neighbor," 13–25.

53. Davies, *Theology of Compassion*, 231.

Realist Dimension of Iconic Phronema

While on the one side of icons is depicted the eschatological reality of this world, on their other side stands the beholder and the entire created world. To extend a meaningful invitation, the theology of icons recognizes the fallen reality of this world. On the one hand, icons extend an invitation to the entire world. When Christ took a human body, he embraced the entire created (material) reality as his body so he may bring salvation to the whole world, not only to the humankind. On the other hand, iconographers use the corruptible materials of this world to depict the ineffable divine reality. Some theologians even believe that the world itself (despite its corruptibility) is an icon of the divine reality.[54] However, it is the responsibility of the faithful beholder to unveil the iconic dimension of the world.[55] Also, it is the responsibility of the faithful beholder to perceive the divine image in every other human being, regardless of how far from God the latter may seem.

Therefore, using an iconic *phronema* in bioethics would necessarily expand the mission of bioethics beyond its current narrow agenda. Bioethics was meant to connect the biological sciences (*bio-*) to the moral heritage of humankind (ethics). The ultimate way of bridging these two dimensions is the icon; only the icon unfolds the ultimate meaning of the creation while profoundly understanding its current fallen status. In perceiving the current world through the lens of icons, the Orthodox Church cannot ignore prevailing iniquities.[56] Corruption and death plague the world. Suffering and injustice are everywhere. Pluralistic perspectives are the norm, while interdependence among various groups is unavoidable. Strangeness in the world is the result of human fallenness rather than pure rationalistic disagreement or cultural diversity. In a globalized world, human vulnerability is frequently exploited, and environmental degradation is threatening the survival of the human race. An iconic *phronema* takes on the responsibility to extend a divine invitation to save the entire created reality. An authentic Orthodox bioethics cannot overlook the plight of the human race and the environment and dwell upon the narrow agenda of mainstream bioethics. An iconic *phronema* has to be hospitable in that it prophetically reminds the world of its mortality and strives with sacrificial and Christ-like love to overcome human

---

54. Chryssavgis, "World of the Icon," 35–43.
55. Clément, "Science and Faith," 120–27; Chryssavgis, "World of the Icon," 35–43.
56. Chryssavgis, "Orthodox Spirituality," 130–38.

alienation from God and from each other. It is only through highlighting the role of compassion, i.e., suffering with the other, as Christ did, that the world may be healed of its currently innate mortality.[57]

As a result, an authentic Orthodox bioethics should be at the forefront of global bioethics to highlight the common anthropological ground among the various experiences of life and death.[58] An Orthodox bioethics should also be activist in that it aspires to the hospitable iconic *phronema* to tend to the needs of the most vulnerable humans. It is missiologically prophetic in that it brings the good news to the entire world by clarifying the misunderstood concepts in bioethics. On the one hand, this mission is propelled by a vulnerable love that is open to dialogue with the different other.[59] On the other hand, it is the responsibility of the royal priests—the followers of Christ—to show the face of Christ in the midst of a politicized bioethics discourse.

For instance, rather than perceiving freedom as the freedom of the market, an Orthodox bioethics emphasizes the ascetic freedom of those who perceive the world as an icon.[60] Similarly, rather than pursuing a bioethics that is a legalistically binding enterprise, an authentic Orthodox bioethics brings the experience of Christ to the world through mercy and compassion.[61] Ultimately, Orthodox theology condemns extreme positions because they imbed distorted premises, such as the idolization of biological life or the concept of individual autonomy in the clinical setting. Both cases negate the divine providence to save all humans and eliminate the Orthodox genuine hope in resurrection at the deathbed.[62] It is therefore the responsibility of Orthodoxy and all religious communities to prophetically teach medicine "to be present to those who are weak by accepting our finitude and vulnerability."[63]

---

57. Khushf, "Illness," 102–20.

58. Hamalis, "Eastern Orthodox Ethics," 1525–35.

59. Duraisingh, "Christian Mission," 207–18.

60. Chryssavgis, "Orthodox Spirituality," 130–38; Hierotheos, "Christian Bioethics," 29–41.

61. Clément, "Orthodoxy and Politics," 1–6.

62. Guroian, *Life's Living*, xiii–xxvii; Soelle, *Suffering*, 151–78.

63. Tham, "Lessons Learned," 223.

The Anthropological Implications of Vulnerability for Secular Bioethics

In this section, I will discuss the concept of human vulnerability as it relates to the prevalent secular bioethics discourse. As a new concept in bioethics, human vulnerability is advocated within a non-religious mindset to bolster the argument for a substantive global discourse in bioethics. The premise of this secular discussion is the fundamental connection between vulnerability and dignity as though they were two sides of the same coin; if humans were not invaluable, there would be no moral concern when they are vulnerable.[64]

Human Vulnerability in a Secular Mindset
What Is Vulnerability?

The word "vulnerability" is related to the Latin verb *vulnerare*, which means wounding, and the noun *vulnus*, meaning wound. Vulnerability refers to the possibility of being easily hurt, influenced, or attacked by others or by natural events. When vulnerability refers to humans, it highlights their fragility and innate finitude. However, being vulnerable in a certain context refers to two related possibilities: a possibility of being harmed and a possibility of being protected from the impending harm, regardless of the nature and severity of the harm itself.[65]

Vulnerability as a concept is usually used in technical contexts to refer to the precariousness of the particular system and the possibility of manipulating or harming it.[66] In medical context, human beings are vulnerable to a certain infection, for instance, because of other comorbidities (susceptibility of their bodies), because of exposure to certain pathogens, and/or because of the fragility of their defense mechanisms. Similarly, but to a lesser extent, military personnel use vulnerability to refer to weaknesses of a certain system which allow for exploitation by the enemy.

---

64. Bayer, "Self-Creation?," 275–90; Marcel, *Existential Background*, 114–35, 136–53; Kass, "Defending Human Dignity," 297–331; Pellegrino, "Lived Experience," 513–39.

65. ten Have, *Vulnerability*, 1–19.

66. ten Have, *Vulnerability*, 20–36.

To challenge mainstream bioethics, Henk ten Have offers a thorough study of vulnerability and its use over the past few decades. He discusses examples of four groups of vulnerable people to highlight several points on the use of the concept of vulnerability.[67] In any society, (1) seniors and (2) homeless people are vulnerable to exploitation and harm because of their life circumstances, especially the unavailability of effective social support systems and necessary protective relations. (3) Some medical research subjects may be vulnerable to harm not only because of their inability to make informed choices but also because of the nature and content of their choices which put their life in jeopardy. At a larger scale, (4) entire countries and cultures may be vulnerable because of geopolitics, global injustices, and environmental degradation, to only name a few detrimental factors. Therefore, ten Have endorses a comprehensive exploration of the term because of its broad applicability and possible normative implications.

Dimensions of Vulnerability[68]

Contrary to the narrow medical use of vulnerability (susceptibility to certain diseases), the above examples unveil a broader understanding of vulnerability. The following three dimensions of vulnerability are notable: (1) Vulnerability is applicable to individuals, groups of people, communities, and countries. At this dimension, although harm manifests at the individual level, vulnerability is not limited to individual persons.[69] (2) There are many types of vulnerability which can affect people at various levels at the same time. Individuals and communities may be vulnerable to physical, psychological, social, economic, and environmental harmful factors. Therefore, it depends on their ability to cope (on the short term) and adapt (on the long term) with these factors to prevent harm. (3) Internal and external factors also play a role in shaping the vulnerability of different individuals and groups of people. One may be exposed to harm, not only because of making wrong choices but also because of numerous external factors which limit the number and quality of available choices. These dimensions warrant an understanding of vulnerability in terms of its dynamics rather than in terms of who qualifies as vulnerable or not.

---

67. ten Have, *Vulnerability*, 1–19.
68. ten Have, *Vulnerability*, 11–19.
69. Also in Macklin, "Bioethics, Vulnerability," 472–86.

Functions of Vulnerability[70]

To have a comprehensive and useful understanding of vulnerability, Henk ten Have advocates a functional, rather than a descriptive, definition. By exploring its functional dimensions, one is able to understand the dynamics that put certain people under the threat of harm rather than indiscriminately labelling certain groups.

Functionally, vulnerability is the result of the following three components together: exposure, sensitivity, and adaptive capacity. (1) In the first place, one should be exposed to some external factor that could harm her. (2) She has to be sensitive to the afflicting factor so that she may be harmed by its effect. And, (3) the afflicting factor is going to be harmful either because she was not able to avoid the looming harm or because she has no ability (or has ineffective ability) to adapt to the changing circumstances.

In general, Henk ten Have explains that vulnerability is understood either from a political or a philosophical perspective. These perspectives differ because they emphasize a certain component of vulnerability rather than the other. A *political perspective* on vulnerability concentrates on the social context of the vulnerable person and highlights the role of external factors in causing harm. Thus, to alleviate human vulnerability according to this perspective, society should limit the exposure of its citizens to external threats. However, a *philosophical perspective* on vulnerability focuses on the innate sensitivity of all human beings to be harmed. Therefore, to protect their vulnerability, society should decrease the sensitivity of its members to harmful factors and enhance their adaptability and resilience to possibly harmful changes in their circumstances.

Globalization and Vulnerability

The discussion of vulnerability is gaining ground especially because of globalization and its mechanisms which are changing the lives of many people around the world.[71] Globalization is exposing the vulnerability of more people because of its effect on two of the above-mentioned components of vulnerability: exposure and adaptability.

---

70. ten Have, *Vulnerability*, 11–19.

71. ten Have, *Vulnerability*, 1–19, 20–36, 149–66; Turner and Dumas, "Vulnerability, Diversity and Scarcity," 663–70.

On the one hand, globalization is forcing more people into borderless exchange dynamics and, in some examples, is limiting the number and quality of their available choices. In the previous chapter, the discussion of human dignity led to the exploration of some of these exchanges under the auspices of medicine, such as surrogate motherhood in India and pharmaceutical research in African countries. In these examples (and many similar ones), not only the dignity of these people is threatened but also their vulnerabilities are exploited because of the numerous faceless relations they are—almost—forced to enter. On the other hand, because of the evolving global economies, more people are seeking better opportunities outside their native communities. Their new circumstances deprive them of their indigenous support systems and alienate them from their protective communal relationships. These evolving circumstances are detrimental to the adaptability of many individuals, leaving them more prone to exploitative relationships and exchanges.

Generally speaking, globalization has revealed that the vulnerability of many individuals is more fundamentally related to their social matrix than to their ability to make "good" choices. This new global reality establishes new responsibilities for physicians and healthcare workers whose ultimate goal is the amelioration of human suffering. Geographical and political boundaries should not stop physicians from tending to the suffering of humans wherever they are,[72] inasmuch as these physicians are able to help. Many examples of such missionary work by individual physicians are inspiring, such as the work of Dr. Paul Farmer.[73] In those same steps, the proliferation of educational programs in global health in developed countries, along with programs that train physicians to practice in limited-resource environments, extends the mission of medical care beyond traditional geographical boundaries.[74]

Intertwined Political and Philosophical Perspectives[75]

To challenge the narrow agenda of mainstream bioethics in a globalized world, Henk ten Have advocates a dynamic relation between the political

---

72. Soelle, *Suffering*, 33–59, 61–86.

73. Farmer, *Pathologies of Power*; Kidder, *Mountains Beyond Mountains*.

74. Bateman et al., "Bringing Global Issues to Medical Teaching," 1539–42; Furin et al., "Novel Training Model," 17–24.

75. ten Have, *Vulnerability*, 1–19, 93–123, 124–48.

and philosophical perspectives on vulnerability. While the social context is gravely important in exposing individuals to various harms (political perspective), human innate vulnerability and resilience are equally important in determining the extent of harm which would befall them (philosophical perspective). Through his analysis, ten Have argues that no one human being is invulnerable, and that it is impossible to eliminate all possible threats. Even science is not able to radically eliminate human vulnerability.[76] Without their innate vulnerability, humans lose their humanity altogether.[77]

Nonetheless, ten Have endorses a positive understanding of human vulnerability rather than its prevailing negative and superficial impression as a sign of weakness. He highlights that communal relationships exist because of human vulnerability. When humans recognize their interdependence and their need for each other, they cooperate and stand with solidarity toward each other. Even human culture is rooted in the recognition of the community members of their vulnerability; consequently, they are motivated to proactively produce a unique cultural heritage to defy the mortality of each individual member. In a few words, a positive understanding of human vulnerability is warranted against its weak façade and is hence able to challenge the narrow agenda of mainstream bioethics.[78] Vulnerability for ten Have is not only an element of the human condition but it has a normative ethical implication that fosters a substantive global discourse in bioethics.

An Ethical Principle to Challenge Ethics Inquiries[79]

It has been argued by several philosophers that ethical inquiries are rooted in human vulnerability. Because of the universal experience of vulnerability, humans reflect on the responsibility of bystanders when harm is about to befall a vulnerable individual. It is in these cases that normative moral demands are discussed.[80] In the same vein, human vulnerability challenges the mainstream bioethical inquiry in a globalized world where

---

76. Barilan, *Human Dignity*, 93–147; Turner and Dumas, "Vulnerability, Diversity and Scarcity," 663–70.
77. Hoffmaster, "What Does Vulnerability Mean?," 38–45.
78. ten Have, *Vulnerability*, 149–66, 207–16.
79. ten Have, *Vulnerability*, 93–123.
80. ten Have, *Vulnerability*, 207–16.

boundaries of responsibility and exploitation are almost effaced. While vulnerability describes the human condition (constant and evolving), it also has a normative ethical dimension that cannot be ignored.[81] First, vulnerability is conditional in that harm is looming, but no harm has yet been inflicted on the vulnerable person. Second, by intervening, it is possible to prevent harm from befalling that person. It is generally arguable that intervening to prevent harm is more morally binding than intervening to accrue a benefit. That is why vulnerability has a normative ethical dimension which should open contemporary bioethical discourse to its global surrounding.

Compatible Orthodox Christian and Secular Understandings of Vulnerability

There are several similarities between the understanding of human vulnerability in the above secular mindset and the previously discussed Orthodox Christian *phronema*. While humans are innately vulnerable according to the philosophical perspective, Orthodox Christian theology concurs and attributes that vulnerability to human mortality.[82] Similarly, the political perspective on vulnerability emphasizes the role of social dynamics in making some people more vulnerable than others. Orthodox theology attributes this to the fallenness of human nature and the ensuing distorted and exploitative relationships among humans. While political systems, from a secular perspective, are necessary to guarantee a peaceful and just social order,[83] Papanikolaou argues that they are necessary because of "a failure on the part of humans to relate to each other as God relates to each one of them."[84] Therefore, when political and economic exchanges slight local and national boundaries and facelessly exploit vulnerable people faraway, sometimes under the auspices of medicine, addressing these emerging vulnerabilities becomes an urgent moral responsibility for a substantive global bioethics.

---

81. ten Have, *Vulnerability*, 1–19.
82. Similar to Judaism, for instance, Heyd, "Jewish Perspective," 203–14.
83. Turner and Dumas, "Vulnerability, Diversity and Scarcity," 663–70.
84. Papanikolaou, *Mystical as Political*, 130.

Human Vulnerability for Secular Bioethics

The Use of Vulnerability in Bioethics Discourse

The use of the concept of vulnerability in bioethics discourse is relatively new.[85] Vulnerability first appeared in the Belmont Report of 1979 in an expert report written by Dr Robert Levine. In 1982, the guidelines promulgated by the Council for International Organizations of Medical Sciences (CIOMS) mentions vulnerability in the context of medical research. The World Medical Association (WMA) did not include vulnerability in the lexicon of the Declaration of Helsinki until the fifth revision of 2000. In these early uses, the notion of vulnerability was not fully explained, and respecting human vulnerability was considered under the principle of respecting human subjects in medical research. Vulnerability was then narrowly perceived as an expression of impaired autonomy.

However, the status of vulnerability in bioethics has changed in 1990s, perhaps because of growing globalization and its detrimental effect on many communities. CIOMS guidelines of 1991 advocate the use of vulnerability as a fundamental ethical principle connected to the principle of respect of persons. The use of vulnerability culminated in the UNESCO *Universal Declaration on Bioethics and Human Rights* of 2005. In this document, respecting human vulnerability is adopted as an ethical principle that is broadly applicable beyond medical research. For the first time, respect of vulnerability was not only an extra consideration in the context of respecting persons and justice; respecting human vulnerability was advocated as an ethical principle with a broad scope.

Conceptually, respecting human vulnerability in its earlier use hinged on one narrow understanding of its root, namely the "limited autonomy" of the vulnerable person. However, revisions of those documents included many more vulnerable groups of people whose vulnerability derives from factors other than their limited autonomous decision-making. These factors included insufficient abilities, intelligence, or education, so that those vulnerable individuals may protect their own beings and interests.

By the same token, the UNESCO's Declaration adopts vulnerability as an ethical principle that combines the previously discussed philosophical and political perspectives. To address innate human vulnerability (philosophical perspective), it is warranted to respect its universal and

---

85. ten Have, *Vulnerability*, 37–60.

unavoidable applicability to every person. However, when certain sociopolitical circumstances expose the vulnerability of some people more than others (political perspective), proactive and active interventions are warranted to protect those who are most vulnerable. Therefore, the scope of vulnerability in the Declaration is broad in that it does not only apply to the context of medical research, but it is pertinent to the provision of health care in general. Also, vulnerability in the Declaration does not only pertain to individuals who are not able to consent, but it is also applicable to families, groups, communities, and populations who are not able, for intertwined social and global factors, to protect their interests and prevent harm.[86]

Challenges to Vulnerability in Bioethics[87]

Notwithstanding its broader use over the past few decades, vulnerability as a concept still faces numerous challenges especially regarding its implementation in bioethics discourse. Yet, these challenges do not deflate the importance of vulnerability as an ethical principle and its normative implications. Challenges to the implementation of vulnerability in bioethics are classified under four categories: its status as an ethical principle, its content, its scope, and its practical implications.

Status: Contrary to its earlier status in official international documents as another consideration to protect human research subjects, vulnerability is advocated as an ethical principle since the promulgation of the UNESCO Declaration. However, as an ethical principle, vulnerability may still be exploited within any political system as a side effect of protecting vulnerable groups. It is arguable that the development of a politics of vulnerability, where certain people qualify as vulnerable, may itself be very harmful; those whose vulnerability is not detected are usually the most vulnerable. Further, when vulnerability ethics concentrates too intensely on protection and human weaknesses, it necessarily undermines human dignity and personal abilities.[88]

Notwithstanding these challenges, vulnerability has a normative moral dimension that qualifies it as an ethical principle which should be balanced against the principles of respecting persons, beneficence, and

86. Also in Solbakk, "Vulnerability," 228–39.
87. ten Have, *Vulnerability*, 37–60.
88. Barilan, *Human Dignity*, 93–147; Solbakk, "Vulnerability," 228–39.

justice. The rise of vulnerability as a principle has been warranted for at least two reasons: first, because of the narrow emphasis by mainstream bioethics on personal autonomy; and second, because of the growing vulnerability of several populations around the world as a result of globalization, sometimes under the auspices of medicine itself (examples were discussed above and in the previous chapter).

Content: The second challenge to vulnerability in bioethics is related to its content. Earlier official use of vulnerability included labelling many individuals and groups as vulnerable; however, it is not always clear in these documents the specific criteria used to do so. In mainstream discourse, especially in medical research, vulnerability refers to the impaired ability of certain individuals to make decisions and protect their own interests. However, autonomous decision making is fundamentally influenced by surrounding social circumstances which may affect the ability to choose and the quality of the choice. Therefore, vulnerability may be related to internal and external forces which influence the ability of certain people to make choices, in addition to their adaptability and resilience.[89] By the same token, some ethicists challenged the philosophical perspective on vulnerability and its universal applicability to all human beings. For instance, and contrary to the above advocated positive connotation of vulnerability, Martha Tarasco Michel does not attribute any positive side to the weakness associated with vulnerability.[90]

Scope: The third challenge to vulnerability in bioethics is its scope. In the UNESCO Declaration, vulnerability does not only apply to individuals but also to families, groups, communities, and even countries. At the individual level, it is understandable that certain groups are vulnerable because of their inability to make autonomous choices. However, in certain contexts, entire groups are systematically disenfranchised because of culture or poverty, for instance, such that their vulnerability cannot be narrowly attributed to their choosing abilities. In general, it may not be easy to unfold all those relevant factors and circumstances that aggravate innate vulnerability. Similarly, when the scope of vulnerability is ever expanding, it may not be meaningful to recruit it at the practical level (see below).

Notwithstanding these challenges, the expansion of vulnerability has at least one advantage. A broader scope raises interest in a more

---

89. In regard to women, for instance, in Macklin, "Bioethics, Vulnerability," 472–86.

90. Michel, "Vulnerability," 29–37.

nuanced understanding of exacerbating conditions rather than in labeling entire groups as vulnerable. At least, by so doing, stigmatizing certain groups of people as vulnerable can be avoided.[91]

Practice: The final challenge to vulnerability in bioethics is related to its practical implications. Understandably, an ever-expanding notion of vulnerability may water down its relevance and applicability in normative contexts. However, at the level of medical research, considering the vulnerability of various persons and groups demands extra moral justification to involve them in research. Further, when enrolled in such research, extra layers of protection should be deployed to avoid exploitation and harm. More important, though, is its relevance to contemporary global dimensions of medical practice. At this level, vulnerability challenges the prevailing narrow perspectives in bioethics and encourages an authentic global outreach in medicine and health provision. Recognizing the universality of vulnerability promotes solidarity and cooperation among all human beings, transforms the nature and scope of medical practice, and fosters global initiatives to improve the health and wellbeing of humankind.[92]

Vulnerability Challenging Bioethics[93]

As discussed before, mainstream bioethics frames vulnerability in terms of individual impaired autonomy. Initially, bioethics discourse evolved in the context of medical research and it was essential to guarantee the autonomy of human participants. However, framing vulnerability narrowly in terms of autonomy severs its fundamental relationship to justice. While decision-making takes place at the individual level, the social background of these decisions is equally relevant.[94]

To illustrate, a bioethics narrowly conceived does not alleviate human vulnerability. For one thing, such bioethics is only occupied with preserving the autonomy of the decision maker. Protection is narrowly perceived: so long as no "outside" influence exists while seeking consent from possibly vulnerable participants, decision making is thought to

---

91. Solbakk, "Vulnerability," 228–39.
92. ten Have, *Vulnerability*, 124–48, 149–66.
93. ten Have, *Vulnerability*, 61–92.
94. Macklin, "Bioethics, Vulnerability," 472–86; Ganguli-Mitra and Biller-Andorno, "Vulnerability in Healthcare," 239–51.

be autonomous. For another thing, a narrow bioethics is caught in the "moment" of seeking consent. Such a narrow perspective disregards all external factors influencing the decision making as long as they do not directly manifest themselves at the moment of consent.

In a few words, a narrow bioethical agenda does not recognize the universal sensitivity to be harmed and is only interested in the momentary exposure to outside influence. Mainstream bioethics inspires interventions that will improve the individual's capabilities to make autonomous decisions without addressing systematic injustices and crippling exploitative relations and cultures outside the moment of seeking consent.

Contrary to its limited role in mainstream bioethics, it is arguable that vulnerability may positively influence the kind and content of bioethics discourse in a globalized and pluralistic world. Vulnerability motivates more cooperation and solidarity among various members of any given community and across national boundaries and ethnic differences.[95] It fosters a serious consideration of the needs of the most vulnerable and motivates everyone to cooperate for the well-being of everyone. Furthermore, recognizing the universality of vulnerability helps healthcare workers to bridge the gap that separates them from their patients and to compassionately care for them.[96]

At a general level, innate vulnerability bridges the gap between individual and social interests by re-introducing and emphasizing other ethical principles such as human dignity, justice, solidarity, and social responsibility. Regarding medical enterprise specifically, recognizing their innate vulnerability, physicians would care for their patients with growing authenticity. They would recognize (as will be further discussed in the next section) that the authentic answer to vulnerability is not to do something; rather, it is to have compassion, i.e., to suffer with, and to be silently present with the suffering other.[97] Furthermore, in his exploration of the meaning of exploitation, Henk ten Have defines exploitation as "self-interested exercise of power."[98] This understanding of exploitation may be witnessed in medicine as an enterprise; medicine itself is exploitative inasmuch as its personnel seek to advance medical knowledge to garner more social power rather than to serve those who are most

---

95. ten Have, *Vulnerability*, 124–48.

96. Thomasma and Kushner, "Dialogue on Compassion," 415–25; Turner and Dumas, "Vulnerability, Diversity and Scarcity," 663–70.

97. Khushf, "Illness," 102–20; ten Have, *Vulnerability*, 93–123.

98. ten Have, *Vulnerability*, 137.

vulnerable. Establishing universal vulnerability as central to bioethical discourse is arguably the antidote of this systematic exploitation (even when no one is individually harmed or exploited).

Next, the discussion will turn to the role which vulnerability can play to foster compassion in medical practice. It is arguable that compassionate care is rooted in the vulnerability of both physicians and patients and is therefore fundamental to change the way medicine is taught and practiced. The next chapter will build on both human dignity and vulnerability in their relationship to hospitality to advocate for solidarity in medicine and healthcare systems. Unlike the argument of other authors who hinge solidarity solely on vulnerability, vulnerability can only be felt at the particular personal level, which necessitates a compassionate and personal touch. However, solidarity is not particular in that it does not relate to specific persons but to a group of them (as will be discussed in the next chapter).

A Systematic Interpretation of Human Vulnerability for Global Bioethics: The Role of Compassion

To further the discussion of human vulnerability, this section will consider the central role that compassion needs to play in contemporary mechanistic medicine to ameliorate human suffering. It may bridge the gap between two equal fellow human beings and help their decision making. From the discussion pursued here, the next chapter will extract practical elements for medical education and training.

Compassion and Mechanistic Medicine

I will start the discussion here by exploring the social standing of modern medicine and its scientific foundations. The goal of this inquiry is to reach the core of medical enterprise, which is death, and then connect it to compassion as the authentic motive of clinical care where two equally vulnerable human beings, physician and patient, meet.

Vulnerability: The Matrix of Medical Care

So far, vulnerability has been established as the universal human predicament with normative ethical demands in medical practice. Since patients approach physicians because of their clearly exposed vulnerability,[99] physicians are expected to ameliorate their suffering. Beyond their professional duties, physicians, as human beings, naturally approach the suffering of their patients with compassion which is the default human response to suffering. However, for many reasons, physicians are lured away from this innate compassionate response and almost mechanically (in some cases) attempt to "fix" their patients. David Hilfiker regrets that medicine as a humanistic enterprise has drifted away from its original goal of serving the poor and marginalized, and has busied its practitioners in a purely scientific (and profitable) search for mechanistic fixes of illnesses and suffering.[100]

Therefore, to establish the cardinal role of vulnerability in medical care and its moral implications, it is necessary to explore the current social standing of medicine and the philosophical foundations of its scientific practice. The social status of medicine and its underpinning theoretical premises influence the way medical practitioners are socialized into the profession and the way they care for their suffering patients.

Medicalization of Society

Over the past few decades, especially in Western but also in non-Western societies, many social aspects have been medicalized.[101] Paul Conrad defines medicalization as "a process by which nonmedical problems become defined and treated as medical problems, usually in terms of illness and disorder."[102] This definition applies to many daily aspects of life in these societies. While earlier examples of medicalization targeted women in general, most recently, medicalization targets more men through commercials and advertisements. By so doing, more medical products for andropause, baldness, and erectile dysfunction are sold to men.[103] Similarly, more adults are diagnosed with attention-deficit/hyperactivity disorder (ADHD), thus uncovering deep dynamics related to medical definitions, consumer demands, and pharmaceutical production.[104] Conrad also

---

99. Pellegrino, "Lived Experience," 513–39.
100. Hilfiker, "Unconscious," 3155.
101. Conrad, *Medicalization of Society*, 3–19.
102. Conrad, *Medicalization of Society*, 4.
103. Conrad, *Medicalization of Society*, 23–45.
104. Conrad, *Medicalization of Society*, 46–69.

discusses in detail similar social trends related to using human growth hormone for idiopathic short stature, aging, and athletic performance. These examples illustrate the growing involvement of medicine in human enhancement enterprise.[105] In the same vein, while homosexuality has been de-medicalized for some time, there are many evolving social and technological factors which may lead to its re-medicalization.[106]

Although it is difficult to measure the amount of medicalization in any given society for several reasons, Conrad contends that it has been rising since 1970s.[107] Many factors play into the medicalization of various aspects of human life at any given time. The availability of safe technologies or interventions may catalyze the medicalization of a certain bodily event; however, the discovery of associated risks may stop the use of these interventions without necessarily de-medicalizing the public perception toward that event. Conrad refers to two examples of such dynamics: hormone replacement therapy and breast augmentation surgeries.[108] When silicone implants, for instance, were used in augmentation surgeries, many women (and their doctors) rushed to use them for reconstruction after breast surgery and for aesthetic purposes. However, when their serious side effects surfaced, many practitioners and patients retreated from their use only for a while. When safer materials became available, the number of augmentation surgeries rose again. In this example, if one were to look solely at the decline in the number of surgeries using risky implants as a sign of de-medicalization, one would miss the point. Breast augmentation surgeries were temporarily at bay because of risk; breast size was practically de-medicalized because of risk, but was still conceptually under the jurisdiction of medicine up until safer alternatives became available.

In general, many social factors played a significant role in fueling medicalization in the United States, which may have been influential worldwide.[109] For the first three decades since the 1970s, Conrad argues, the medical profession, social movements, and inter- or intra-organizational conflicts fueled the engines of medicalization. However, most recently, biotechnology, consumer demands, and managed care play a

---

105. Conrad, *Medicalization of Society*, 70–96.
106. Conrad, *Medicalization of Society*, 97–113.
107. Conrad, *Medicalization of Society*, 117–32.
108. Conrad, *Medicalization of Society*, 117–32.
109. Conrad, *Medicalization of Society*, 133–45.

significant role in propelling the emergence and expansion of medical markets.

The Power of Medicine

The example of medicalization highlights the power of medicine in shaping society and defining social goods. On a general note, it seems that medicine aims at defeating death and obliterating its grip on human life. It has even been argued that medicine occupies a central role in controlling the dying process in society using its powers. More people are dying in hospitals and under direct medical supervision than they were a few decades ago. At this same general level, economics and politics shape the practice of medicine at different levels: from the allocation of resources, to funding certain research inquiries, to the shift away from a social understanding of death to an individual decision in the name of personal autonomy. Seemingly, medicine shapes the social understanding of the normal human body and mobilizes resources to obliterate the abnormal.[110] All these aspects reinforce the biopolitics of modern societies and dictate a certain social appreciation of human life and goods. Not only does medical knowledge and its practitioners have political powers in any given society; afflicted patients (through their demands) and non-human organisms (such as super-bugs) also have similar powers because of their influence on the political affairs of their surroundings.[111]

To curb modern trends of increasingly medicalized society, many critics highlight numerous relevant issues. On the one hand, medicine is not the only social good able to improve health. Other disciplines and social interventions may have comparable benefits in improving the quality of life and longevity, such as public health measures and enhanced access to healthy food.[112] On the other hand, it is out of arrogance on the side of medicine to claim that medicine has the right answer to death and dying.[113] Because humans are innately mortal, medicine has so far failed to fend off death (if at all possible); also, it cannot dictate the meaning

---

110. Bishop, *Anticipatory Corpse*, 1–27; Conrad, *Medicalization of Society*, 133–45, 146–64.

111. Schillmeier, *Eventful Bodies*.

112. Jones, *Peril and Promise*, 229–46.

113. An International Project of the Hastings Center, "Goals of Medicine," S1–27.

of death and the best human response to its inevitability. Simply, these dilemmas are outside the jurisdiction of scientific medicine.

By the same token, to defend against the overreach of medicine over human bodily existence, critics discuss other ways of understanding human ailment. When technological biomedicine was deepening the sense of alienation among patients, biopsychological and then biopsychosocial approaches were adopted to humanely serve patients.[114] Ultimately, a holistic bio-psycho-socio-spiritual approach through hospice care was the answer to an ever-growing interventional medicine and to the marginalization of death.[115] However, it has been argued that this increasingly inclusive circle of interests falling under the auspices of medicine is fueling the power of medicine even more and unveiling the totalizing (and perhaps, totalitarian) power of medicine in society.[116]

On the contrary, religious communities and theologians may have a different approach to the growing powers of medicine. For instance, D. Gareth Jones, a scientist by training, rightly argues that Christian theology and communities should contribute to society through demythologizing science and medicine. The universal idolization of scientific medicine blurs the uncertainties of medicine and human body and attributes to medicine—in the collective mind of society—goals which medicine and its practitioners cannot meet.[117]

In what seems contrary to D. Gareth Jones's perspective, Engelhardt adopts an unjustifiably demanding role from the Christian physician. He contends that: "The Christian character of health care should be salient, in that health care professionals must *accompany patients in facing death* and therefore should *also support them in preparing to stand at the dread judgment seat of Christ.*" Later in the same article he states: "In the newly established laicist secular public domain, there is no room for Christian health care professionals to appear as Christian professionals and thus challenge the secular character of the public domain. In particular, Christian health care professionals are not, like the unmercenary physicians of yore, to pray with and help dying patients to *repent and prepare for death and judgment before Christ's dread judgment seat*" (emphasis added).[118]

---

114. Marcum, "Reflections," 392–405.
115. Callahan, "Death, Mourning," 103–15.
116. Bishop, *Anticipatory Corpse*, 1–27, 227–84.
117. Jones, *Peril and Promise*, 203–28.
118. Engelhardt, "Christian Bioethics," 99 and 105, respectively.

Engelhardt in these examples demands from Christian physicians what should be the responsibility of the community to which the patient belongs. Physicians are not priests to take care of what the priest (and the religious community) should be doing, only because the patient happens to be dying in a hospital ward. While trying to fend off the "secular" medicine intervention in every aspect of human life, Engelhard seems to seek to put even more power into the hands of physicians.

Therefore, it is warranted for religious communities in general, and the Orthodox Christian community in particular, to demythologize scientific medicine and emphasize the uncertainty of human knowledge and life. To do so, questioning the goals of medicine and its theoretical underpinnings is paramount; this is in concurrence with other religious and secular voices.

Theoretical Underpinnings of Scientific Medicine

There are three levels at which theory plays a great role in shaping medical practice and social perception toward sickness and dying.[119] Although modern medicine denies having a *metaphysical dimension*, "material and efficient causation" (what Marcum calls, "mechanistic monism") stands at its heart. Scientific medicine perceives the human body as a machine that is governed by a chain of processes.[120] This perception reduces the human body to juxtaposed organs working within different interacting systems where function rather than purpose is the focus of medical epistemology. As such, *medical epistemology* depends on objective scientific knowledge that is necessarily impersonal and is dissociated from the personal experience of the diseased body.[121] Therefore, scientific medical knowledge had to be derived from the dead body in which the particularity of the human experience of illness is reduced to the universality of bodily functions (and their pathologies). The act of medical knowledge itself is then a violent political act which is innately connected to the social power of medicine.[122]

---

119. Cassell, *Nature of Suffering*, 3–16.

120. Bishop, *Anticipatory Corpse*, 1–27; Marcum, "Reflections," 392–405.

121. Marcum, "Reflections," 392–405.

122. Bishop, *Anticipatory Corpse*, 1–27, 28–118; Bishop's argument is aligned with the work of Michel Foucault and Richard Zaner and is in congruence with Khushf, "Illness," 102–20.

These reductionistic medical metaphysics and epistemology have clear *ethical and social* consequences on the practice of medicine.[123] On the one side, patients are defined through the loss of their social function rather than through a particular human-centered purpose. It is difficult to acknowledge that while disease and death motivate medicine to care for patients, medicine is used to politically control the dying process and arrogantly dictate the meaning of death.[124] For instance, medicine defines pain in a reductionistic way that hurts patients and is overly demanding on its practitioners. Pain in biomedicine is a series of neuronal signals which travel along certain routes and cause the associated discomfort. However, more studies are showing that particular human experiences and socio-cultural contexts shape the experience of pain in a way that demands "'reclaiming' pain from the exclusive jurisdiction of medicine." This is necessary to relieve medicine from an unrealistic public demand to guarantee a painless human existence.[125]

On the other side, to stop the overuse of medical technology and face death, liberal societies took the easy route. Rather than questioning the goals of medicine and its social role, social forces—including medicine and law—shifted the responsibility near death toward the patient. Whether the patient is hooked to different machines in the ICU or under holistic care in a hospice, she is sovereign over the course of her dying process, through decision making, advanced directives, or relatives with power of attorney.[126] However, rather than empowering patients, too much emphasis on autonomy causes the abandonment of patients by their care-givers.[127]

Furthermore, in a mechanistic understanding of disease and dying, emotional detachment at the personal level prevails.[128] It is thought that physicians should be emotionally detached from their patients to avoid any interference (because of emotional concern) in correct diagnosis and treatment. This approach to the ethics of the clinical encounter deprives physicians of their humanness and reduces their role to that of a

---

123. Thomasma and Kushner, "Dialogue on Compassion," 415–25; Cassell, *Nature of Suffering*, 3–16; Kass, *Life, Liberty*, 277–97.

124. Bishop, *Anticipatory Corpse*, 1–27, 119–40; An International Project of the Hastings Center, "Goals of Medicine," S1–27.

125. Bendelow and Williams, "Transcending the Dualisms," 162.

126. Bishop, *Anticipatory Corpse*, 119–40, 197–226.

127. Welie, *In the Face of Suffering*, 227–72.

128. Marcum, "Reflections," 392–405.

machinist who is well-versed in fixing the ailing organ or system. As a result, not only does the disease alienate the patient from her own body, but the emotionally detached practitioner also perpetuates this alienation.[129] A detached practice of medicine does not only affect patients but perhaps also fuels physicians' dissatisfaction and exacerbates their alienation from patients. Perhaps this is where physicians' burnout is seeded.[130]

Death at the Core of Medicine Leading to Compassion

The paradox of death manifests in human life every day. On the one side, death is destructive of every meaning because it puts an end to any human value and prospect. On the other side, death is the foundation and motivator of every human cultural and scientific product: culture and science aim at defeating death and its nihilistic presence in human life. More specifically, medicine is motivated by death to overcome death— the eternal human dream—inasmuch as it is propelled by social and political forces to control those who are dying.[131] However, it is out of arrogance when medicine claims to know the overall good of society or attempts to dictate the meaning of aging and death.[132] Clearly, within the mortal condition of humans, preventive medicine is confusing in that it exaggerates the—actual or future—abilities of medicine to defeat death. Similarly, because of growing unrealistic public expectations for death-defying medical technology, humans are perplexed about their responsibility in causing their own disease and death and the ways they may mourn their withering life or the life of their departed loved ones.[133] Therefore, Callahan argues, to genuinely appreciate the role of death in human life, it is important to explore the nature and meaning of life and health in the context of innately mortal life. Medicine alone cannot provide satisfactory answers because these inquiries fall outside the jurisdiction of medicine.[134]

---

129. Hilfiker, "Unconscious," 3155.

130. Halpern, "What Is Clinical Empathy?," 670–74.

131. Bishop, *Anticipatory Corpse*, 1–27.

132. An International Project of the Hastings Center, "Goals of Medicine," S1–27; Bishop, *Anticipatory Corpse*, 1–27, 119–40.

133. Bishop, *Anticipatory Corpse*, 285–313.

134. Callahan, "Death, Mourning," 103–15; Bishop, *Anticipatory Corpse*, 1–27.

More specifically, to humanely confront suffering and dying, medicine has to unearth the original and deepest motivator of its practitioners—before they became practitioners of medicine—namely the call of the suffering other. In the clinical context, the encounter between physician and patient is transformative to both parties, although it happens between relative strangers. It is the compassionate care by the physician, rather than a cold professional encounter, that closes the gap which separates them.[135]

For the patient, this encounter is initiated because of the symptoms which disrupted her life story; her goal is to repair the brokenness of, and alienation from, her ailing body.[136] Through naming the disease, prognostics, and a treatment plan, the particular patient re-writes her own life story with evolving new meanings to her existence. The encounter itself is central to the healing process inasmuch as the physician "silently" listens with compassion and addresses the—existential—anxiety and fear associated with bodily and medical uncertainty.[137]

For the physician, this encounter is originally motivated by a call of the suffering other even before this physician decided to pursue medical education. The physician, as a human being, has answered the call of a suffering other even before she became a physician. When humans encounter a suffering other, they respond by first being there with her before even offering anything to relieve her suffering. Some of these people respond by pursuing medical training to relieve suffering. The response is transformative and itself causes suffering on the side of the aspiring physician. Encountering suffering disrupts the life story of the aspiring physician and directs her toward pursuing medical education despite all the necessary self-disciplining and long-term commitment. Jeffery Bishop presumes that, for most of those who aspire to become physicians, there is an encounter with a suffering other; this encounter demands their transformation and is usually captured in their personal statements submitted for admission to medical school. In short, Bishop argues that the only answer to suffering is suffering-with, i.e., compassion, which starts long before medical practitioners encounter patients in the clinic.[138]

135. Benner, "When Health Care Becomes a Commodity," 119–35.

136. Cassell, *Nature of Suffering*, 94–114; Bishop, *Anticipatory Corpse*, 285–313.

137. Bishop, *Anticipatory Corpse*, 285–313; Fuks et al., "Narratives, Metaphors," 301–13; Zaner, "On Evoking," 655–66.

138. Bishop, *Anticipatory Corpse*, 285–313.

By the same token, Bishop thoroughly analyzes the clinical encounter and criticizes the individualistic claim that physicians (and in general all humans) are unable to know the suffering of the other. According to Bishop, this claim may be motivated by the fear of entering into the suffering of the other and the fear of the transformative power of being-with-the-suffering-other. At a deeper level, learning how to be with the suffering other is primordially communal. Those who have perceived the call of the suffering other themselves have learned how to answer such call by the virtue of belonging to a community; that community answered their call of dependency while they were growing up. In other words, by growing up in a caring community, human beings are sensitized to recognize suffering and to answer the call of those who suffer; some people answer by *becoming* physicians. Thus, certain humans *become* physicians because they first embraced their own vulnerability and learned from their surrounding community how to answer the call of those who suffer. This is a reminder that vulnerable embodiment is prior to, and is at the root of, ethical inquiry and normative moral demands.[139] Psychopaths would not *become* successful physicians who humanely address suffering (although they may still act like ones), perhaps because they have not learned how to answer the call of the suffering other through genuine care.[140]

Unfortunately, after matriculating in medical school, aspiring physicians are lured away from their original response of being-with-the-suffering-other toward a functional and machinist answer to the bodily cause of suffering.[141] Therefore, Bishop argues, contrary to the totalizing power of medicine (through universalizing assessment methods, i.e., statistics and measurements), the call of a particular suffering-stranger requires a practice of genuine human presence. An authentic answer to suffering is hence a suffering-with, a compassionate and transformative encounter between two vulnerable human beings.[142]

---

139. Bishop, *Anticipatory Corpse*, 285–313.

140. Dougherty and Purtilo, "Physicians' Duty," 426–33; Svenaeus, "Empathy," 293–99.

141. Bishop, *Anticipatory Corpse*, 1–27, 285–313.

142. Bishop, *Anticipatory Corpse*, 285–313.

Compassion and Human Suffering

Human Suffering

To understand the role of medicine in ameliorating human suffering, it is warranted to shine some light on suffering itself and what makes humans suffer in the context of ailment. Eric Cassell defines suffering broadly as "the state of severe distress associated with events that threaten the intactness of person."[143] Clearly, the human being as a whole is at the center of any sense of suffering, which highlights its multidimensional nature.

At the bodily level, pain is not the only component of suffering.[144] Even when patients suffer from physical pain, the legitimacy of their pain should be first accepted by others, whether physicians or family members.[145] Further, persons may suffer because of the loss of control (e.g., incontinence), disruption of their physical abilities (e.g., losing their vision), and change in their future plans (e.g., attending a daughter's wedding).[146] Other factors also play a role in the experience of suffering including, but not limited to, gender identity and past religious experiences.[147] At these dimensions, suffering is precipitated because of the embodied experience of life. All human projects and plans are embodied, such that any disruption in bodily abilities will change the relationship with the surrounding world. In other words, diseases cause suffering because they alienate humans from the world order which they lived before falling ill. As a result, the meaning of human life itself is disrupted, demanding a reconsideration of one's priorities and future projects. This change in meaning and priorities manifests during illnesses (especially chronic and life-threatening ones) as a serious spiritual or existential crisis.[148] In short, the experience of suffering may start as burdensome pain and then reach a sense of absurdity and disconnectedness from community.[149]

---

143. Cassell, *Nature of Suffering*, 33.

144. van Hooft, "Suffering," 125–31.

145. Bendelow and Williams, "Transcending the Dualisms," 139–65; Cassell, *Nature of Suffering*, 30–47.

146. Cassell, *Nature of Suffering*, 48–65.

147. Black, "Gender, Religion," 1108–19.

148. van Hooft, "Meaning of Suffering," 13–19; Soelle, *Suffering*, 9–32, 61–86, 151–78.

149. Hierotheos, "Christian Bioethics," 29–41; Cassell, *Nature of Suffering*, 30–65; Connelly, "Avoidance of Human Suffering," 381–91; McKenny, "Physician-Assisted Death," 145–58; Mendiola, "Overworked," 129–43.

Since childhood, compassionate communities are the source of meaning for any event in life; therefore, disconnectedness leaves the patient in a state of meaninglessness which fuels suffering.[150]

In seeking medical care, one paradox shows up: patients suffer not only because of their disease and its prognosis but because of the medical treatment which they receive (such as chemotherapy).[151] Their suffering starts when symptoms disrupt their life enough to seek medical attention. When a disease is diagnosed, and its prognosis is outlined, the treatment they have to undergo may itself have taxing effects, such as fatigue, nausea, and hair loss after chemotherapy for instance. Therefore, in the light of this paradox, further investigation of the goals of medicine is warranted to realign these goals with human needs under the duress of disease and its treatment.

Treating Diseases, Bodies, or Patients[152]

As previously discussed, medicine has evolved over the past few decades using a mechanistic approach to diseases and human body. Within this narrow framework, medicine intends to prevent ailments when possible, and to heal diseases or ameliorate their symptoms and associated suffering when healing is not possible. Medicine also aspires to preventing premature death and to helping to pursue a peaceful one.[153] Most importantly, when treating a patient as a whole, practitioners ought to alleviate associated suffering, or at least not add to it. To do so, practitioners ought to recognize the multiple dimensions involved in any disease (beyond bodily symptoms) by considering the particular narrative of the patient.[154]

However, in medical school curricula, knowing patients as persons to address their suffering is not relevant to a pure scientific-mechanistic understanding of diseases. In general, persons are not objectively knowable through scientific methodologies of assessment and measurement; rather, it is only through experiential relationship that physicians may

---

150. Cassell, *Nature of Suffering*, 30–65; Connelly, "Avoidance of Human Suffering," 381–91; Soelle, *Suffering*, 9–32; Gustafson, *Treasure in Earthen Vessels*.
151. Cassell, *Nature of Suffering*, 30–47.
152. Cassell, *Nature of Suffering*, 115–57.
153. An International Project of the Hastings Center, "Goals of Medicine," S1–27.
154. Fuks et al., "Narratives, Metaphors," 301–13.

be able to know their patients.[155] Unless doctors perceive themselves as (important) protagonists in the life narrative of their patients, they cannot fathom how the diagnosis and prognosis they utter are received as a "life sentence" by their patients.[156]

When a physician breaks the news of a serious disease to her patient, the latter enters into a crisis mode to reevaluate his being in the world. This being is only experienced through an embodied existence whose intactness and integration is imperiled by the disease. Many dimensions and roles constitute who the human individual is, and they are frequently threatened because of diseases. Any human being has a past and a life experience, has roles to play, has relationships with herself and with society, and has a transcendental dimension (whether spiritual, religious, or philosophical).[157] While understandably medicine has to ameliorate suffering, medicine has no authority or experience in dealing with some of the disrupted dimensions of the patient's life. However, to avoid deepening suffering at those levels, practitioners have a duty to know about them by entering into an experiential relationship with their patients.[158] In the context of suffering, the only way to know patients more is to suffer with them, to encounter them with compassion.[159] In the words of Stan Van Hooft: "Perhaps all the meaning that suffering can have is that it teaches us to care for others."[160]

Compassion: An Answer to Suffering

In general, compassion is suffering with other fellow humans, and then being moved to alleviate that suffering.[161] It derives from the suffix *com-*: with, and *passion*: suffering, *pathos* (from Greek, refers to pain, and desire). Therefore, compassion may not be very popular because it is connected to suffering, a generally negative experience. Besides, many

---

155. Bishop, *Anticipatory Corpse*, 285–313.
156. Cassell, *Nature of Suffering*, 66–80; Fuks et al., "Narratives, Metaphors," 301–13.
157. Cassell, *Nature of Suffering*, 30–47.
158. van Hooft, "Suffering," 125–31.
159. Cassell, *Nature of Suffering*, 30–47.
160. van Hooft, "Meaning of Suffering," 19.
161. van Hooft, "Meaning of Suffering," 13–19; Jones, "Opening the Doors," 4–20.

people try to avoid being objects of compassion (where they are treated with compassion), because this reminds them of their vulnerability.[162]

Suffering itself has a negative connotation even if all human cultural heritage attempts to embed individual suffering in a rather hopeful bigger picture. Encountering another fellow human who suffers is a reminder of the observer's own vulnerability and precarious existence. The observer may then choose to avoid the suffering of another out of self-preservation.[163] More specifically, avoiding human suffering seems to be influential in shaping libertarian trends in bioethics as previously discussed. Mainstream bioethics frequently emphasizes the moral strangeness of human beings and the essentially procedural way of addressing moral conflicts. Because of such emphasis, autonomous decision making is quintessential for moral medical research and practice while excluding the intersubjective connection between physicians and patients (black-box-ness).[164]

Nonetheless, compassion, as a long-established human virtue, proves the opposite, namely that intersubjectivity between human beings is possible.[165] Through compassionate encounter with each other, persons do not meet as relative strangers. They already know so much about each other because of their ever growing collective (and nowadays global) shared meanings. At a very basic level, when listening with a compassionate ear, many linguistic cues divulge a great deal of information about the life narrative of the speaker. Furthermore, contrary to prevailing individualistic emphasis on privacy, personal inner life is sometimes much clearer to an outsider than it is to the pertinent person herself. Personal knowledge is experiential in that it cannot be completed in one encounter; humans are changing all the time and only one aspect of their life is revealed each time.[166] In a few words, it is only through compassion that humans can connect to each other and unveil the host of things that are common to them all, especially their vulnerable embodied existence.[167]

162. Comte-Sponville, "Compassion," 103–17.

163. Connelly, "Avoidance of Human Suffering," 381–91; Thomasma and Kushner, "Dialogue on Compassion," 415–25.

164. Welie, *In the Face of Suffering*, 159–200, 227–72.

165. Thomasma and Kushner, "Dialogue on Compassion," 415–25; Marcum, "Reflections on Humanizing Biomedicine," 392–405; Oreopoulos, "Compassion and Mercy," 539–42.

166. Cassell, *Nature of Suffering*, 158–75, 214–36.

167. Hoffmaster, "What Does Vulnerability Mean?," 38–45; Turner and Dumas, "Vulnerability, Diversity and Scarcity," 663–70.

When exploring compassion *per se*, many philosophers emphasize its dual nature, as an emotion and as a virtue. In its affective nature, compassion starts as an emotion of sympathy toward another fellow human who is in distress. Yet, as a virtue, compassion answers the normative demand of the suffering other through an action to ameliorate her distress.[168] While sympathy shares in the emotional status of its object (such as joy, sadness, hatred . . . etc.), compassion always shares with the sadness, fear, or distress of the suffering fellow human. In this sense, compassion is a complete virtue because it always bears with the other person her suffering. Recognizing the suffering of another is not enough to have compassion: a mere knowledge of human weaknesses and what hurts may be used to torture other people.[169] Furthermore, compassion is universal; a compassionate beholder does not judge the morality of the suffering other, so she is open to all those who suffer regardless of their background and values. Thus, a compassionate beholder does not regard the suffering of another person with indifference. True compassion even sensitizes the person to every suffering creature in the world, not only the human race.[170]

Contrary to compassion, pity negatively affects suffering.[171] Pity is a feeling of sadness instigated by the sadness of the suffering other. It does not necessarily move the beholder to ameliorate the distress of the fellow human; it is rather self-centered and disrespectful. It hinges on a sense of superiority on the side of the beholder who is not necessarily moved to action. Thus, "where pity is abstract, loquacious, and generalizing, compassion is concrete, silent, and specific."[172] Compassion starts from a sense of love and joyous hope toward equal fellow humans.[173] Although it is initiated because of suffering, compassion extends horizontally toward fellow humans who share their equal vulnerability. Compassion builds on mutual respect between fellow humans and arguably propels morality in any given society. It has also been argued that compassion at the social level nourishes a sense of solidarity among strangers.[174]

168. ten Have, *Vulnerability*, 93–123.

169. Thomasma and Kushner, "Dialogue on Compassion," 415–25; Dougherty and Purtilo, "Physicians' Duty," 426–33; Comte-Sponville, "Compassion," 103–17.

170. Comte-Sponville, "Compassion," 103–17.

171. Comte-Sponville, "Compassion," 103–17.

172. Comte-Sponville, "Compassion," 114.

173. Davies, *Theology of Compassion*, 212–24.

174. Davies, *Theology of Compassion*, 232–53; Comte-Sponville, "Compassion," 103–17.

Notwithstanding the importance of compassion in nurturing social solidarity, compassion is a particular and person-oriented virtue. Hence, social compassion or solidarity needs to be built on a more universal (encompassing and socially oriented) moral concept. This concept, I will argue in the next chapter, is hospitality. Hospitality builds on the universality of human dignity and vulnerability, and uses the sociality of gratitude and the particularity of compassion to nourish solidarity.

Compassion: A Duty?

Because of the affective component of compassion, Kant argues that compassion cannot be a duty: humans do not have a moral duty to encounter others with compassion. This is similar to love, for instance, where one cannot decide, or be forced, to love another human being. However, compassion is similar to love in that feeling compassion or love can be nourished within any given society. Compassion and love are nurtured and encouraged through various methods, especially through role modeling and mindful practice.[175]

Nonetheless, perceiving compassion as a duty in medical practice is not unfounded. While one cannot be forced to encounter every other fellow human with compassion, clinical medicine may demand compassion. At least, this is because of the enormous difference in power between physicians and patients, and because of the enormous risk and historical antecedents of exploitation in their encounter. Moreover, medicine is practiced within a complicated web of systemic relations which could affect the physicians' ability to show compassion toward their patients. It is from this standpoint that Dougherty and Purtilo argue that compassion is a duty. For them, medical systems (and any suggested changes to their operations) should be judged not only according to their efficiency but also according to how much they squeeze compassion out of the practice of medicine within them.[176] In the end, physicians cannot encounter their patients with indifference because the notion of "non-compassionate competent physicians" is fundamentally antithetical.[177]

---

175. Comte-Sponville, "Compassion," 103–17; Thomasma and Kushner, "Dialogue on Compassion," 415–25.

176. Dougherty and Purtilo, "Physicians' Duty," 426–33.

177. Comte-Sponville, "Compassion," 103–17.

Compassion in Medicine

It has been discussed earlier that, generally speaking, human beings tend to avoid suffering and perceive compassion with suspicion. This is similarly noticeable, paradoxically though, among medical trainees and recent graduates whose assumed goal is to ameliorate human suffering and illness. Therefore, to re-establish the place of compassion in medical practice, one should first emphasize that healing is holistic inasmuch as both patients and physicians embrace the fullness of their humanity rather than mechanistically (and reductionistically) attempt to fix the broken party, i.e., the patient.[178] Furthermore, notwithstanding the importance of physicians being competent in their technical knowledge of medicine, medical knowledge on its own is not enough for healing. By merely reading available medical information, patients are not able to heal themselves. The personal presence of another human, a physician, who knows how to wisely use her medical knowledge and experience to treat this particular patient is quintessential. However, to use medical knowledge "wisely", it is necessary to genuinely know the patient herself.[179] This has been argued so far to be possible only through compassion.[180]

In general, for their encounter to bring healing, physicians should also experience, and perhaps expose, their own vulnerability and weaknesses. The "mysterious" relationship between physicians and patients is the foundation of any sought healing.[181] Fundamentally, healing is not only about how much doctors are able to control patients and "fix" their sick bodies; it is also about the ability of physicians to confront the uncertainty of both the human body and medicine with self-mastery and humility.[182] Similar to any compassionate encounter, physicians, as well as patients, change as human beings. When physicians decidedly avoid the compassionate side of their encounter with patients, they put their own satisfaction and the efficacy of their art in jeopardy. By so doing, physicians detach themselves from their patients and risk the loss of the deeper humane meaning of their profession.[183]

---

178. Cassell, *Nature of Suffering*, 66–80.

179. Cassell, *Nature of Suffering*, 81–93; Oreopoulos, "Compassion and Mercy," 539–42.

180. Svenaeus, "Empathy as a Necessary Condition," 293–99.

181. Cassell, *Nature of Suffering*, 66–80; Marcum, "Reflections," 392–405.

182. Cassell, *Nature of Suffering*, 66–80, 214–36.

183. Thomasma and Kushner, "Dialogue on Compassion," 415–25; Connelly,

Here is where Bishop's exploration of the core of medicine leads. Bishop argues that the original encounter of the physician-to-be as a human being with another suffering fellow human is transformative to the former in a lasting manner. The physician-to-be compassionately answers the call of a fellow suffering human through her personal presence in the first place, rather than through a (mechanical) action to cure the disease. However, because of this "inert" (in that it does nothing) personal encounter, the beholder is inspired to transform into a physician through a long process of suffering (because the new plan disrupts her life plan until that moment). The aspiring physician has initially learned how to care through being a receiver of care from the surrounding community. In other words, compassionate care is interwoven into the very being of the medical practitioners because it transformed them to become who they are.[184]

On the darker side, two factors may jeopardize compassion in medicine. First, an instrumental use of compassion in medical practice may empty it of its deeper authentic connection between two fellow human beings. Compassion can be used to measurably "improve" treatment outcomes, but it will thus be sapped of its transformative power. By the same token, when compassion is used instrumentally in medicine it perpetuates the power inequality in clinical practice between physicians and patients. With instrumental compassion, powerful physicians preserve their position rather than expose their vulnerability as equals to their fellow human patients. The most serious danger to compassion is in limiting its implications to the physician-patient encounter. By only thinking of compassion in terms of the encounter of two individuals, its social dimension (similar to that of health, illness, suffering, and healing) and its universal implications will wither.[185]

Second, medical school curricula avoid discussing and teaching (about) compassion, perhaps because of compassion's unclear and immeasurable definition and practical implications.[186] However, by so doing, medicine lures its novices away from their original compassionate experience in exchange for "measurable" and evidence-based scientific

---

"Avoidance of Human Suffering," 381–91; van Hooft, "Meaning of Suffering," 13–19; Welie, *In the Face of Suffering*, 201–26.

184. Bishop, *Anticipatory Corpse*, 285–313.
185. Hooker, "Understanding Empathy," 541–52.
186. Hooker, "Understanding Empathy," 541–52.

practice.[187] Parallel to the formal curriculum that avoids "compassion" and suffering,[188] there exists a hidden curriculum that equally shapes future physicians. At the core of this hidden curriculum is the standardization of the dead human body and the objectification of patients to gain medical knowledge. The next chapter will discuss in more detail the hidden curriculum in medical education and possible practical interventions to nurture compassion.

Conclusion

Building on the Orthodox bioethical *phronema*, this chapter discussed the second concept for a common ground in global bioethics. Respecting human vulnerability builds on the prophethood of Christ, which exposes the mortality of humankind when estranged from God, the only source of life. Human sickness, suffering, and death are the result of human ancestors breaking their communion with God. The resulting alienation from God, others, and self could only be bridged through divine compassion: suffering death with humans, to raise the humankind. This same *phronema* is applicable to medical care by recognizing the innate and universal vulnerability of all humans, including medical practitioners. Therefore, this chapter highlighted the relevance of universal human vulnerability, from religious and secular perspectives, to shape the ethical discourse in a globalized world. By studying the nature of suffering and the role of compassionate personal presence as the primordial answer to suffering, it was possible to uncover the importance of compassion in motivating certain people to becoming physicians. It was also emphasized that, because vulnerability shows at the personal level, compassion is the authentic answer to suffering when two vulnerable human beings meet, especially physician and patient. It is through compassion that physicians can cross the artificial boundaries between objective medical science and subjective encounter with particular patients.

In the next chapter, the role of global solidarity in shaping medical systems, especially near the end of life, will be discussed. It will be argued that solidarity sprouts from hospitality as it relates to human dignity and vulnerability, and that it needs the universality of gratitude and the

---

187. Bishop, *Anticipatory Corpse*, 285–313; Connelly, "Avoidance of Human Suffering," 381–91.

188. Cassell, *Nature of Suffering*, 30–47; Pellegrino, "Lived Experience," 513–39.

particularity of compassion to shape globally sensitive medical systems and education.

6

The Application of Dignity and Vulnerability to Hospitality

End of Life Care in Global Bioethics

After establishing the importance of human dignity and vulnerability in bioethics, this chapter elaborates on the third of the three concepts advocated for an inclusive Orthodox Christian bioethics and a substantive global discourse. The understanding of hospitality and its relation to dignity and vulnerability will be discussed within Orthodox Christian theology and secular bioethical discourse. This relationship will have practical implications in ethical dilemmas near death.

Hospitality in Orthodox Bioethics: Theological and Anthropological Perspectives

This section will explore hospitality within an Orthodox Christian hermeneutics and its practical ramifications as a basis for solidarity among strangers in health care.

A Christocentric Hermeneutics for Hospitality

Christ the Priest

In the previous chapters, the kinghood and prophethood of Christ were explored in Orthodox theological *phronema* to connect them to respecting human dignity and to protecting human vulnerability, respectively. The study of Christ's kinghood and prophethood unveiled their fundamental relationship to two concepts, gratitude and compassion, which are central to shaping the practice of medicine in a globalized world. However, by introducing the third function of Christ, his priesthood, a robust common ground is established for a substantive global bioethics, at least from an Orthodox Christian perspective.

The priesthood of Christ is epitomized in his universal mission to restore the communion between God and the entire creation. Through his incarnation, he acquires a created body, uniting divinity and humanity in his person and bridging the gap between the creator and the created world. The liturgical celebration is performed on the premise of a hospitable invitation extended to the entire world to come into communion with God in the body and blood of Jesus Christ. Unambiguously, Christ is the one who offers the oblation and the one who is offered in the liturgy for the salvation of the world (The prayer of the Cherubic hymn in the Orthodox Liturgy attributed to St John Chrysostom).[1] In other words, through his incarnation, Christ revives the original human mission of being the bridging microcosm between the divine and the created world (as understood in the work of St Maximus the Confessor, AD 580–662).[2]

Royal Priesthood and Hospitality

The priesthood of Christ fashions the royal priesthood of believers (1 Pet 2:9) and the worldly mission of the entire Orthodox Church according to the divine hospitality as it manifests in the liturgy.[3] Hospitality in its Greek origin, *philoxenia*: the love of the stranger, is central to this worldly mission since it aspires to the bringing of estranged humanity back to God through Christ's incarnation. Christ loved the alienated human race (alienated because of their fallenness) and welcomed them back to his kingdom through his providential work. Thus, St Paul exhorts the early Christian community in Rome saying: "Welcome one another . . . as Christ has welcomed you" (Rom 15:7).

---

1. Bouteneff, "Christ and Salvation," 93–106; Meyendorff, "Unity of the Church," 30–46.

2. Harakas, "Integrity of Creation and Ethics," 27–42; Bouteneff, "Christ and Salvation," 93–106.

3. Yannaras, *Freedom of Morality*, 89–107.

In terms of the Christian mission to the world, divine hospitality substantiates two important aspects. First, God is still working in the world outside the boundaries of the church through his own mystical methods. The Holy Spirit who abides in the world leads this mission (John 14:26). Second, in the church, God has fully revealed his divine economy, in words and in deeds, which puts more responsibility on the shoulders of the faithful when engaging the world outside the church.[4] Therefore, in the Eucharist, the church recognizes her own identity and mission toward the world, not as an entity in opposition to an—allegedly—inimical world, but as a hospitable and priestly missionary led by the Holy Spirit to bring the entire creation back to God.[5]

In a world full of different religious and philosophical identities, Orthodox Christians live among strangers who, Christians believe, are equally dignified but vulnerable neighbors; they all are dignified, because God has also created them in his image, and they all are vulnerable because they are also descendants of the same fallen humanity. As previously argued, Orthodox Christian bioethics should be perceived within this inclusive hospitable *phronema* which aspires to the place of icons in the Orthodox theology.

The Hospitable Dimension of Icons

For a globally sensitive Orthodox Christian bioethics, an iconic *phronema* is warranted. In the previous two chapters, the other two dimensions of this iconic *phronema* were discussed: eschatological and realist. However, a third dimension is necessary to have a complete picture of that *phronema*, i.e., the hospitable dimension. While the eschatological dimension of icons offers a bright destination for humans, the realist dimension recognizes the fallen condition of humanity. To cross from one dimension to the other, a hospitable—and hopeful—leap is necessary to bridge the ontological gap that separates them. Icons stand as windows open toward, and constantly inviting, the world, a converted and microcosmic

---

4. Trakatellis, "Orthodox Churches in a Pluralistic World," 1–10; Clément, *On Human Being*, 108–25.

5. Harakas, "Church and the Secular World," 167–99; Khodr, "Church and the World," 33–51; Yannoulatos, *Facing the World*.

beholder, embedded in a hospitable community, then extends the invitation to the entire world, in bioethics and in all other aspects of life.[6]

Hospitality Shaping the Christian Ethos

As previously mentioned, the Greek origin of hospitality, *philoxenia*: the love of stranger, is the term that shapes the argument of this book. However, a working definition is necessary to explore the practical ramification of loving the stranger. Parker Palmer offers the following definition of hospitality: it means "inviting the stranger into our private space, whether that be the space of our own home or the space of our personal awareness and concern."[7] Hospitality is the "bond between utter strangers" that leaves a friendly space for the stranger to discover herself without the fear of being judged according to preset expectations. A hospitable host expresses in her welcoming to a stranger their common humanity and recognizes the worth of the stranger solely for being a human. Hospitality between strangers does not require growing an intimate friendship between the two (although this may happen) because hospitality is fundamentally built on common humanity. On the contrary, the inhospitable host renders the stranger invisible, or visible but on harsh trial for who she is. Further, in English, *hospes* (the origin of hospice and hospital) semantically refers to the unity between host and guest recognizing their unity despite their apparent otherness. Although strangers meet in a public space, the resources available at a hospitable encounter are available in a private space, whether physical or emotional. As a result, a hospitable encounter does not only benefit the stranger who receives a physical or emotional shelter (hospitable space), but even the host accrues significant benefit from welcoming others. A host is propelled to perceive his space through new eyes; even his relationship with God and the world is deepened and expanded when practicing hospitality.[8]

More specifically, hospitality has been shaping the Christian ethos and mission in the world for many centuries.[9] Initially, Christians aspired to the divine hospitality which welcomed the chosen people and they extended it, according to the divine command, toward the marginalized and

---

6. Guroian, "Seeing Worship as Ethics," 332–59.
7. Palmer, *Company of Strangers*, 69.
8. Palmer, *Company of Strangers*, 56–70.
9. Kirk, "Hospitality," 104–17; FitzGerald, "Hospitality," 161–77.

voiceless, including the orphans, widows, and passersby. When exploring Christian hospitality, authors frequently refer to the advice offered in the letter to the Hebrews (13:2): "Do not forget to entertain strangers, for by so doing some have unwittingly entertained angels."[10]

Therefore, a hospitable ethos is integral to an authentic Christian mission at any given time,[11] and it has been inspired by the various books of the New Testament, although it is not literally mentioned in any of them. Through the mission of Jesus Christ, the feast of the heavenly kingdom opens up to the entire world, obliterating all the traditional boundaries that previously separated different races and ethnicities.[12] In his letters, the apostle Paul encourages Christians to welcome to their own the strangers whom they encounter. By so doing, the new humanity, recreated in the incarnate Christ, can experience the divine grace in abundance.[13] Similarly, in his two-volume work, Luke emphasizes the hospitable host-guest relationship as central to the universal mission of Christ in his incarnation. For Luke, gathering around a table for meals is the leitmotif around which God's hospitality is extended toward the entire world.[14]

Within an ethos rooted in hospitality, Christians continued to welcome strangers and care for them for many centuries, taking various shapes. In the fourth century, Christians established hospitals (*xenodocheion*, house of strangers) which became precursors for modern-day hospitals. St Benedict's monastic communities cared for strangers and passersby as an essential duty of their order. Most recently, many Christians unwaveringly endangered their lives to protect some Jews from being executed during the Holocaust and vehemently advocated for a better treatment of the refugees.[15]

By the same token, it has been argued that hospitality is necessary to mitigate the environmental crisis detrimental to all humans. Hospitality demands an ascetic approach to the world by consuming less resources in order to leave enough space for the voiceless and distant stranger for

10. Owono, *Hospitality to Strangers*, 1–6.

11. Bretherton, "Tolerance, Education," 80–103; Bretherton, *Hospitality as Holiness*, 121–59.

12. Koenig, *New Testament Hospitality*, 15–51.

13. Koenig, *New Testament Hospitality*, 52–84.

14. Koenig, *New Testament Hospitality*, 85–148.

15. Bretherton, *Hospitality as Holiness*, 121–59; see also Hobbs, "Hospitality in the First Testament," 3–30.

her to flourish.[16] Similarly, several Christian voices defend in theological terms the unavoidable global dimension of bioethics, especially to care for the most vulnerable whose well-being is dependent on others.

Hospitality is also strongly present in other religious and cultural practices, which gives it a universal normative implication in every society.[17] In Judaism, for instance, hospitality hinges on a respect of the embodied experience of humans along with an underpinning religious taboo against violating the stranger's body. In Jewish ethos, communal hospitality is paramount to preserve bodily integrity of its members and of every stranger as created in the image of God.[18]

Hospitality and Ethics

Beyond its particular importance to a Christian ethos, hospitality has a profound presence in secular ethical discourse. Derrida argues that ethics is itself hospitality. Without a hospitable perspective toward the stranger, i.e., a recognition of her presence and dignity, there will be no need for ethical discourse; if a stranger does not exist (or is not recognized), no moral responsibility toward her is established. More specifically, morality hinges on the premise that two strangers (or groups of them) recognize both the presence of a dignified other and an embedded moral obligation toward the most vulnerable of the two, especially when one of them can help. Therefore, a hospitable recognition of the dignity and vulnerability of a stranger other is the foundation of any moral discourse among strangers. Without hospitality, strangers do not have moral demands on each other; to be moral, one has to be hospitable toward strangers.[19]

To adopt hospitality in a pluralistic society, one ought to grapple with its broad moral demand and possible risky implications. On the one hand, Levinas's radical hospitality is demanding in that it gives the guest an authority over the physical and emotional space of the host, thus switching their roles. Hospitality is also demanding in its scope. Adopting a radical hospitality prevents the use of reasonable criteria to limit its

---

16. Wirzba, "Priestly Approach," 354–62.

17. Bretherton, *Hospitality as Holiness*, 121–59; Hobbs, "Hospitality in the First Testament," 3–30. More details on hospitality in different religious traditions are included in Kearney and Taylor, *Hosting the Stranger*.

18. Barilan, "From Imago Dei," 231–59.

19. Owens, *Hospitality to Strangers*, 7–31.

beneficiaries which may risk emptying it of any meaningful moral implication. Further, when a host obliterates her boundaries (physical and emotional), she risks her well-being by possibly welcoming malevolent intruders. Therefore, however important hospitality is to morality, it cannot offer unnegotiable directions for all moral inquiries. Hospitality is rather important to question different perspectives and to pose ethical inquiries in any social discourse among strangers, without necessarily advising final policies.[20]

Tolerance, Hospitality and the Public Space

To overcome the demands of hospitality in pluralistic societies, tolerance is advanced to achieve peaceful social order. By tolerating differences with strangers, one does not have any moral imperative to engage in dialogue, to care for them in duress, or to actively protect their interests when they are vulnerable. Thus, while tolerance may guarantee a minimal state of social peace among strangers, it hinders the possibility of nurturing a coherent and caring community of strangers. In facing the vulnerability of dignified humans, tolerance is morally inert, while hospitality is engaging and caring.[21]

Building on a deeply rooted heritage of hospitality, Christians are exhorted to go beyond tolerance and to engage with others within a hospitable public space. Similar to God welcoming fallen humans through the priestly mission of Christ, Christians have a moral obligation toward the most vulnerable and marginalized. By their pursuit of an eschatological unity with all humans, Christians should foster a hospitable dialogue with others wherever they are in order to improve the lives of the vulnerable. Through hospitality, Christians and all others have the opportunity to genuinely stand within their particular traditions, and at the same time, respect the otherness of the stranger.[22] By so doing, the anthropological similarities among strangers, especially their dignity and vulnerability, prove to be overwhelming compared to their differences. Furthermore, through hospitality, benefit accrues to both parties; the stranger is cared

---

20. Noble and Noble, "Hospitality as a Key," 47–65.

21. Bretherton, "Tolerance, Education," 80–103; Also, Bretherton, *Hospitality as Holiness*, 121–59.

22. Bretherton, "Tolerance, Education," 80–103; Bretherton, *Hospitality as Holiness*, 121–59.

for in the midst of her vulnerability, and the hospitable caregiver recognizes his own vulnerability and his need for others.

At the political level, Christians have a moral responsibility to establish a hospitable public space that is welcoming and caring to strangers. Parker Palmer argues that such a hospitable environment is "pre-political" in that its existence is fundamental for a flourishing political life. Christian churches have a vested interest in supporting such political environment since both Christianity and politics pursue the unity of humans. Although both Christianity and any secular political system pursue different understandings of unity, they both attempt to overcome human alienation by emphasizing the connectedness and interdependence among all humans.[23] Palmer likewise contends that a Christian—private—identity and spiritual life is not separable from the way Christians live and interact with strangers in the public space. Christianity is epitomized, rightly contends Palmer, in a sincere search for human commonalities rather than in a narcissistic fixation on differences.[24]

Therefore, it is incumbent on the church to create an internal safe environment where people can learn how to hospitably meet strangers and how to engage in a meaningful and flourishing public life with other strangers.[25] Through their hospitable involvement in public life, Christians may bring hope to their community, by emphasizing the goodness embedded in a caring social milieu.[26] In the same vein, by taking hospitality seriously, Christians bring to heart their responsibility toward the voiceless and marginalized in a globalized world where exploitation and injustices prevail.

Hospitality in Health Care[27]

In the particular context of medicine, hospitality is fundamental for an ethical practice in health care where vulnerable strangers constantly seek help. As it has been previously discussed, physicians and patients do not

---

23. Palmer, *Company of Strangers*, 17–33; Bouteneff, "Christ and Salvation," 93–106, concords with Palmer's idea from a theological perspective building on St Maximus the Confessor.

24. Palmer, *Company of Strangers*, 56–70.

25. Palmer, *Company of Strangers*, 90–152.

26. Palmer, *Company of Strangers*, 153–65; And: Koenig, *New Testament Hospitality*, 124–48.

27. Owens, *Hospitality to Strangers*, 7–31.

only meet as moral strangers; rather, they meet as utter strangers within faceless institutions where powerful technologies almost control life and death.

When a physician and a patient meet, they both willingly enter the space of each other as strangers. However, without hospitality, care cannot evolve. Medical care is embedded within a hospitable encounter within which the physician recognizes the dignity of her patient and his vulnerability as it is exposed due to illness. Furthermore, hospitality in the physician-patient relationship helps them both to remedy the uncertainty of the human body and medical knowledge. When a cure is not certainly attainable because of bodily and medical precariousness, hospitable care frames the encounter in order to bring healing in an unfamiliar environment. More specifically, hospitality in the clinical encounter is asymmetrically reciprocal. When the patient enters the unfamiliar territory of illness and healthcare institutions, her physician becomes her host because of his knowledge and familiarity with the institution. In contrast, the patient invites her physician into the private space of her body, thus posing as a host to a novice physician: the physician is novice in terms of the patient's embodied experience of illness. In other words, while the patient needs her hospitable physician to seek health, the physician needs his patient's hospitality to understand and heal her affliction.

In short, when physicians and patients encounter each other with hospitality, they both recognize their common vulnerability and henceforth genuinely care for each other, though in asymmetrical ways. Therefore, hospitality plays a cardinal role both in shaping a moral encounter between physicians and patients and in fashioning medical systems that are hospitable to the most vulnerable and marginalized, locally and globally.

Hospitality as an Inclusive Basis for Solidarity among Strangers

Hospitality as a Basis for Solidarity

Christian ethos of hospitality aspires to the primordial hospitality of God. Divine love was not only the *raison d'être* of the entire created world out of nothingness: divine hospitality toward fallen humanity brought the entire world back to its creator. The divine hospitality was embodied in the person of Jesus Christ who incarnated (taking a human body) and stood in solidarity with all humans through bearing the anguish of death on the cross. His divine love brings humanity, and the entire creation, back to life and reconciles it with the creator through his resurrection.

Despite the alienation of human beings from their creator, Jesus Christ took on a human body and suffered as an expression of solidarity with humans. He willingly entered the created realm as a "guest" to bring his alienated human "hosts" back to where they originally belong: his divine kingdom, where Christ is the host (Eph 1:9–10; Col 1:17–22).[28] In a few words, despite the ostensible façade of alienation among humans, a genuine Christian hospitality demands an active solidarity with strangers. Because they experience the solidaristic hospitality of Christ, Christians bear a grave responsibility to highlight the commonalities among humans rather than their differences.

Other authors have argued that compassion toward the vulnerable is the basis for solidarity in any given society.[29] However intuitive this may sound, it is arguable that solidarity is rooted in hospitality rather than in compassion for several reasons. On the one hand, it was argued that hospitality is the basis for empathy and compassion. Without a hospitable attitude toward a distressed stranger, the beholder cannot establish an intersubjective rapport to empathically recognize her suffering and to then be moved by compassion (suffering with) to relieve her distress. Thus, empathy and compassion are primordially rooted in hospitality toward a particular other.

Furthermore, solidarity is relatively more universal than compassion. Solidarity does not need a specific and concrete other to move the person into action. In medical care, it was previously argued (chapter 5) that compassion may be faultily used to distract the ethical discourse from the systemic problems afflicting health systems. However, by adopting solidarity, policy changes to mend systemic injustices in healthcare planning and delivery are possible without sacrificing the healing interpersonal compassion in the clinical setting. A solidarity that is rooted in hospitality helps shape a universal approach to bioethical dilemmas that takes both the personal and the global dimensions of health care seriously.

---

28. Bouteneff, "Christ and Salvation," 93–106.

29. ten Have, *Vulnerability*, 207–16; Davies, *Theology of Compassion*, 232–53; Comte-Sponville, "Compassion," 103–17.

Solidarity in Ethics and Public Life

To shape public policy, it is important to understand the role of solidarity in ethics and public life, locally and globally. Similar to many other intuitive concepts, solidarity may prove difficult to define. Like love and friendship, solidarity is broad enough of a concept to bear a broad spectrum of meanings. Unlike love and friendship, which are personal and private in their perception, solidarity has a more public applicability. Most people recognize their need for solidarity in times of crises when their vulnerability is most exposed; however, it would be challenging to pinpoint its nature. It may be perceived as an emotion, an ethical or political ideal, or a personal virtue. Some critics even deem solidarity to be an empty concept especially in regard to public policy or social ideals.[30]

Prainsack and Buyx define solidarity as "enacted commitments to accept costs (financial, social, emotional, or otherwise) to assist others with whom a person or persons recognize similarity in a relevant respect." They explain that solidarity has three tiers: interpersonal solidarity (individuals recognizing their commitment toward other individuals); group solidarity (collective commitment to the well-being of others); and solidarity as contractual, legal, or administrative norms (societal and governmental commitment to the welfare of every citizen).[31]

Although solidarity has only recently emerged in bioethical discourse, Prainsack and Buyx trace its ancient history back to Roman law. In modern history, solidarity is associated with the French revolution under the guise of *fraternité* (fraternity-brotherhood) although it did not literally appear in formal documents until 1848. Henceforth, solidarity was used among the members of trade unions and Marxist-socialist groups as a uniting force against evolving powerful capitalist and individualistic ideals. Because of industrialization, drastic social changes gave rise to an organic solidarity in Western societies due to growing specialization in production processes and unfolding interdependence among various groups. Organic solidarity stands in contrast with a mechanistic solidarity which prevailed in the preceding era wherein close-knit and like-minded members of a community "mechanically" supported each other in an agricultural society. Unlike communitarianism which may emphasize the collective well-being of a community at the expense of individual interests, solidarity respects individual rights as central to

30. Prainsack and Buyx, *Solidarity in Biomedicine*, 1–42.
31. Prainsack and Buyx, *Solidarity in Biomedicine*, 52–57.

collective prosperity,[32] where everyone submits her unique talents for the service of others.[33]

The influential presence of solidarity in Western societies (especially Europe) did not only hinge on the growing secular mentality following the French Revolution. Rather, a deeply rooted religious solidarity continued to be dominant despite the rift between Roman Catholic and Protestant Churches. For Christians in the West, solidarity among strangers was rooted in their similarities as fellow humans created according to the divine image, despite their disputes.[34]

Unlike the virtue of charity which embeds asymmetry between the involved parties, solidarity is built on symmetric relationships among individuals for the sake of their collective well-being. Thus, solidarity is necessarily connected to social justice and the common good without sacrificing individual well-being. In general, a Christian concept of solidarity in the West has emerged as reminiscent of Christian love (*agape*) in an increasingly secular society without necessarily sacrificing the core meaning and motive of that love.[35]

Moreover, in a globalized world full of disparities, Christians in Western countries should adopt solidarity as a way of living.[36] Similar to Christian thinkers who embraced liberation theological premises as a way to advocate for the poor and marginalized in developing countries, Western Christians are invited to repent (experience *metanoia* as a change of mind) in order to be loyal to an authentic Christian ethos. In this vein, Rebecca Peters encourages privileged Western Christians to espouse a "gospel of solidarity" instead of the "gospel of prosperity" which they have adopted for a long time. While a gospel of prosperity perceives Western privileges as a divine blessing, a gospel of solidarity questions the systemic, political, and historical reasons behind the inequities prevailing in other countries.

As a result of this *metanoic* change in mentality, Western Christians would assimilate an ethics of accountability that moves them away from

---

32. Prainsack and Buyx, *Solidarity in Biomedicine*, 1–18; Peters, *Solidarity Ethics*, 17–32.

33. Jaeggi, "Solidarity and Indifference," 287–308.

34. Prainsack and Buyx, *Solidarity in Biomedicine*, 1–18; Peters, *Solidarity Ethics*, 17–32.

35. Peters, *Solidarity Ethics*, 17–32.

36. Peters, *Solidarity Ethics*, 1–15, 33–47; Ryan, "Beyond a Western Bioethics?," 158–77.

charity toward a more concrete, and global, sense of social justice. Peters describes her solidarity ethics as a "liberation theology for the privileged." In order to motivate Christians to adopt her theological agenda, Peters recognizes the challenges associated with this profound change: first, the challenges of examining one's own personal and collective privileges, and second, the challenges of establishing relationships across traditional dividing lines. Nonetheless, Peters entreats privileged Christians to assume solidarity ethics through a sincere commitment to building—perhaps risky—relationships, whereby trust and care may grow out of mutual vulnerabilities. Consequently, solidarity will move the privileged to engage in structural changes to ameliorate global inequalities.[37]

In the bigger scheme of public life, Peters contends that an ethics of solidarity, though rooted in the Christian ethos, is open to dialogue with other value systems, religious or non-religious. Even if rooted in religious ethos, solidarity defies any threat of theocratic or exclusivist trends; it rather expands the public space to become ultimately global in scope. Such counter-cultural ethics is fundamental to confronting the unjust neo-liberal understanding of globalization which is precipitating economic disparities and environmental crises.[38]

By the same token, other authors cultivate solidarity as a corrective measure to public and global policies that are solely built on distributive justice, especially those related to healthcare resources. Although Ruud ter Meulen does not deprecate the role of a right-based concept of justice, he believes that solidarity complements the shortcomings of such justice by emphasizing the relational dimension of social goods such as health care. Therefore, in health care at least, solidarity is quintessential, not merely because of mutual interest in the well-being of others, but rather, out of a humanitarian association built on respect and solidaristic responsibility.[39]

Solidarity in Health Care

For many decades in Europe, solidarity has been at play in the provision of health care. However, it has been recently used in several contexts related to health including public health policies, justice in healthcare

---

37. Peters, *Solidarity Ethics*, 69–91, 111–20.
38. Peters, *Solidarity Ethics*, 111–20.
39. ter Meulen, "Solidarity, Justice," 517–29.

systems, and humanitarian aid during international crises. Contrary to the American ideal of solitude,[40] solidarity highlights the divergence between health systems in the US and other European countries. Although the development of healthcare systems in Europe took different routes depending on the unique political, economic, social, and historical circumstances of each country, the underpinning motif of all these systems remains a collective responsibility to care for everyone.[41] However, due to recent medical advancements and their rising cost, the sustainability of these systems and their underpinning solidarity were brought to the surface.

The surfacing debate over solidaristic healthcare systems, Prainsack and Buyx contend, helps reshape scholarly and public discourses. Such debate unveils the importance of inter-individual and communal relationships for social prosperity and for overcoming traditional impasses in bioethical debates. For example, Prainsack and Buyx explore the practical implications of solidarity in health databases,[42] precision and individualized medicine,[43] and transplantation and organ donation.[44]

At a global level, solidarity has more implications because of the prevailing disparities in health care and in other health-related resources.[45] Solidarity at the global level extends the circle of moral responsibility beyond national boundaries and highlights the anthropological similarities despite the prevailing cultural plurality. For instance, in a multilayered ethical dilemma similar to the migration of healthcare workers from low-income countries to more developed ones, using solidarity to lead the debate is informative. When personal and transnational interdependence is highlighted, global solidarity can motivate different national governments to cooperate in overcoming health inequalities and diseases that afflict the most vulnerable around the world.[46] Over the past two decades, global solidarity was influential in shaping the global bioethical

---

40. Welie, *In the Face of Suffering*, 159–200.

41. A detailed exploration of solidarity in the healthcare systems of various European countries is discussed in ter Meulen, Arts, and Muffels, *Solidarity in Health and Social Care in Europe*.

42. Prainsack and Buyx, *Solidarity in Biomedicine*, 97–122.

43. Prainsack and Buyx, *Solidarity in Biomedicine*, 123–44.

44. Along with Prainsack and Buyx, *Solidarity in Biomedicine*, 145–68, on organ donation, Saunders, "Altruism or Solidarity?," 376–81.

45. Illingworth and Parmet, "Solidarity for Global Health," ii–iv.

46. Eckenwiler, Straehle, and Chung, "Global Solidarity," 382–90.

discourse especially in adopting the UNESCO *Universal Declaration on Bioethics and Human Rights* in 2005. Although solidarity is not directly mentioned in this document, it is arguable that this document amounts to a solidaristic covenant between various nations.[47]

Challenges to Solidarity

Although solidarity is gaining ground in bioethical debates, locally and globally, one should not ignore the possible challenges to the concept and the limitations of its applicability. Conceptually, solidarity may be vague and could mean different things to different people. Solidarity may not always refer to a positive thing; criminals may show solidarity to each other but not for the well-being of their community. Similarly, a subtle sense of exclusion may lurk behind solidarity; by showing solidarity toward a certain group of people, one may, intentionally or unintentionally, exclude other groups of people. Nonetheless, a decidedly exclusive perception toward others cannot be considered solidaristic, no matter how helpful it is to its beneficiaries. Therefore, solidarity cannot be considered a normative concept *per se* because of all the subtleties which may disguise under its mantra. Therefore, a serious consideration of the historical and social context of solidaristic policies and their frequent re-evaluation are warranted to guarantee their intended solidaristic aspirations.[48]

Practically, solidarity is costly and risky. Thus, its applicability is contingent upon factors other than the good intentions of its advocates. For instance, perceiving similarity with a vulnerable group depends on how costly it is to offer them help, in terms of financial, emotional, political, and national resources. Solidarity, similar to its foundational hospitality, is risky since building trust among strangers takes a great deal of time and effort.[49] For instance, these issues have recently surfaced because of the refugee crisis spreading through Europe. Recognizing similarities with the refugees proved to be very costly in some of the hosting countries, not only financially but also in terms of national and cultural identities.[50]

In the same vein, several examples of exploitation under the disguise of solidarity are detrimental to their victims. Advocates of offshore

47. Gunson, "Solidarity and the Universal," 241–60.
48. Prainsack and Buyx, *Solidarity in Biomedicine*, 43–96.
49. Prainsack and Buyx, *Solidarity in Biomedicine*, 169–86.
50. Noble and Noble, "Hospitality as a Key," 47–65.

commercial gestational surrogacy in the US frame this practice as a solidaristic sisterhood across national boundaries. They contend that, through this practice, adoptive mothers help gestational mothers in developing countries escape their exploitative conditions. However, such rhetoric glosses over pervasive transnational injustices and disguises an exploitative relationship behind a solidaristic façade.[51]

In general, although people cannot be obliged to show solidarity toward others, it is warranted to nurture a hospitable environment which unveils similarities rather than accentuates differences. Here comes the role of the anthropological similarities advocated in this book. By emphasizing the universality of human dignity and vulnerability, it becomes possible to advocate for an inclusive solidarity in global bioethics. Such solidaristic framework will have local, national, and international implications regarding the provision of medical and health-related resources. More specifically, to foster solidarity among healthcare professionals, Prainsack and Buyx argue, it is necessary to nurture an educational environment that emphasizes similarities among various stakeholders.[52]

This is the goal of the following two sections, namely, to explore how to establish a hospitable environment, in academic medicine and in clinical practice, that can nourish solidarity in health care, locally and globally. Regardless of the possible challenges facing a global solidaristic approach to health care, solidarity is pregnant with hope in the goodness of the human society. Whereas human fallenness brings alienation and enmity, solidarity brings hope in a better human condition.

Hospitality and Dignity: The Role of Gratitude in Global Bioethics

To stand in solidarity with patients across the globe, gratitude is an important value in shaping medicine. In chapter 4, gratitude was advanced as a fundamental value in shaping the personal relationship between physicians and patients. In this section, gratitude will be extended beyond that particular clinical encounter to address the environment of medical practice within its broader social context. Since gratitude was derived from a socially constructed understanding of human dignity, its hospitable application in medical care should transfigure both involved

---

51. Fixmer-Oraiz, "Speaking of Solidarity," 126–64.
52. Prainsack and Buyx, *Solidarity in Biomedicine*, 169–86.

parties, physicians and patients. The leitmotif of the solicited change is hospitable openness toward each other.

Physicians and Healthcare Workers

Out of gratitude toward their current and previous patients, physicians, healthcare workers, and systems should be humbly open to patients, especially regarding the following themes. Such openness fosters reasonable expectations of medicine among patients along with public appreciation of the limitations of medicine and human life.

Social Dimensions of Medicine and Health

Physicians and healthcare systems should be humbly open about the broad spectrum of factors affecting health beyond access to medical services. They should be at the forefront of social movements to advocate for mending any public misconceptions and national and international injustices affecting health.

Over the past few decades in the US, physicians have evolved to become strangers to their patients due to many social changes. Because of ingrained social injustices, physicians pursue medical training in a social context that is drastically different from their own. While they mostly come from a privileged background, their initial exposure to patients takes place in inner-city hospitals with underserved populations.[53] Many of these physicians grow numb to the social injustices that are detrimental to these patients, including homelessness,[54] along with many other racially and culturally rooted injustices.[55] Consequently, when physicians unconsciously classify their patients according to their social worth, patients' health may be unnecessarily jeopardized. Unveiling these biases is warranted for a more solidaristic health care system.

Further, recent studies in the humanities unequivocally unveil the social and cultural construction of individual's experience of pain and suffering.[56] Hence, physicians have a vested interest in understanding and explaining these socially and culturally constructed experiences of

53. Rothman, *Strangers at the Bedside*, 127–47.
54. Hilfiker, "Are We Comfortable," 1375–76.
55. Black, "Jake's Story," 293–307.
56. Leder, "Toward a Phenomenology of Pain," 255–66.

suffering. When relieved from a powerful public demand for a painless human existence, physicians will have a broader set of tools to control pain. Similarly, when patients seek treatment for their affliction in a sophisticated and bureaucratic medical system, it is important for providers to recognize the epistemic injustice that befalls them. Patients are the weakest party within the medical system: they are forced to seek medical care (since no one would ever like to be sick) and, because of its science-centered mentality, medicine is more interested in what is objectively verifiable than in the patient's experience of her ailment.[57]

At a more general level, the social hype related to recent medical advancements has fueled an expensive "research imperative" which has a dire local and global social cost.[58] In the same vein, the influence of money and outside forces on the medical agenda is rarely integrated into medical training and practice, although it may negatively affect the health of patients.[59] Along with the rising cost of medical care, especially in Western countries, healthcare disparities are widening and increasingly disadvantaging the most vulnerable communities. At a global level, the burden of diseases unduly disadvantages poor nations and is exacerbated by offshore and laxly regulated pharmaceutical research (among other injustices) that narrowly benefit the already privileged citizens of the world.[60]

Hidden Curriculum in Medical Training and Practice

The hidden curriculum of medical training and practice is another aspect that needs to be unearthed for an authentically solidaristic practice of medicine. Rather than being mere educational institutes with a clearly defined teachable curriculum, medical schools are arguably moral communities and learning environments for adult learners. In such an environment, not only what students are taught is important, but also what they learn while immersed in the demanding context of medical education. Therefore, Frederic Hafferty explains that a medical curriculum consists of formal, informal, and hidden components which

---

57. Carel and Kidd, "Epistemic Injustice," 529–40.
58. Callahan, *What Price Better Health?*
59. Hergott, "View from Fiesole," 147–48; Bascom, "Sketches from a Surgeon's Notebook," 17–33.
60. Macklin, *Double Standards*.

influence the professional development of future physicians. The *formal* component of the curriculum stands for the concepts, behaviors, and skills directly taught to the students in the classroom. The *informal* component includes all the educational opportunities that help mold future physicians through their interaction with other colleagues and faculty members. However, the *hidden* component of the curriculum includes those systemic and social elements embedded in medical care which insidiously influence the development of students' professional identities. Those elements include institutional policies, evaluation activities of students and faculty, resource allocation decisions, and institutional slang.[61] Unsurprisingly, the hidden curriculum of an institution does not only shape students; a similar hidden curriculum is embedded in faculty development activities. Both curricula equally influence each other.[62]

In an educational milieu that is partly shaped by a hidden curriculum, medical atrocities cannot be prevented solely through comprehensive ethical training. While formal ethical training hones the morality of already-moral adult learners, its presence as part of the formal curriculum does not guarantee its efficacy. Thus, a narrow perception of medical ethics as a set of teachable skills does not suffice to nurture a moral professional identity in physicians. Rather, a broad perspective that addresses the school's cultural milieu is paramount.[63] Therefore, to build a solidaristic health system that delivers to vulnerable patients, medical schools should not narrowly underscore formal instruction in cultural competence, for instance: rather they ought to sensitize their students to the broader social context at the root of health disparities through formal, informal, and hidden aspects of their curricula.[64]

Furthermore, out of gratitude toward, and transparency with, future generations of physicians, medical schools and systems have to empower incoming students to be agents of change and to resist the negative aspects of the hidden curricula. A medical school, it is argued, unveils its hidden curriculum and helps students resist it through a longitudinal program that starts in the pre-clinical years and continues throughout their training. It is necessary to (1) prime students on what they will perhaps encounter on the rounds and among colleagues, and (2) sensitize

61. Hafferty, "Beyond Curriculum Reform," 403–7.
62. Hafler et al., "Decoding the Learning," 440–44.
63. Hafferty and Franks, "Hidden Curriculum," 861–71.
64. Paul, Ewen, and Jones, "Cultural Competence," 751–58.

them to identify their own motivations and actions within a powerful environment that demands tame conformation. (3) Students should be then encouraged to analyze their experiences along with other students in a safe environment. (4) They should finally be supported to choose their behaviors and attitudes in a way that cultivates their best possible professional identity.[65]

While these aspects of the hidden curriculum have been extensively studied in medical schools in the US, similar aspects are surely at play in schools around the world. Hence, a serious global effort to unearth their unique implications on the professional identity of future physicians is warranted.

Medicine Is Not a Science

The relationship between medicine and science is very important for a satisfactory practice of medicine for both patients and physicians. However, because of the lure of modern science, it is necessary to openly and publicly discuss this relationship to correct any public misconceptions and unrealistic expectations of medicine.

In the face of human fragility, scientific medicine may sooth any sense of uncertainty that accompanies serious illness.[66] However, the clinical practice of medicine does not narrowly follow a simplistic understanding of science; practitioners have to use the general scientific medical knowledge of pathology and apply it to the particular patient's case. Hence, practical reasoning, or *phronesis* in Aristotelian terms, is vital for the practice of medicine, which is not a pure science nor a technical art (skill-centered).[67] The importance of practical reasoning is substantiated during the apprenticeship of medical novices; clinical judgement is honed through narrative case studies using various approaches including thorough exploration of medical history and skeptical dissection of clinical and laboratory findings. This pedagogical model highlights the unviability of standardized or computerized medical algorithms because of the uniqueness of each case, even when patients are afflicted with the

---

65. Holmes et al., "Harnessing the Hidden Curriculum," 1355–70.

66. Montgomery, *How Doctors Think*, 13–28.

67. Montgomery, *How Doctors Think*, 29–41; Henry, Zaner, and Dittus, "Moving beyond Evidence-Based Medicine," 292–97.

same disease.[68] Several pedagogical tools depart from scientific standards, such as (1) using informal and contradictory rules, (2) emphasizing complexity and flexibility through challenging maxims, and (3) ingraining ritualized hierarchies according to clinical experience rather than exam achievements.[69]

Because of the uniqueness of each patient, medical practice dissociates from a simplistic understanding of scientific causality. While it is possible to explain the pathology and symptoms of a certain disease after it happens using linear causality, more difficult questions remain unanswered, such as what are the specific reasons behind the particular patient's affliction at the time it happened? At a deeper level, and what matters for most patients, arises the question of "why me?" which unveils several anthropological dimensions defying any possible scientific answer.[70]

Furthermore, while adopting a scientific façade may assuage human fear of uncertainty through "quantified uncertainty," pure scientific inquiry into diseases equally harms patients and physicians by overlooking their deeper yearning for human rapport. By shaping their profession on scientific objectivity, physicians pronounce death as their insidious, but inevitable, enemy, and easily hide behind a procedurally ethical, but anthropologically indifferent, professional practice. In the same vein, by hiding behind science, physicians avoid questioning the certainty of medical science, especially when biomedical advancements overshadow lurking uncertainties. Hence, a detached practice of medicine arguably impairs the ability of some physicians to make sound medical judgements.[71] Emotional detachment from their patients has serious ramification on physicians' professional and personal lives, such as dissatisfaction with their practice, emotional detachment from family and friends, and exaggerated sense of invulnerability which becomes detrimental when they fall ill.

By the same token, patients are possibly harmed because of overoccupation with scientific facts. While some patients may choose not to be fully informed about the scientific details of their illness, all patients deeply yearn to assuage their fear of an uncertain future. Along with their

---

68. Montgomery, *How Doctors Think*, 42–53.
69. Montgomery, *How Doctors Think*, 103–53.
70. Montgomery, *How Doctors Think*, 57–99.
71. Halpern, *From Detached Concern to Empathy*, 39–65.

fear of losing control, patients seek the assurance of non-abandonment of their physicians, friends, and family members. Hence, even when physicians are not qualified to answer the teleological questions rising near death, they have a moral obligation to acknowledge the anguish of their patients when facing a serious illness.

On the side of physicians, when they are overly occupied with medical science, they may neglect the relational dimension of their profession. Their deeper yearning for a friendlier relationship with their patients is rarely acknowledged in the prevailing "medicine of strangers." However, a "medicine of neighbors" does not demand building friendships with every patient (though not totally excluded); rather, it recognizes, through its embedded hospitality, the humanity of both strangers: physician and patient. At a global level, a "medicine of neighbors" recognizes the neighborliness of all patients, regardless of how far apart, physically or culturally, they seem.[72]

Narrative Medicine

To build a neighborly and hospitable medicine, it is essential to understand the important role that narrations play in shaping the clinical encounter. Works of literature, it is arguable, are indispensable resources for physicians to imagine the inner lives of their patients. Because of their brief encounter, physicians are not able to unveil all the personal, emotional, and historical particularities of their patients. Therefore, it takes a leap of imagination for physicians, with the help of fictional literature, to address the unique experience of particular patients in cases of devastating diseases or looming death.[73]

Furthermore, in medical education, narrative medicine has been introduced to highlight the relational dimension that shapes the story of both physicians and patients. By developing their narrative competencies as neophytes, future physicians can recognize, absorb, and interpret their patients' verbal and nonverbal communication bits. At a deeper level, physicians and patients evolve to humbly recognize their shared humanity and more openly share their personal struggles.[74] As a result of hospitable openness toward each other, physicians change as much as

72. Montgomery, *How Doctors Think*, 157–207.
73. Connelly, "Whole Story," 150–61.
74. Charon, "Narrative Medicine," 261–70.

their patients heal. Physicians assuage the fears of their patients through naming their disease, proposing a prognosis, and promising to not abandon the patient during her ordeal. In certain cases, only attentive and compassionate listening to the patient's story can unveil the meaning of her ordeal and bring about healing to her entire person.[75]

In general, the positive role of the humanities in medical education, Jeffery Bishop argues, should not be measured using narrow scientific standards. The use of the humanities in medicine, including narrative medicine, reminds physicians of their original call into medicine: a call of a suffering other which initially exhorted them to pursue medical education.[76] Contrary to a simplistic preoccupation with measurable efficacy, healing accrued in hospitable encounters may not meet the rigorous standards of evidence-based medicine. The most that a humanistic encounter may prove is that both physicians and patients are vulnerable humans awaiting the consolation of each other.

Patients

Out of gratitude to the services that physicians and medical systems offer to them, patients are expected to play a hospitable role toward their providers at various levels. On the personal level, patients need to recognize the dignity and vulnerability of their physicians. The ordeal of becoming a physician is not easy to comprehend by outsiders. Despite the public fascination in medical technology in the US for instance, very little is said about what doctors actually go through before they acquire their prestigious social status. Along with the many years of training, self-disciplining, and delayed gratification, physicians are trained in less-than-perfect environments where their embodied humanity is constantly harassed (more details in the next section). Physicians are always short on time, sleep, and family activities, and they are expected by their patients to not have emotions in the face of suffering and death.

However, articles in popular newspapers and magazines can tone down medical jargon and explain the inner works of medicine to the public. By so doing, these articles expose public misconceptions about physicians and re-establish their human side in the public eye. In an article in *The Atlantic*, for instance, Meghan O'Rourke reviews a wide

---

75. Zaner, "On Evoking," 655–66; Fuks et al., "Narratives, Metaphors," 301–13.
76. Bishop, "Rejecting Medical Humanism," 15–25.

array of books that narrate the human side of physicians, in the making and in practice. She unpacks the practice of medicine in the US to the general public and highlights some of the reasons behind the difficulties of communication between physicians and patients. She explains the duress which physicians must endure when their time is constantly running short, when faceless insurance representatives or hospital bureaucrats have to validate their professional decisions, and when their practice is constantly under the microscope for possible legal prosecution. O'Rourke ultimately argues that it is necessary to reform the medical system in the US not only for the sake of better healing services to patients, but equally for the sake of physicians.[77] Therefore, an important public discourse should evolve to highlight the challenges of becoming a physician and practicing medicine. This is to counter the public perception of physicians which feeds on commercials-saturated celebrity-physician-led talk shows or an increasingly negative—and unrealistic—portrayal of physicians in movies.[78]

To counterbalance the unrealistic public demand on physicians and medical systems, it has been recently argued, even by physicians, that patients have to be actively involved in their own care. Proponents do not advocate this involvement from an individualistic and autonomous perspective; rather they recognize the vulnerability of physicians as human beings and encourage patients to be partners in their care because they have equal epistemological authority with their physicians. As a physician himself, Jerome Groopman initiates his lay readers into the world of physicians, how they think and how they make medical decisions. He argues that many of the errors that doctors fall prey to are not because of ignorance of clinical facts. Rather, physicians are sometimes misguided by their emotions and temperaments, by their ingrained prejudices toward certain patients, by their falling into cognitive traps,[79] or because of outside financial interests in their medical decisions.[80]

Hence, it is important for physicians to honestly acknowledge the uncertainty of their medical knowledge and the fallibility of their human skills.[81] Similarly, it is important for patients to recognize those limita-

77. O'Rourke, "Doctors Tell All."
78. Flores, "Mad Scientists," 635–58; Flores, "Doctors in the Movies," 1084–88.
79. Groopman, *How Doctors Think*, 27–5.
80. Groopman, *How Doctors Think*, 203–33.
81. Groopman, *How Doctors Think*, 101–55; Also in; Hilfiker, "Allowing the Debilitated to Die," 716.

tions, to not demand of medicine what it cannot deliver, and to gracefully ask for a second opinion whenever necessary.[82] Groopman envisions an open (hospitable) relationship between physicians and patients/families, whereby patients help their physicians hone their expertise through honest feedback and increasing self-awareness.

Fundamentally, patients play a crucial role in guarding the well-being of their physicians, in two examples at least. First, when physicians commit medical errors for any reason, patients/families can prevent them from becoming second victims; they can facilitate the healing of physicians through reconciliation, especially considering the fact that the culture of peer-reviewed medicine does not have a place for absolution.[83] By being open to human vulnerability and lurking mistakes, patients/families understand the possibility of error and harm, without downplaying the need for systemic interventions to prevent future errors. Furthermore, physicians experience an abundance of guilt and shame throughout their training and practice, so an act of kindness on the side of patients/families brings a great relief. Second, and equally important, patients are not defined by their illnesses. They are rather active members of society who can shape the politics of medical care delivery through democratic and civil-society initiatives. Patients and their families can stand in solidarity with their physicians and other marginalized patients through demanding systemic and educational changes that take the well-being of both patients and physicians seriously.

Hospitality and Vulnerability: The Role of Compassion in Global Bioethics

To stand in solidarity with strangers across the globe, compassion is central to the practice of clinical medicine. In chapter 5, compassion was discussed as the proper answer to the suffering other and defended as a basis of profound changes in medical education and physicians' self-awareness. In this section, two important themes are discussed, namely, the vulnerability of physicians and the role of compassion in medical education. This is the final step before bringing the different threads of this book together to discuss end of life care in the final section.

---

82. Groopman, *How Doctors Think*, 177–202.
83. Bascom, "Sketches from," 17–33.

The Humanness and Vulnerability of Physicians

When hospitality shapes the encounter between strangers, the vulnerability of both parties surfaces. A hospitable host recognizes her anthropological similarities to her guest, specifically their common dignity as humans and their shared and inevitable vulnerability. Although her vulnerability may not be readily obvious at that encounter, a self-conscious host is aware of her ingrained vulnerability which will show up sooner or later. Ultimately, hospitality is the basis of compassion toward the vulnerable other.[84]

During the medical encounter, physician's vulnerability is not always clear both to the physician herself nor to her patients. Ironically, being a medical professional does not give practitioners any immunity against diseases and suffering.[85] However, the vulnerability of physicians, though unjustifiably ignored, manifests in many ways, during medical training and practice, through their unconscious avoidance of human suffering, and through their high rate of burnout and suicide. It is therefore arguable that by consciously accepting to suffer-with (have compassion toward) their patients, their practice of medicine is built on a robust and fulfilling basis.

Vulnerability of Physicians

As embodied experiences, medical training and practice expose the vulnerability of physicians at different levels.[86] Medical training and practice are embodied in that a great deal of violence afflicts both the bodies of physicians and patients. Through their constant interaction with patients, physicians may acquire or spread infections which might harm them, their families, and many other patients. Within healthcare institutions, strict "embodied" procedures are put in place to prevent the spread of those infections, the simplest of which are hand sanitization and mandatory yearly vaccination against influenza. Similarly, resuscitating a dying patient epitomizes the violence done to her body by the physician's body.

---

84. Frakes, "When Strangers Call," 79–99; Owens, *Hospitality to Strangers*, 1–6.
85. Owens, *Hospitality to Strangers*, 7–31.
86. Poirier, "Medical Education," 522–52; Hoffmaster, "What Does Vulnerability Mean?," 38–45.

Furthermore, the demands of medical practice are taxing on the bodies of physicians starting in medical school. Students and residents in training complain of sleep deprivation, unhealthy eating habits, and a sense of uncleanliness after many hours of work.[87] They are flooded with scientific medical information that needs to be absorbed through one's own skin.[88] In the same vein, several trainees highlight the insidious role of discrimination in shaping the culture of medicine during their training and practice. Racial and gender discrimination afflict the educational environment (hidden curriculum) for many physicians in training and influence their own perceptions toward patients when in practice.[89]

Moreover, physicians struggle with power dynamics and personal relationships during their training and beyond. Very early in their training, medical students start feeling their separation from the world of lay people, including family and friends, because of the demands and nature of their studies. Also, the culture of medicine nourishes extreme competitiveness that precipitates their anxiety and sense of isolation from peers and teachers. Not only are medical students and residents at the bottom of medical hierarchy, but they sometimes find themselves at the mercy of abusive teachers and patients. While it is illogical to consider a vulnerable and sick patient a threat to medical trainees, the complexity of power relationships in medicine may justify to some trainees to have several distorted perceptions and behaviors.[90]

For instance, Terry Mizrahi argues that internal medicine residents develop an attitude of getting rid of patients that seems necessary for them to survive their training with the least possible damage. This attitude, she contends, results from a socialization process in which both other colleagues and patients play a central role rather than "exemplary" faculty members. It is a "hidden" subculture among trainees which motivates them to classify patients according to their social and medical worth within the unique and underprivileged social context of urban academic medical centers (unlike the trainees' mostly privileged backgrounds). Because of this socialization process, physicians experience lasting effects on their relationship with patients and on their career choices.[91]

---

87. Poirier, "Medical Education," 522–52; Poirier, *Doctors in the Making*, 72–94.

88. Poirier, *Doctors in the Making*, 45–71.

89. Poirier, *Doctors in the Making*, 95–124. Several examples unfold in Takakuwa, Rubashkin, and Herzig, *What I Learned in Medical School*.

90. Poirier, *Doctors in the Making*, 95–153.

91. Mizrahi, *Getting Rid of Patients*.

The most hidden side of physicians' vulnerability is that related to their emotions and how those affect their practice of medicine.[92] Because of the exhausting demands of their training, physicians start to lose their empathy toward patients when they first encounter them in third year medical school. This is partly attributed to their fatigue and sense of disorientation in the hospital's strange and disorganized landscape. Compared to the organized environment of the classroom, patients in real life never follow textbook rules or shift schedules. During this chaos, trainees become focused on survival while unconsciously integrating many negative emotions. Fear of harming patients,[93] shame of previous mistakes or near-misses,[94] and sadness and grief for losing a patient,[95] are among the most influential emotions experienced in training. While a bit of concern to not make mistakes is essential for the safety of patients, too much fear may be paralyzing. Similarly, while grieving a patient is a normal human reaction, the ignoring of this grief by colleagues and faculty members is detrimental to the practice of medicine. Both extremes, numbness to human suffering and debilitating sorrow, may lead to physician burnout.[96]

These negative emotions grow their roots in an environment that seems hostile to its dwellers. As mentioned above, because of the complex power dynamics within this environment, powerless trainees victimize their patients and classify them according to their social and medical worth. Because trainees in urban medical centers come from different cultural, ethnic, and educational backgrounds compared to their patients, it is very difficult for them to empathize in the hostile and demanding environment of the hospital. After years of self-disciplining and delayed gratification, physicians encounter patients who are perceived to be manipulative of the system or self-destructive through over-eating, alcoholism, or drug addiction. Thus, when the suffering of those patients does not make sense from the perspective of privileged and disciplined physicians, empathy and compassion are rarefied and the ability to heal is shattered.[97]

---

92. Ofri, *What Doctors Feel*.
93. Ofri, *What Doctors Feel*, 64–94.
94. Ofri, *What Doctors Feel*, 124–39.
95. Ofri, *What Doctors Feel*, 98–121.
96. Ofri, *What Doctors Feel*, 143–69; Granek et al., "Nature and Impact," 964–66.
97. Ofri, *What Doctors Feel*, 6–22.

Avoidance of Suffering

One of the detrimental results of a demanding training is a tendency among physicians to avoid suffering. Although humans generally tend to avoid suffering when possible, the detrimental effect of such avoidance in the context of medical care cannot be ignored. When physicians avoid their patients because of how much they are suffering, patients feel abandoned by their physicians, and the quality of care they receive is notably compromised. Ultimately, when medical cure is not available, healing through powerful personal presence is not achievable.

However contrary to their professional ideal, physicians tend to avoid suffering because of their unacknowledged vulnerability. Physicians may identify with patients, may feel inadequate in facing complicated diseases, or may have unresolved emotional issues stirred by certain patients. At a deeper level, physicians may struggle with their own fear of dependence, suffering, and death,[98] which are fueled by unrealistic appreciation of medical advancements and an ingrained image of "a lone and heroic physician."[99] Therefore, when physicians avoid their suffering patients and abandon the opportunity of healing through personal rapport, they fail to connect with their inner vulnerable self; that is what makes it even more difficult for them when they inevitably fall ill.[100]

Burnout and Compassion Fatigue among Physicians

As vulnerable humans, physicians are prone to burnout because of the demands of their jobs and their mitigated ability to cope with them. Burnout afflicts normal people in their demanding jobs perhaps because of prevailing negative attitudes, ineffective communications with colleagues, and inadequate self-awareness. Burnout is detrimental to both physicians and patients because it compromises the well-being of physicians and their ability to care for themselves and others. Burned out physicians tend to perform less on the job because of emotional exhaustion, cynicism, and a sense of detachment (depersonalization), along with a sense of ineffectiveness and lack of personal achievement (negative

---

98. Connelly, "Avoidance of Human Suffering," 381–91.
99. Poirier, *Doctors in the Making*, 125–53.
100. Montgomery, *How Doctors Think*, 157–75.

self-evaluation).[101] Some specialties pose a higher risk of burnout compared to others, such as orthopedic surgery.[102] During their training and beyond, orthopedists and other specialists are more prone to burn out, depression, errors, and unprofessional behaviors because of their sense of loneliness and the absence of an effective support system.[103]

Furthermore, as they are constantly exposed to suffering and dying patients, physicians may be prone to compassion fatigue because of compromised boundaries. It might be difficult to strike a healthy balance between compassion and self-care in a time-restrained work environment.[104] Because of burnout and compassion fatigue, physicians are more susceptible to substance abuse behaviors and have higher suicidal risk compared to the general population.[105] Therefore, to preserve the well-being of physicians, it is the responsibility of their departments and institutions, and even more broadly of the entire health system, to address their challenges.[106] Although individual well-being programs are useful in some cases, a social and cultural discourse is crucial to publicly discuss the premises of medicine and its goals and limitations.

In short, the well-being of physicians and patients may be severely compromised when medicine is solely perceived as a scientific venture rather than a call to compassionately care for suffering patients using scientific knowledge.

The Role of Compassion in Medical Education

Compassion as a Basis for Satisfying Physicianship

It has been previously argued that compassion is the initial motivation for those who pursue medical education. It is because of the call of a suffering other that some people decide to become physicians and

---

101. Vachon, "Care of the Caregiver," 379–93.

102. Daniels, DePasse, and Kamal, "Orthopaedic Surgeon Burnout," 213–19.

103. Shapiro, Zhang, and Warm, "Residency as a Social Network," 617–23; Bruce, Congalen, and Congalen, "Burnout in Physicians," 272–78.

104. Gallagher, "Compassion Fatigue," 265–67; Vachon, "Care of the Caregiver," 379–93.

105. Mavroforou, Giannoukas, and Michalodimitrakis, "Alcohol and Drug Abuse," 611; Gold, Sen, and Schwenk, "Details on Suicide," 45–49.

106. Atallah et al., "Put on Your Own Oxygen Mask," 731–35.

extend their compassionate service toward other suffering strangers.[107] Thus, compassion, it is argued, is the basis of the medical enterprise and its primordial moral motive rather than any outside source of morality, whether religious, secular, or market-driven.[108]

Despite the recent advancements of medicine, its practice continues to hinge on *phronesis* (practical wisdom) which balances the general scientific rule with the particular condition of patients. Phronesis then demands a personal transformation of the practitioner as she initially answers, affectively more than cognitively, the call of a suffering and vulnerable other.[109] Therefore, it has been argued that the presence of a suffering stranger is the first normative demand asking for the sympathy of the practitioner. Sympathy in this case is a precondition of morality.[110] However, hospitality is endorsed in this book as the precondition for sympathy; to sympathize with a stranger, one should be first open to her. Through hospitality, the physician recognizes the dignity and vulnerability of her patient and is then moved in sympathy to have compassion (suffer with) and to offer help. On the contrary, when physicians meet their patients as objects, they objectify themselves and hinder the healing process even when a cure is available. Hence, a compassionate relationship between physicians and patients brings healing to physicians inasmuch as it brings it to patients. The satisfaction of both physicians and patients depends on their hospitable and compassionate interaction.[111]

For a long time, concerned detachment was the ideal of medical practice. Sir William Osler argued in 1889 that detachment (equanimity) is the ideal of medical practice to prevent physician's burnout and clinical errors, and to provide scientifically sound clinical judgement.[112] A professional ideal of emotional detachment from patients grew out of exaggerated emphasis on the scientific and objective side of medicine;[113] such detachment has tangible negative consequences on the well-being of patients.[114] Although their unchecked emotional involvement with their

107. Bishop, *Anticipatory Corpse*, 285–313.
108. Welie, "Relationship between Medicine's," 175–98.
109. Fuks et al., "Foundation of Physicianship," 114–26.
110. Welie, *In the Face of Suffering*, 125–57; Welie, "Sympathy as the Basis," 476–87.
111. Owens, *Hospitality to Strangers*.
112. Halpern, *From Detached Concern*, xi–xvi.
113. Halpern, *From Detached Concern*, 15–38; Also in Brincat, "How Medical Training," 199–210.
114. Halpern, *From Detached Concern*, 1–13.

patients may influence their reasoning processes, physicians need their empathic abilities to better understand their patients. Initially, physicians need to humbly validate the patient's story and believe her symptoms,[115] so that they may balance against the unavoidable epistemic injustice that frequently befalls vulnerable patients in a complicated medical system.[116] Through empathy, physicians use their imagination to better comprehend their patient's experience and to offer accurate diagnosis and suitable treatment options to fit the patient's needs.

In medicine, empathy is a kind of "emotion-guided activity of imagination" or "emotional reasoning" that uses emotional connections with another human being to better understand her experience. Although emotions in clinical practice may be risky, physicians need to be self-aware to avoid projecting their own emotions and to fine-tune their imagination. By so doing, physicians serve their patients through better diagnosis, more accurate understanding of patient's autonomous decisions, and ultimately a satisfactory healing experience to both patients and physicians.[117] Even empirical studies have shown better clinical results when physicians treat their patients with compassion.[118]

At a deeper level, patients do not heal solely because they autonomously make their own medical decisions. Patients make decisions that are partly shaped by the ways physicians frame their diagnoses and by how much their physicians are emotionally involved in their care. While understandably protecting patient's autonomy is quintessential for their well-being, non-interference and leaving them alone to sort through their options amount to abandonment, which hinders their healing. In other words, empathic rapport with patients preserves their autonomy, however counterintuitive this may sound from an objective scientific perspective. As Jodi Halpern puts it: "Empathy can help patients recover the ability to imagine a livable future."[119] Ultimately, a hope of healing grows out of the presence of a hospitable and compassionate other.

To bring a hope of healing to the patient, a compassionate care giver (a physician, a family member, or a friend) needs to appropriately address

115. Ekstrom, "Liars, Medicine," 159–80.

116. Carel and Kidd, "Epistemic Injustice," 529–40.

117. Halpern, *From Detached Concern to Empathy*, 67–99; and in Halpern, "What Is Clinical Empathy?," 670–74.

118. Del Canale et al., "Relationship between Physician Empathy and Disease," 1243–49.

119. Halpern, *From Detached Concern to Empathy*, 11, 101–27.

suffering as it unfolds. Suffering after a dire diagnosis passes through three phases: a mute phase, an expressive phase, then the evolvement of a new identity (a healed self). Comparatively, to show compassion to the suffering person, compassion should pass through similar phases: (1) a silent empathy; (2) an expressive empathy that helps find a voice to the voiceless (giving a diagnosis helps the patient and her support system to transform her life story using new words and reimagined meanings); and (3) a new identity (a healed self that has its own renewed and hopeful voice). Along with the transformative healing that the patient experiences, the compassionate person who cares for her also experiences similar transformation by identifying with his compassionate self. The problem in medical education and practice resides here: the physician is rarely given the opportunity to be in touch with her compassionate self. Many reasons are to blame, including overly emphasized scientific and objective medicine and paternalistic benevolence, rather than a sense of common vulnerability between physicians and patients.

Furthermore, to empathize with her patient, a physician needs the patient to empathize with her as well since she also experiences distress when she constantly has to deliver bad news or has to be in the presence of dying patients.[120] Patients have to acknowledge the vulnerability of their physicians for the latter to be compassionate with them in return; an entitled patient repels her doctor who would thus, when forced, only offer a lip service to compassion. When Ivan Ilyich recognized the distress of his servant Gerasim, he re-evaluated his life anew and accepted death as natural, contrary to the cultural ideal he thus far lived. Ivan started to heal when he found himself in the presence of a caregiver who recognized the universal human reality, death, without being apologetic about bringing it up.[121]

In summary, although healing may be narrowly thought of as a physician's responsibility, it is clear that healing is achieved within a social context where physicians, along with other friends and family members, bring hope and meaning to the suffering patient. Consequently, medical education should focus on training physicians within a healing-centered environment.[122] Such environment does not only emphasize the vulnerability of patients but also recognizes and cultivates a sense of

---

120. Reich, "Speaking of Suffering," 83–108.

121. Reich, "Speaking of Suffering," 83–108; Charlton and Verghese, "Caring for Ivan Ilyich," 93–95.

122. Pellegrino, "Toward a Reconstruction of Medical Morality," 65–71.

vulnerability among physicians for a truly transformative and healing clinical relationship.

Compassion in Medical Education

After establishing compassion as crucial to a satisfying practice of medicine for both physicians and patients, it is warranted to explore the ways to "teach" or cultivate compassion in medical education.

One important starting point for this quest is the bravery to question what has been taken for granted in medical education and to make necessary changes even if they break with long standing practices. Several philosophical and historical inquiries were explored in this book so far; however, many inspiring scholars have already used philosophical methods to rethink the efficacy of academic practices and their influence on medical trainees.[123] Similar scholarship should be continued within medicine to equip future generations of practitioners with necessary tools for a healing practice of medicine. While science has overtaken the public and professional perception of medicine, compassionate care for vulnerable patients remains the core of healing. Physicians should recognize their professional identity as scientific healers rather than medical scientists.[124] However effective empathy and compassion are, there remains a danger of using them as another tool to perpetuate physicians' power, thus emptying them of their personal and human dimension.[125]

Thus far, several factors that interfere with compassionate care have been discussed. Some factors are related to the simplistic understanding of medicine as science rather than a scientifically inspired healing venture. In identifying medicine with science, suffering is avoided, in training and practice, because it is not measurable nor objectively verifiable. Similarly, the hidden curriculum in medical institutions may shape trainees, practitioners, and faculty members in a way that is indifferent to vulnerable patients. Extreme competitiveness, exhausting workload, and overlooked embodied and emotional experiences of trainees dry up their reservoir of compassion and foster a sense of individualistic heroism as central to their professional identity. Further, social and cultural

---

123. For instance, Hodges et al., "Medical Education," 563–71; Kuper, Whitehead, and Hodges, "Looking Back," e849–60.

124. Boudreau, Cassell, and Fuks, "Healing Curriculum," 1193–201.

125. Hooker, "Understanding Empathy," 541–52.

disparities between trainees in urban medical centers and their patients may impede any sense of similarity, thus shattering the very basis of compassion.

Other factors related to medical education further phase out compassion as irrelevant to the practice of medicine. The environment in pre-medical education initiates aspiring physicians into the competitive environment of medicine through competitive organic chemistry courses, MCAT preparatory courses and exam, and illusionary compassionate volunteering (though mandatory) activities. Even admission officers in medical schools appreciate more robust scientific achievements than compassionate personal attributes.[126] In the same vein, after admission to medical school, students are quickly initiated to medicine's mode of thinking. Through the anatomy lab experience, for instance, students integrate the importance of their eyes/vision to verify normalcy and ailment more than using their listening ears to understand the patient's experience.[127] Cadavers and their anatomy, unconsciously, become more real for medical decision-making than a personal encounter with a suffering patient. Objective and depersonalized scientific knowledge is enshrined, early in medical training, as the epitome of medical care.[128]

Furthermore, the emotions of medical students are lastingly shaped during their anatomy lab experience. There, students are socialized into medicine by integrating a basic emotional rule, namely, detachment. Through humor, an emotional distance is established between students and cadavers; a distance that is replicated within every future encounter with patients. Similar to the instrumental use of human cadavers to gain medical knowledge, students instrumentally treat patients to advance their career,[129] while feeding the prevailing denial of death in medicine.[130]

By the same token, medical knowledge is transferred between teachers and students by the way of classifying patients according to their diseases, rather than by investing in a humane healing encounter.[131] Such pedagogy saps the student's reservoir of compassion because it pushes

---

126. Spiro, "Empathy: An Introduction," 1–6; Morowitz, "Pre-Med as a Metaphor," 70–75.

127. Spiro, "Empathy: An Introduction," 1–6; Spiro, "What Is Empathy" 7–14.

128. Landau, ". . . And the Least of These," 103–9.

129. Hafferty, "Cadaver Stories," 344–56. More details are introduced in his book *Into the Valley*, especially, 53–152.

130. Robbins, "Confronting the Cadaver," 131–40.

131. Reiser, "Science, Pedagogy," 121–32.

them to classify patients: some as deserving sympathy (because their diseases are scientifically intriguing), while others are blamed for their afflictions (such as an alcoholic patient diagnosed with liver cancer).[132]

In general, many educators have ventured into the territory of teaching compassion in medical school and have highlighted relevant points regarding the efficacy of their interventions. It is broadly admitted that teaching empathy and compassion starts early on in life within a compassionate family and a caring community.[133] It has also been explained that applicants to medical schools have usually been moved by a suffering other to become physicians.[134] Therefore, the role of medical education is to nourish existing compassion rather than ingrain it in a previously fallow land.[135] However, Henk ten Have and Bert Gordijn warn of a broader challenge to teaching empathy. They contend that in a globalized world, it is not the sole responsibility of academic medical centers and bioethics to nourish compassion in future generations of healthcare workers. Because of growing inequality, political manipulation, and growing nationalistic interests, fostering compassion becomes a collective social-global responsibility.[136]

It is suggested that admitting students who show more compassion, through their pre-admission activities and/or in a personal interview, is warranted.[137] However, because of the environment of medical training and practice, students' compassion may be sapped if no effective interventions were implemented to prevent it.[138] Similarly, other educators emphasize the positive influence of good and compassionate role models on shaping compassionate students.[139] However, such approach presumes a homogeneously compassionate faculty and expects students to acquire a compassionate attitude through "osmosis." Hence, an engaging discussion between faculty and students, in a leisure-like and safe context,

---

132. Peschel and Peschel, "Selective Empathy," 110–20.
133. Cavanagh, "Rediscovering Compassion," 317–27.
134. Bishop, *Anticipatory Corpse*, 285–313.
135. Charlton and Verghese, "Caring for Ivan Ilyich," 93–95.
136. ten Have and Gordijn, "Empathy and Violence," 499–500.
137. Glick, "Empathic Physician," 85–102; And in Ekstrom, "Liars, Medicine," 159–80.
138. Davis, "What Is Empathy," 707–11; Pence, "Can Compassion Be Taught?," 189–91.
139. Ekstrom, "Liars, Medicine," 159–80.

about their distressing experiences with patients and other colleagues, is necessary.[140]

Some of the most implemented educational interventions among students are those that foster a healthy personal curiosity in patient's experience and suffering. Unfortunately, many physicians do not recognize the dearth of compassion in medical practice until they themselves fall ill and are treated as patients. When they experience, first-hand, what their patients endure, physicians recognize the harm caused by the ideal of equanimity.[141] Therefore, to correct their detachment from patients, physicians have to cultivate a hospitable openness and personal (rather than pure scientific) curiosity toward their patients to better understand their ordeal.[142] Rita Charon and many other educators suggested that nourishing narrative abilities among students has a positive effect on the latter's compassionate rapport with patients. Through a curious approach to patients, physicians read the verbal and nonverbal communication bits and use them to mitigate the uncertainty of the human body and medical knowledge. Encouraging students to write medical histories from the perspective of their patients helps them imagine and participate in their ordeal. In addition, educators have used stories to foster a meaningful discussion about patient suffering and physician experience.[143] Some even suggest using stories written by faculty members to teach self-reflection and explore unconscious prejudices toward patients.[144]

Moreover, through openness to patients, physicians embrace their own compassionate selves and inner emotional lives. Activities that foster reflection and self-awareness, whether as part of medical curriculum or within their religious or broader community, help students unveil their inner selves and suppressed emotions. Self-awareness shields students within the demanding practice of medicine against burnout and compassion fatigue.[145] Similarly, by teaching students to accept their

---

140. Spiro, "What Is Empathy?," 7–14; Wear and Zarconi, "Can Compassion Be Taught?," 948–53; Ponce, "Can Compassion Be Taught?," 189–91.

141. Spiro, "Empathy: An Introduction," 1–6.

142. Halpern, *From Detached Concern*, 129–47; Connelly, "Avoidance of Human Suffering," 381–91.

143. Lateef, "From Data to Stories," 50–55.

144. Farrell et al., "Autoethnography," 974–82; Charon, "Narrative Medicine," 261–70.

145. Poirier, *Doctors in the Making*, 154–70; Connelly, "Avoidance of Human Suffering," 381–91; Lu, "Why It Was Hard," 454–58; Burks and Kobus, "Legacy of Altruism," 317–25.

own vulnerability as integral to their embodied professional experience, they are better equipped to encounter patients with emotional honesty and healing personal presence.[146] Flexible clinical demands on students provide enough time for reflection and personal engagement with patients.[147] Also, developing interview skills to be patient-centered rather than symptoms-centered nourishes the students' compassionate rapport with their patients.[148]

Hospitality and End of Life Care in Global Bioethics

This final section will discuss the moral issues related to end of life care and two of its options, euthanasia and physician-assisted suicide (PAS) on the one hand, and palliative and hospice care on the other. The brief discussion will use the moral mindset developed in this book to argue against euthanasia and PAS and to advocate an earlier and broader use of palliative and hospice care to attend to those close to their death. The discussion is not meant to be exhaustive of all the arguments relevant to these practices; however, it highlights that end of life care, along with other pressing global ethical issues, should be seen through a broader, and more inclusive perspective to overcome impasses in ethical discourse.

The Hospitality Case against Euthanasia and Physician-Assisted Suicide

Over the past few decades, euthanasia and PAS have gained ground in liberal societies and were legalized (or introduced for voting) in some countries and states. Regardless of their technical differences, euthanasia/PAS are introduced as a legal option under the banner of "death with dignity" or "a right to die." Yet, it has been previously discussed that the peculiar understanding of human dignity and rights in this context is controversial. Both opponents and proponents of euthanasia/PAS use human dignity to advance their arguments, though each building on a different understanding of the concept.[149]

---

146. Poirier, "Medical Education," 522–52.
147. Pence, "Can Compassion Be Taught?," 189–91.
148. Benbassat and Baumal, "What Is Empathy?," 832–39.
149. Mendiola, "Overworked," 129–43.

Proponents of euthanasia/PAS use dignity in its "attributed" sense to justify an—almost—absolute patient freedom to end her life. This sense hinges on the respect one can garner within her community. However, because of illness and invasive medical interventions, a person may feel that her life is so deformed and is not worth living anymore. She hence has the right to end her life while still having her dignity and ability to decide. To protect her vulnerability against the encroachments of medical technology, the argument goes, autonomous decision-making is her shield. In short, proponents of euthanasia/PAS use a narrow sense of human dignity and vulnerability to justify an overly individualistic autonomous decision making.

However, their argument does not square with a deeper questioning of their premises within the hospitable framework advanced in this book. Other relevant senses of dignity were discussed previously. Along with the "attributed" sense, dignity refers to the "innate" and inalienable worth of humans for merely being humans. Also, "inflorescent" dignity manifests in achieving human excellence through going above and beyond what every person is expected to do.[150] Further, "residual" dignity is the value communities bestow on individuals even when they have not acquired (or are not able to acquire) any human excellence. It is a universally recognized sense of dignity that manifests in respecting dead people and ritually burying them.[151]

Ultimately, any understanding of human dignity presupposes a human community that equally dignifies each member (regardless of their achievements). A community ingrains in its members a communal identity through embracing every member with dignity; a community extracts its sense of dignity from the dignity with which it embraces every member.[152] In medical care, patients do not have consensus on the meaning of dignity close to their death. Dignity has a subjective and dynamic meaning that evolves over time. While some patients value independence near death, others perceive dignity in preserving meaningful relationships, in relative freedom from distress and pain, and in being surrounded with a respectful, calm, and safe environment.[153]

---

150. Sulmasy, "Dignity and Bioethics," 469–501.

151. Barilan, *Human Dignity*, 93–147.

152. Rosen, *Dignity*, 63–128, 129–60.

153. Guo and Jacelon, "Integrative Review," 931–40; Oechsle et al., "Symptom Burden," 313–21.

Furthermore, proponents of euthanasia/PAS contend that human vulnerability in the face of death is mendable through autonomy. However deeply connected vulnerability and autonomy are, autonomy cannot stand on its own without recognizing the importance of human vulnerability for a healthy development of autonomy. Fundamentally, humans strive to be autonomous, but they will always be dependent on others as members of a human community.[154] As previously argued, vulnerability is deeply rooted in the mortal human condition in a way that only compassionate neighbors can mend. In contrast to one's own autonomy—and responsibility—stands the vulnerability of the other. Therefore, the moral question should be "HOW to act as a compassionate neighbor toward the vulnerable other" rather than "WHO is vulnerable around me," because ultimately everyone is vulnerable.[155] Consequently, a relational turn in bioethics has recently materialized to correct the over-individualistic discourse. More voices express the importance of relations in shaping a meaningful and substantial discourse in bioethics within a changing world, locally and globally. Yet, such emphasis on relationships does not have to come at the expense of individuality and autonomous decision-making.[156]

At a general level, it is important to understand the context within which arguments for euthanasia/PAS have evolved. Because of recent medical advancement and multiplication of—sometimes—effective technological interventions, euthanasia/PAS grew as a protest against the encroachments of a powerful medicine on the dying process and its unnecessary prolongation.[157] Many authors have detailed the changes brought by medicine to the dying process in the US from the side of medical practitioners, such as Haider Warraich's *Modern Death: How Medicine Changed the End of Life*.[158] Other studies have shown the role of medical advancements in aggravating a public denial of death,[159] even among physicians who constantly encounter death. Without

---

154. Hettema, "Autonomy," 493–98; Eibach, "Protection of Life," 58–77; Pellegrino, "Lived Experience," 513–39.

155. Welie, *In the Face of Suffering*, 125–57; Also in Pelluchon, "Taking Vulnerability Seriously," 293–312.

156. Jennings, "Reconceptualizing Autonomy," 11–16.

157. ten Have and Welie, *Death and Medical Power*.

158. Warraich, *Modern Death*.

159. Thursby, *Funeral Festivals*, 116–25. A more detailed account of this denial is explored in the seminal work of Becker, *Denial of Death*.

acknowledging death as integral to the human condition, doctors may be easily tempted to extend life as long as medical technology permits,[160] especially when they forget that they also are vulnerable and inevitably mortal.[161] Acknowledging death is not only crucial for medical care, but is similarly vital for a meaningful living.[162] By the same token, not only death shapes how humans live, but how humans live and perceive life (at its different stages) also shapes how they die.[163]

Therefore, it is warranted to invoke a substantial social discourse to articulate a contemporary *Ars Moriendi*. The goal should be to establish a communal, non-relative,[164] understanding of the good death, not as an individualistic confrontation with death, but as a communal embracing of human mortality.[165] Along with elaborating on an *Ars Moriendi* for modern times, a robust discourse should also explore the meaning of old age, especially when medicine and public health interventions have extended longevity alongside chronic illnesses and long-term disabilities. Hence, a dialectic balance between frailty and strength is inevitably at play with advanced age.[166] However, one of the hurdles for a sensitive discussion of aging in modern society is the prevailing bourgeois morality, specifically in Western countries, which values the accumulation of wealth and health and perceives bodily decline as a failure.[167] Such distorted morality is still at play even when it is used to oppose age discrimination in the workforce. When proposing an equal footing for all workers regardless of their age, devaluation of physical decline lurks within the discussion. Similarly, by defending euthanasia/PAS in the name of dignity, a morality that negatively perceives aging underpins the discussion and may insidiously foster an obligation to end one's own life before it lapses from its dignified status to a senile embarrassment.[168]

Ultimately, a great deal of communal imagination and hospitality is necessary to reach a meaningful *Ars Moriendi* to confront a globalized

160. Gawande, *Being Mortal*.
161. Bishop, "Finitude," 19–31; Tucker, "Culture of Death Denial," 1105–8.
162. Imhof, "From the Old Mortality," 1–29; Kateb, *Human Dignity*, 174–217.
163. Harrington and Sulmasy, "Spiritual Preparation," 87–106.
164. Lantham, "Pluralism," 33–46.
165. Ridenour and Cahill, "Role of Community," 107–30; Dugdale, "Conclusion: Toward a New Ethical," 173–91.
166. Gadow, "Frailty and Strength," 235–43.
167. Cole, "'Enlightened' View of Aging," 115–30.
168. Burt, "Legal Reform," 99–113.

and aggressive practice of medicine.[169] Most importantly, a social adoption of hospitality toward aging patients should open the bioethical discourse to those aspects of suffering and dying that are usually overlooked because of advanced interventions. A hospitable health care embraces palliative and hospice care for every mortal human being, even those who are not yet on their deathbed.

The Hospitality Case for Hospice Care

Historically and linguistically, hospitality to strangers was at the roots of the first hospital and contemporary hospice movement. Although in both cases Christian ethos inspired welcoming those who suffer and caring for their needs,[170] hospitality toward strangers is valued among various religious and value systems for the same reasons. Because she recognizes her own innate dignity and vulnerability, a hospitable host acknowledges her moral responsibility toward a valuable but stranded stranger and is moved to stand in solidarity with him.

The hospice movement evolved in the late 1960s because of the efforts of Cicely Saunders, who established the first hospice of St Christopher in London in 1967. Her work to address the human suffering in a time of increasingly aggressive medicine was intended to counterbalance the rising voices to legalize euthanasia/PAS in Europe. While palliative medicine refers to the medical interventions to ameliorate physical suffering, hospice care addresses all physical, psychological, social, emotional, and spiritual aspects to facilitate a peaceful death to the patient and a healing mourning environment to her family. This multi-dimensional approach to suffering gave rise to the concept of "total pain" advocated by Saunders; many scholars since then have emphasized a holistic approach to suffering and chronic illness.[171]

At the end of life, human vulnerability is most exposed because of its rootedness in innate mortality. Although physical pain, especially persistent pain, feeds one's sense of vulnerability, other elements of suffering are crucial near death, such as the burden of self-care, the disruption of daily activities, and the fear of death, loneliness, and uncertainty. It is

---

169. Burt, "Legal Reform," 99–113; And Rosel, "Growing Old Together," 199–233.

170. Bretherton, *Hospitality as Holiness*, 160–95.

171. Clark, "'Total Pain,'" 727–36; Clark, "From Margins to Centre," 430–38; Saunders, "Evolution of Palliative Care," 7–13.

therefore very important for hospitable physicians to recognize the human anguish near death and its many intricacies to facilitate the healing of the whole person.[172] Furthermore, health systems and medical schools should be hospitable to the premises and practices of palliative and hospice care to ingrain them in the new generations of practitioners. Palliative and hospice care have gained grounds in medical education over the past few decades, but its integration has not changed the way medicine perceives its goals. As with other useful tools, palliation is used as a tool to improve patients' satisfaction within an ever-powerful medicine, rather than as a way to nourish physician-patient human rapport. Unfortunately, using palliative medicine instrumentally deprives physicians of the opportunity to perceive accompanying patients near death as a privilege: a privilege that has a healing effect on them and on how they perceive their own lives.[173]

Furthermore, education in palliative medicine is still limited and far from occupying a central role in the practice of medicine regardless of the specialty. Physicians tend to perceive death as their enemy and use every available tool to fend it off. Further, in the US, Medicare and other insurance companies reward aggressive interventions with higher reimbursement than more peaceful (palliating) care. In medical schools, palliative medicine is not integrated into the curriculum in a way that advances healing more than aggressive intervention. Rather, palliative and hospice care is usually introduced in pre-clinical lectures when students are not in direct contact with suffering patients.[174]

Nonetheless, several attempts to expose new practitioners to aging and death were successful. Even a theoretical seminar on old age had a positive, long-term effect on the attitude of medical students toward the elderly and their health needs.[175] Yet, a more sophisticated pedagogical intervention in the pre-clinical years may have a profound influence. It has been suggested that broadening the perspectives of medical students to include psychological, social, cultural, and spiritual determinants of health may counterbalance a narrow-minded interventionist

172. Bosch-Barrera and Bota, "Vulnerability at the End," 167–87; Williams, "Chronic Illness," 40–67.

173. Lynn, "Travels in the Valley," 40–53; Connelly, "Avoidance of Human Suffering," 381–91.

174. Rizzo, "Major Issues," 34–59.

175. Wilson and Hafferty, "Changes in Attitudes," 993–99; Wilson and Hafferty. "Long-Term Effects," 319–24.

understanding of medical care. Further, it is necessary to unveil the hidden curriculum in medical institutions, which disproportionately rewards physicians for more interventions, to immunize students against such mentality through constant reflection and self-awareness.[176]

Moreover, while it is necessary to train more practitioners in palliative medicine to meet the growing need,[177] it is equally important to encourage all specialties to introduce palliative medicine early. In a chronic illness, for instance, consulting with a palliative care team to establish the goals of care is warranted rather than waiting until all effective medical interventions are exhausted.[178] To avoid unnecessary and debilitating interventions, physicians ought to visit the goals of care, early and frequently, to adjust them as the disease progresses.

Since suffering and death do not only afflict those who are sick but may also compromise the well-being of their family members and friends, a public health approach to dying and bereavement is warranted. It is argued that a public health approach to bereavement increases the availability of community services outside the umbrella of sophisticated medical institutions.[179] By moving bereavement from the private to the public space, human mortality becomes more salient in society, thus offering a better opportunity to address suffering at various levels.[180] Further, by moving bereavement to the public space of strangers, a public discussion would challenge the community to find a common ground on which to build its own palliative care. The province of Kerala, in India, for instance, proves that developing a hospitable and healing palliative care system does not require lavish resources. Rather, a social acknowledgement of universal vulnerability close to death nurtures a sense of communal solidarity to shape palliative and hospice care within its available resources and reach everyone who is in need.[181] Extensive work has been done to advocate approaching palliative and hospice care from a public health perspective; however, the detailed arguments in favor and the projected advantages of such approach are beyond the scope of this book.[182]

176. Barnard et al., "Preparing the Ground," 499–505.
177. Institute of Medicine, *Dying in America*.
178. Barrett, "Good Death," 27–33.
179. Rumbold and Aoun, "Bereavement and Palliative Care," 131–35.
180. Callahan, "Death, Mourning," 103–15; Callahan, "End-of-Life Care" 114–20.
181. Abraham and Jithesh, "Kerala Experience in Palliative Care," 14–29.
182. See for instance, Van den Block et al., *Palliative Care for Older People*, and Cohen and Deliens, *Public Health Perspective*.

Unfortunately, the presence of palliative and hospice care in schools of public health in the US is meager. Very few schools of public health expose the new generation of practitioners and policy makers to the details and intricacies imbedded in palliative care. This will make it even more difficult for the growing number of patients and their family members to heal in a system that ignores death and its scathing presence.[183] Moreover, policies that demand evidence of the effectiveness of palliative care, similar to other medical interventions, do not recognize the difficulties associated with research in patient- and family-centered care near death.[184] When healing is subjectively constructed to serve the specific needs of a patient in her social context, it is very difficult to measure the healing effect of the personal presence of a hospitable and compassionate healthcare worker. Notwithstanding the importance of rigorous research in palliative medicine,[185] by unnecessarily emphasizing an evidence-based practice, palliative care lapses into the status of another tool in the hands of medicine, again, ignoring the importance of personal presence in healing a wounded humanity.[186]

Obviously, close to death, religious communities play a significant role. Because of their long-standing reconciliation with death, regardless of their specific metaphysics, religions provide their believers with tools to heal. Despite their vulnerabilities, believers are healed, not because of a dogmatic-theoretical explanation of diseases and death, but because of a ritualized presence of other believers with the dying person and her family. By the same token, it is warranted that religious leaders and theologians engage in substantive discussion with physicians and healthcare workers who belong to their communities. Such discussion helps tailor the healing approach of both the community and the providers to the specific needs of dying patients and their families.[187] Ultimately, preparation for death should not be left till the very end of life when death is imminent. Rather, confronting death requires unceasing living toward dying within a caring community.[188]

---

183. Lupu et al., "Few U.S. Public Health Schools Offer Courses," 1582–87.
184. Normand, "Setting Priorities," 431–39.
185. Riffin et al., "Identifying Key Priorities," e15–21.
186. Bishop, *Anticipatory Corpse*, 253–78.
187. Hinshaw et al., "Spiritual Issues in Suffering," 7–14.
188. Guroian, *Life's Living*, 81–105; also Guroian, *Ethics after Christendom*, 175–99.

Conclusion

Building on the Orthodox bioethical *phronema*, this chapter discussed the third anthropological concept for a common ground in global bioethics. Hospitality is fundamentally related to both human dignity and vulnerability discussed in the previous two chapters. The reconciliation between the creator and the creation materialized through the incarnation of Jesus Christ. By becoming human, the Second person of the Trinity performed the mission which humans failed to pursue, i.e., bridging the existential gap between the divine and created realms. His priesthood shapes the royal priesthood of every believer and underlines the responsibility of the church to find a common ground in a social-global order of strangers, especially in medical practice and ethics. It was therefore argued that hospitality toward the strange other is ingrained in the Christian ethos and demands standing in solidarity with others, especially in dire times of illness. Building a solidaristic healthcare system does not only provide care for everyone who is in need, but also shapes the entire enterprise of medicine through sincere openness toward new practitioners and the public. Through a hospitable openness in medicine, a more satisfactory and humane care would evolve. These ideas were briefly used to discuss ethical dilemmas at the end of life. Approaching dying patients and their families with hospitality preserves their dignity and tends to their vulnerability. Not only then do patients receive care that is centered on their needs, but also physicians then practice a personally fulfilling and ultimately healing medicine.

7

Conclusion

In this book, anthropology has been argued to be a possible ground for consensus in a global and pluralistic bioethical discourse. From an Orthodox Christian perspective, anthropology derives from Christology to understand the genuine human condition and its eschatological potential. Thus, an Orthodox Christian hermeneutics was explored to highlight a social construction of universal human dignity and innate vulnerability. When both dignity and vulnerability were explored, it became clear that they are embedded in a human community that is able to protect dignity against the circumstances that expose vulnerability. In the medical encounter, it was also emphasized that the dignity and vulnerability of physicians should be recruited as central to a healing relationship.

Therefore, human dignity and vulnerability were connected to what was argued as the basis of ethics among strangers, namely, hospitality (*philoxenia*): the love of the stranger. The core relationship between hospitality, dignity, and vulnerability in Orthodox hermeneutics derives from the triadic christological mission of priesthood, kinghood, and prophethood, respectively. When a physician encounters her patient with hospitality, not only the physician but also the entire medical enterprise is challenged to stand in solidarity with vulnerable patients regardless of how different or distant they may seem. A hospitable physician recognizes the dignity and vulnerability both in herself and in her patient, challenging her to a healing rapport using gratitude and compassion. Both gratitude and compassion shall change, it was argued, the way medicine is taught to new students and the way it is practiced, locally and globally. The example of end of life care is used to illustrate how such a *phronema* may change the way a society cares for dying patients and their families.

In the introductory chapter, the layout of this book and its ultimate goals were discussed within a universal mission of the Orthodox Church in a pluralistic and globalized world. The cultural and scientific context where medicine developed in Western countries is relatively foreign to Orthodox Christianity; however, Orthodox Christians today, those who live in the East or the West, have to deal with the consequences of recent medical advancements and related ethical dilemmas. Furthermore, since some of these moral issues afflict vulnerable humans across the world, the Orthodox Church should engage in a vehement advocacy to protect them, building on her claimed catholic (universal) mission.

Nonetheless, Orthodox Christian bioethicists have yet to engage in this global dimension of bioethics: not only have Orthodox bioethicists avoided engaging the international dimension of medical practice, but they have also avoided, for the most part, discussing the social determinants of health beyond the access to medical care.

In line with the majority of Orthodox bioethicists, this book explored the Orthodox Christian heritage to unveil a unique *phronema* for an Orthodox bioethics. However, this book goes a step further in that it seeks an inclusive and dialogical bioethics which highlights the responsibility of Orthodox Christianity in a pluralistic world. While those bioethicists established what is unique about Orthodox bioethics, this book pursued the commonalities with other religious and secular value systems. Therefore, in contrast with Tristram Engelhardt, who (philosophically, but in theological garments) rejects the possibility of ethical common ground, the argument advanced here established this common ground using an authentic Orthodox theological anthropology. The advocated common ground derives from a common anthropological experience of life, suffering, and death, rather than from a rational consensus on ethical principles. To address evolving global bioethical issues, this book challenged the universal mission of the Orthodox Church that is rooted in the personal truth of Jesus Christ as the only savior of humanity from death.

Chapter 2 discussed the hermeneutics on which Orthodox theology can actively engage in bioethical issues at the global level. This hermeneutics aimed at developing a patristic *phronema* that is relevant to the mission of the Orthodox Church in global bioethics. Building on an inclusive anthropology, the Orthodox Church should bear the responsibility to find a common ground with other groups (regardless of how different they may seem in their ethos) so that the church may be consistent with her universal eschatological-eucharistic identity and mission.

Discussing the hermeneutics of Orthodox theology involved an exploration of its theological premises for an Orthodox Christian bioethics. The first premise was related to the historical encounters between Orthodox Christianity, on the one side, and Western Christianity and post-modern ideas where contemporary medicine has developed, on the other. This brief historical background was essential to understand the internal dynamics of theological and hermeneutical evolution of Orthodoxy regarding modernity and post-modernity.

The second premise of this hermeneutics explored the theological tenets which support an active and inclusive involvement of Orthodox Christians in global bioethics. Building on the triadic mission of Christ, Orthodox Christianity establishes an inclusive global bioethics and a common ground with other value-systems. As God and man, Jesus Christ was the king, the prophet, and the priest; this three-fold calling fashions an authentic mission of the Orthodox Church in a globalized world. The core relationship between hospitality, dignity, and vulnerability is established in their respective derivation from Christ's priesthood, kinghood, and prophethood.

In order to bring practical insights to the study of global bioethics, the previous hermeneutical premises were used to unfold the anthropological tenets shaping humanity's mission in the world. The first tenet was related to the Orthodox Christian understanding of the *Imago Dei* which contradicts the modernist and post-modernist narrow understanding of humans as rational beings. Because of the ancestral sin, the divine-human relationship was shattered, and consequently sin fostered alienation, corruption, and death in the world.

The second tenet of this anthropology explored the role of Orthodox Christian embodied spirituality and asceticism in fashioning the lives of the believers and their mission in the world. It was argued that embracing one's own vulnerability is the first step toward standing in solidarity with other vulnerable humans and recognizing that the human experience of vulnerability and death unites them more than their rational agreement.

Starting from a missionary anthropology, eschatology serves as the interpretive lens for a *phronema* that shapes the Orthodox Church's responsibility in today's world. Inspired by the economy of the Holy Spirit, Orthodox Christians may hospitably extend their liturgical experience of the *eschata* (the last things) and engage in a transfiguring mission in the world. Because of what happened at Pentecost, this mission puts the onus of finding a common ground, in bioethics at least, on the shoulders of Christians. When extending the liturgy beyond the liturgy, and by taking the "sacrament of the brother [and sister]" seriously, Christians recognize the unity of the entire universe in its createdness and in its longing toward God. Adopting this inclusive *phronema* challenges Christians to transfigure the world through a pastoral, missionary, and prophetic way of living.

Chapter 3 discussed the current status of bioethical discourse within the pluralistic and complex global context. It highlighted the prevailing trends in secular and religious bioethics over the past few decades. Ultimately, this chapter advocated an inclusive iconic *phronema* for Orthodox bioethics which helped find a common ground for global bioethics.

To situate the advocated inclusive *phronema* and substantive discourse within the contemporary global scene, an exploration of the pluralistic context of contemporary bioethics was initiated. Several factors shape the contemporary global context for medical practice, including communication and movement, consumerism and ecological crises, and the effacement of national boundaries and power. These changes highlight the universal responsibility toward those who are most disadvantaged, especially in regard to health and bioethical dilemmas. Arguing against "culture-war" and "clash-of-civilizations" perspectives toward the current world order, this chapter adopted a dynamic understanding of human culture and identity. The discussion highlighted the responsibility of Christians to be neighbors of everyone else, near and far.

Through a brief historical analysis, this chapter also demonstrated how mainstream bioethics developed over the past few decades. While its first pioneers perceived a global (comprehensive and international) version of ethical inquiry into life sciences, bioethics in the US evolved as an individualistic and procedural enterprise. However, because of recent global developments, a deeper scrutiny into medical practices, and a broader approach to health and illnesses, a global and multi-disciplinary bioethics evolved in academia and at the international governmental level. However, a broader adoption of a global bioethics ethos is warranted; this book advocated a deeper involvement by Orthodox Christians in this global ethos. It challenged Orthodox Christians (and all Christians) to actively stand in universal solidarity with the vulnerable and marginalized, at least as pertinent to health disparities.

Secular bioethical discourse was not the only salient discourse over the past few decades. Some religious voices in bioethics were influential in shaping the public discourse. However, religious bioethicists approached the prevalent secular discourse in two different ways. On the one hand, some religious bioethicists are entrenched in the prevailing individualistic and procedural bioethical discourse, although they offer a different—religious—ideology. On the other hand, other bioethicists venture from within an original religious mindset into a broader territory in bioethics. While the former group advocates a bioethics in religious garment, the latter group perceives bioethical dilemmas through different lenses. The latter group is usually open to substantive dialogue with other value systems because of its acknowledgement of a unifying human experience of illness, suffering, and death.

Two examples were discussed under the first approach in religious bioethics: Robin Gill's *Health Care and Christian Ethics* and Dennis Macaleer's *The New Testament and Bioethics: Theology and Basic Bioethics Principles*. Comparatively, two authors are discussed as representative of the other approach in religious bioethics: Allen Verhey's *Reading the Bible in the Strange World of Medicine* and Lisa Sowle Cahill's *Theological Bioethics: Participation, Justice, and Change*. Despite their different religious traditions, Verhey and Cahill are both critical of the prevailing individualistic mindset and both advocate an activist involvement in public life. To protect the health and well-being of the vulnerable, Verhey advocates for compassion and Cahill aspires to a social ethics to eliminate health disparities.

Inspired by the examples of Verhey and Cahill, the argument of this book proceeds in favor of an inclusive and globally oriented Orthodox Christian *phronema* in bioethics. The discussion briefly explored the work of a few notable Orthodox theologians and bioethicists to situate the book's argument within the broader Orthodox theological scene. Ultimately, the goal was to extend a liturgical Orthodox identity beyond the traditional boundaries of the church and to challenge believers to address contemporary ethical dilemmas. A detailed critique of Engelhardt's version of Orthodox Christian bioethics is offered to demonstrate how he departs from the inclusive theological bioethics advocated in this book.

Consequently, an iconic Orthodox Christian *phronema* for bioethics was advanced to engage in global bioethics. In Orthodox theology, icons stand as windows that bridge the existential gap between the created and divine realms. Icons extend a hospitable and constant invitation to the created world in the person of a faithful beholder who belongs to a community. It was argued that the eschatological, realist, and hospitable dimensions of the icon are important in shaping an inclusive bioethics. While the eschatological dimension brings hope in a glorified eschatological reality, the realist dimension is cognizant of the fallen, mortal, and vulnerable reality of this world. In its hospitable dimension, an icon gives hope to the world through those who in faith take its universal mission seriously. This *phronema* emphasizes the serious responsibility that the Orthodox Church should bear to find a common ground for substantive dialogue in global bioethics.

In chapter 4, the discussion concentrated on the first concept advocated for an Orthodox Christian bioethics and as a basis for a common ground in global bioethics, namely, human dignity. The foundations of human dignity were discussed in Orthodox theology and in secular bioethics. Through this discussion, gratitude was promoted in health care as the first concept in a substantive and globally sensitive bioethics. Ultimately, gratitude can play a major role in shaping medicine in its clinical and systemic enterprises.

This chapter started by reiterating the theological principles discussed in the second chapter to defend an Orthodox Christian understanding of human dignity as cardinal to a constructive engagement in a global bioethical discourse. Within a Christocentric hermeneutics, human dignity was initially argued to derive from the creation of humans in the image and according to the likeness of God. Hence, respecting human dignity was advocated by emphasizing the dignity's embodied and communal experience in times of sickness and suffering; this contrasts with a misplaced emphasis on respecting autonomy as equal to respecting dignity.

To build a common ground, human dignity was then explored within the prevalent philosophical framework of contemporary secular bioethics. This book established a non-religious support for the use of human dignity in bioethical discourse. The narrow understanding of human dignity as solely related to autonomy was deemed insufficient for a substantive global discourse.

A detailed historical development of the concept of human dignity and some of its philosophical and practical difficulties were explored. Dignity has several meanings and its innate and inalienable sense was emphasized as central to an ethos that is respectful to all humans. Furthermore, the relationship between human dignity and human rights emphasized the importance of respecting human dignity as a social ethos whereby human rights are used as a tool (rather than as an ideology) to guarantee a decent life for everyone. Dignity was consequently discussed from the vantage point of health and illness especially because of its special presence within an aggressive practice of medicine. Dignity and vulnerability were shown to be organically connected in confronting human fragility in front of illness and death.

To further the discussion of dignity in global bioethics, the practical dimensions of respecting human dignity were considered. Gratitude was argued to be the proper virtue for a dignified humanity. In return for a socially constructed and bestowed dignity (a social gift), gratitude fashions any given community, and should therefore fashion medicine as an enterprise and as a clinical encounter. Because of globalization, human lives are more entangled than ever before. Further, medical practice and research today overlook traditional boundaries and have, in several cases, harmed the dignity of many people around the world. Over its recent history, medicine has benefited from the sacrifice of many practitioners and patients, therefore it has to show gratitude not only toward those who have passed but also toward current contributors to its knowledge and development. Physicians have to be grateful even to their own patients whom they serve. Hence, a brief discussion of gratitude and its moral repercussions was pursued in religious, philosophical, and psychological perspectives.

Chapter 5 elaborated on the second of the three concepts central to the advocated Orthodox Christian bioethics and the common ground for global bioethics. The understanding of human vulnerability was discussed within the Orthodox Christian theology and secular bioethical discourse as it derives from the universal embodied experience of all human beings. The goal of discussing vulnerability was to promote compassion as central to the practice of medicine. In combination with gratitude, compassion shall fashion a solidaristic medicine through medical education and systemic changes to care provision.

This chapter starts by briefly exploring a theological understanding of human vulnerability within Orthodox Christian hermeneutics and its practical ramifications to ameliorate human suffering. In christological terms, human vulnerability is related to Christ's prophetic mission which announces that God is the only source of life. Humans are vulnerable because of their mortality which was the result of their alienation from God since Adam and Eve's sin. Illness, suffering, and death result from the state of estrangement, away from God, others, and self. Therefore, the role of Christ's incarnation in mending the state of alienation and its consequent vulnerability and mortality was discussed. To re-establish the broken relationship between God and the universe, Christ took a human body and compassionately suffered with humans through the anguish of death on the cross; it was his compassionate providence that redeemed humans from their mortality.

While Orthodox Christianity positively perceives medicine and its practitioners, theologians warn against enshrining medicine as a savior of humanity. Rather than vehemently fighting death, embracing one's own vulnerability, in an ascetic and spiritual life, is the way to bear the vulnerability of others and then redeem the entire creation.

To advance a common ground, the concept of human vulnerability was then discussed as it relates to the prevalent secular bioethical discourse. Because of its growing presence in secular discourse, vulnerability can play a central role in shaping a common ground in global bioethics. The premise of a secular adoption of vulnerability is its fundamental relation to human dignity as if vulnerability and dignity were the two sides of the same coin; if humans were not invaluable, one should not be concerned when they become/show as vulnerable.

Therefore, a central presence of vulnerability challenges the narrow agenda of mainstream bioethics, especially in regard to its intertwined philosophical and political perspectives. Its recent adoption in the UNESCO *Universal Declaration on Bioethics and Human Rights* opens the door for more international cooperation among nation-states to improve universal human health.

In general, vulnerability has a normative ethical dimension that challenges everyone to care for those who are vulnerable wherever they are. By embracing universal vulnerability, contemporary bioethical discourse would espouse a broad and solidaristic agenda among various communities, nations, and racial groups. Furthermore, recognizing the universality of vulnerability helps healthcare workers to bridge the gap that separates them from their patients and to compassionately care for them.

Therefore, to further the discussion on human vulnerability, this chapter considered the central role that compassion, i.e., suffering with, needs to play in medicine. In the face of a mechanistic medicine, compassion helps bridge the gap between two equal fellow humans and helps them to make relevant and personally fulfilling decisions. The ultimate goal of this inquiry was to find the deepest motivator for medicine and its practitioners. Death proved to be at the core of medicine, not as a foe to be defeated but as the universal experience that motivates some—equally vulnerable but compassionate—people to become physicians.

To achieve this goal several themes had to be explored. The first theme dealt with the presence of vulnerability in the matrix of medical care. Although all humans are vulnerable because of their mortality, patients are especially vulnerable because they are forced to seek healing in the strange land of medicine. The land of medicine was then explored at various levels: its social standing and its underpinning theoretical premises, which both influence how physicians are socialized into the practice of medicine and how they care for their suffering patients. The second theme was related to the motivation behind becoming a physician. Through a deeper questioning of medical care, it was revealed that compassion toward the suffering and dying is what motivates some people to pursue medical training and become physicians. It is only through suffering with others, i.e., compassion, that an encounter between two vulnerable strangers can be transformed into a healing relationship.

Furthermore, to fully understand the role of compassion in healing, a third theme was discussed, namely, the meaning of human suffering. Suffering was shown to be more than physical pain. In the case of suffering, the goal of medicine is not only treating the underlying disease or fixing the ailing organ; rather it is healing the whole person whose relation to the world and self is disrupted. However, in medical schools, this holistic approach to healing is thwarted for future practitioners and it should be re-established as paramount to the entire enterprise of medicine. Even if some aspects of suffering fall outside the jurisdiction of medicine, practitioners should acknowledge them to prevent further suffering.

In chapter 6, the role of global solidarity in shaping medical systems, especially near the end of life, was discussed. After establishing the importance of human dignity and vulnerability in bioethics, this chapter elaborated on the third of the three concepts advocated for an inclusive Orthodox Christian bioethics and a common ground for global bioethics. The core relationship of hospitality with dignity and vulnerability was discussed within Orthodox Christian theology and secular bioethical discourse. Ultimately, solidarity sprouts from hospitality as it relates to dignity and vulnerability. Solidarity needs the universality of gratitude and the particularity of compassion to shape globally sensitive medical education and systems. All the threads of this book were then brought together to discuss end-of-life care within the advocated inclusive *phronema* and substantive bioethics.

This chapter started with exploring hospitality within an Orthodox Christian hermeneutics and its practical ramifications as a basis for solidarity among strangers in health care. In christological terms, hospitality (*philoxenia*, the love of the stranger) derives from Christ's priesthood through which Christ bridged the existential alienation between the divine and created worlds. In the Eucharist, the church extends the priesthood of Christ and recognizes her own identity and mission toward the world as a hospitable and priestly missionary to bring it back to God. Therefore, hospitality was found to be integral to the Christian ethos and even to non-religious ethical discourse. Without hospitality, a moral agent is not able to recognize the presence of a stranger other and cannot bear any moral responsibility toward her. However, with hospitality, the stranger is recognizable and thus has a moral demand upon the beholder.

Consequently, hospitality is cardinal to fostering a healthy public space where strangers meet and thrive. Similarly, hospitality is important to the physician-patient relationship since they meet as strangers and each one of them has to enter into the personal space of the other to heal and be healed.

At a broader level, hospitality is the basis of solidarity among strangers when utter strangers are willing to accept a cost for assisting others who are similar to them. Solidarity was shown to be deeply rooted in human history and Christian ethos. Most recently, solidarity shaped the provision of health care in European countries and has also inspired the UNESCO *Universal Declaration* to address rising global bioethical issues. Notwithstanding possible challenges to its relevance at the global level, solidarity is pregnant with hope in the goodness of human society. Whereas human fallenness breeds alienation and enmity, solidarity brings hope in a better human condition.

To establish the practical ramifications of the core relationship between hospitality, dignity, and vulnerability, the discussion addressed first the role of gratitude then that of compassion in global bioethics.

First, to stand in solidarity with patients across the globe, gratitude was previously argued to be an important value in shaping medicine. In chapter 4, gratitude was advanced as a fundamental value in framing the personal relationship between physicians and patients. In chapter 6, gratitude was extended beyond the particular clinical encounter to address the environment of medical practice within its broader social context. Since gratitude was derived from a socially constructed understanding of human dignity, its hospitable application in medical care should transfigure both involved parties, physicians and patients. The leitmotif of the solicited change is hospitable openness toward each other.

On the one side, out of gratitude toward their current and previous patients, medical practitioners and systems must be humbly open regarding several important elements of the practice of medicine. This openness helps foster reasonable expectations from medicine among patients along with a public appreciation of the limitations of medicine and human life. These elements include the social dimension of medicine and health; the hidden curriculum in medical training and practice; the unscientific nature of medical practice; and the role of narration in fostering a satisfactory and healing medical practice.

On the other side, patients can arguably play an active role in their health and in molding a healing practice of medicine. By standing in solidarity with their physicians, patients recognize the vulnerability and dignity of physicians and appreciate the ordeal they had to live to become physicians. Patients are therefore able to heal their physicians when reconciliation is necessary. They are also able, as active citizens, to shape the medical system so that it serves the well-being of patients and physicians at the same time.

Second, to stand in solidarity with strangers across the globe, compassion was previously advocated as central to the practice of clinical medicine. In chapter five, compassion was discussed as the proper answer to the suffering other and was defended as a basis for profound changes in medical education and physicians' self-awareness. However, to model a global bioethical discourse, two important themes were discussed, namely, the vulnerability of physicians and the role of compassion in medical education.

On the one hand, the vulnerability of physicians is not always clear in a science-oriented and technology-dependent medical practice. However, when hospitality inspires the encounter of physicians and patients, physicians become deeply aware of their own vulnerability and can thereafter practice a fulfilling and healing medicine with authenticity. The vulnerability of physicians was demonstrated through the discussion of several themes including their embodied experience of training and practice, their struggle with power and negative emotions, their avoidance of suffering patients, and their risk of burnout and compassion fatigue.

On the other hand, compassion has an important role in shaping a healing practice of medicine. It was argued that compassion is the basis for a satisfactory physicianship contrary to the prevailing concerned detachment (equanimity) ideal. Thus, by cultivating a sense of vulnerability among aspiring physicians and nourishing their compassion toward suffering patients, medicine is transformed into a truly healing encounter. Unfortunately, medical students are socialized into the medical profession in an environment that harasses their innate and motivating compassion. Nonetheless, many pedagogical interventions have been proven to foster hospitality toward patients and openness toward one's own inner compassionate self.

Finally, chapter 6 brought the different threads of this book together to briefly discuss the moral issues pertinent to end-of-life care. Against arguments in favor of euthanasia and physician-assisted suicide, a broader adoption of palliative and hospice care in medical practice, especially for patients close to their death, was promoted.

While many liberal individualistic arguments are recruited to defend euthanasia and physician-assisted suicide, the *phronema* developed in this book questioned many of the premises of these arguments such as the meaning of autonomy and dignity. Eventually, it is argued, a social discourse to establish an *Ars Moriendi* that is pertinent to contemporary global reality is warranted. Therefore, a broad presence of palliative and hospice care in medical practice is necessary to achieve healing even when death is imminent. Through palliative and hospice care, the suffering and anguish near death are addressed within a holistic mindset by mutually hospitable physicians and patients. Further, through a hospitable health system, solidarity becomes the motivator of every effort to ameliorate human suffering, whether through public health interventions or broad medical training in suffering and dying. Ultimately, because of their long-standing experience with death, religious communities can play a central role in nourishing a humanistic practice of medicine at a global level.

In the final analysis, although the developed *phronema* may not offer final answers to all pressing global bioethical issues, it is able to raise new questions, especially those related to moral responsibility. This hospitable *phronema* shifts the global ethical discourse toward a new territory where all value systems can meet to initiate a meaningful and substantive ethical discourse.

Bibliography

Abou Mrad, Nicolas. "The Witness of the Church in a Pluralistic World: Theological Renaissance in the Church of Antioch." In *The Cambridge Companion to Orthodox Christian Theology*, edited by M. Cunningham and E. Theokritoff, 246–60. Cambridge: Cambridge University Press, 2008.

Abraham, Aneena A., and V. Jithesh. "The Kerala Experience in Palliative Care: An Ethical Exploration from the Public Health Perspective." *Asian Bioethics Review* 4 (2012) 14–29.

Agadjanian, Alexander, and Victor Roudometof. "Introduction: Eastern Orthodoxy in a Global Age-Preliminary Considerations." In *Eastern Orthodoxy in a Global Age: Tradition Faces the Twenty-First Century*, edited by V. Roudometof, A. Agadjanian, and J. G. Pankhurst, 1–26. Walnut Creek, CA: AltaMira, 2005.

An International Project of the Hastings Center. "The Goals of Medicine: Setting New Priorities." *Hastings Center Report* 26 (1996) S1–27.

Andorno, Roberto. "Global Bioethics at UNESCO: In Defence of the Universal Declaration on Bioethics and Human Rights." *Journal of Medical Ethics* 33 (2007) 150–54.

Andorno, Roberto, and Antonio Pele. "Human Dignity." In *Encyclopedia of Global Bioethics*, edited by H. ten Have. Cham: Springer, 2016.

Andreopoulos, Andreas. "A Modern Orthodox Approach to Spirituality." *Spiritus: A Journal of Christian Spirituality* 11 (2011) 10–23.

Annas, George J., and Michael A. Grodin. "The Nuremberg Code." In *The Oxford Textbook of Clinical Research Ethics*, edited by E. J. Emanuel et al., 136–40. Oxford: Oxford University Press. 2008.

Ariès, Philippe. *Western Attitudes toward Death: From the Middle Ages to the Present*. Baltimore: Johns Hopkins University Press, 2010.

Atallah, Fouad, et al. "Please Put on Your Own Oxygen Mask before Assisting Others: A Call to Arms to Battle Burnout." *American Journal of Obstetrics and Gynecology* 215 (2016) 731–35.

Athanasios, Metropolitan of Hercegovina. "The *Eschata* in Our Daily Life." In *Living Orthodoxy in the Modern World*, edited by A. Walker and C. Carras, 37–49. Crestwood, NY: St. Vladimir's Seminary Press, 1996.

Avakian, Sylvie. "The Mystery of Divine Love in the Apophatic Theology of Bishop George Khodr." *Theological Review* 33 (2012) 39–68.

Barilan, Y. Michael. "From Imago Dei in the Jewish-Christian Traditions to Human Dignity in Contemporary Jewish Law." *Kennedy Institute of Ethics Journal* 19 (2009) 231–59.

———. *Human Dignity, Human Rights, and Responsibility: The New Language of Global Bioethics and Biolaw*. Basic Bioethics. Cambridge, MA: MIT Press, 2012.

Barnard, David, et al. "Preparing the Ground: Contributions of the Preclinical Years to Medical Education for Care Near the End of Life." *Academic Medicine* 74 (1999) 499–505.

Barrett, Pamela M. "A Good Death: Changing the Script for End-of-Life Care." *Frontiers of Health Services Management* 27 (2011) 27–33.

Bascom, George S. "Sketches from a Surgeon's Notebook." In *Empathy and the Practice of Medicine: Beyond Pills and the Scalpel*, edited by H. M. Spiro et al., 17–33. New Haven: Yale University Press, 1993.

Basil, Bishop of Sergievo. "Living in the Future." In *Living Orthodoxy in the Modern World*, edited by A. Walker and C. Carras, 23–36. Crestwood, NY: St. Vladimir's Seminary Press, 1996.

Bateman, Catherine, et al. "Bringing Global Issues to Medical Teaching." *Lancet* 358 (2001) 1539–42.

Bayer, Oswald. "Self-Creation? On the Dignity of Human Beings." *Modern Theology* 20 (2004) 275–90.

Beauchamp Tom L. "The Belmont Report." In *The Oxford Textbook of Clinical Research Ethics*, edited by E. J. Emanuel et al., 149–55. Oxford: Oxford University Press, 2008.

Beauchamp, Tom L. and James F. Childress. *Principles of Biomedical Ethics*. 7th ed. Oxford: Oxford University Press, 2013.

Becker, Ernest. *The Denial of Death*. New York: Free Press, 1973.

Beecher, Henry K. "Consent in Clinical Experimentation: Myth and Reality." *JAMA* 195 (1966) 34–35.

Behr, John. *Becoming Human: Meditations on Christian Anthropology in Word and Image*. Crestwood, NY: St. Vladimir's Seminary Press, 2013.

Bekos, John. "Memory and Justice in the Divine Liturgy: Christian Bioethics in Late Modernity." *Christian Bioethics* 19 (2013) 100–113.

Benbassat, Jochanan, and Reuben Baumal. "What Is Empathy, and How Can It Be Promoted during Clinical Clerkships?" *Academic Medicine* 79 (2004) 832–39.

Bendelow, Gillian A., and Simon J. Williams. "Transcending the Dualisms: Towards a Sociology of Pain." *Sociology of Health & Illness* 17 (1995) 139–65.

Benner, Patricia. "When Health Care Becomes a Commodity: The Need for Compassionate Strangers." In *The Changing Face of Health Care: A Christian Appraisal of Managed Care*, edited by J. F. Kilner, R. D. Orr, and J. A. Shelly, 119–35. Grand Rapids: Eerdmans, 1998.

Berkwitz, Stephen C. "History and Gratitude in Theravada Buddhism." *Journal of the American Academy of Religion* 71 (2003) 579–604.

Bishop, Jeffrey P. *The Anticipatory Corpse: Medicine, Power, and the Care of the Dying*. Notre Dame: University of Notre Dame Press, 2011.

———. "Finitude." In *Dying in the Twenty-First Century: Toward a New Ethical Framework for the Art of Dying Well*, edited by L. S. Dugdale, 19–31. Cambridge: MIT Press, 2015.

———. "Rejecting Medical Humanism: Medical Humanities and the Metaphysics of Medicine." *The Journal of Medical Humanities* 29 (2008) 15–25.
Black, Helen K. "Gender, Religion, and the Experience of Suffering: A Case Study." *Journal of Religion and Health* 52 (2013) 1108–19.
———. "Jake's Story: A Middle-Aged, Working-Class Man's Physical and Spiritual Journey toward Death." *Qualitative Health Research* 11 (2001) 293–307.
Bobrinskoy, Boris. "God in Trinity." In *The Cambridge Companion to Orthodox Christian Theology*, edited by M. Cunningham and E. Theokritoff, 49–62. Cambridge: Cambridge University Press, 2008.
Boingeanu, Corneliu. "Personhood in Its Protological and Eschatological Patterns: An Eastern Orthodox View of the Ontology of Personality." *Evangelical Quarterly* 78 (2006) 3–19.
Boleyn-Fitzgerald, Patrick. "Gratitude Toward Things." In *Perspectives on Gratitude*, edited by D. Carr, 112–25. London: Routledge, 2016.
Bono, Giacomo, and Christopher Odudu. "Promoting the Development of Gratitude to Build Character and Improve Society." In *Perspectives on Gratitude*, edited by D. Carr, 185–98. London: Routledge, 2016.
Bosch-Barrera, Joaquim, and Juan Vidal Bota. "Vulnerability at the End of Life: A Medical Perspective." In *Human Dignity of the Vulnerable in the Age of Rights*, edited by A. Masferrer and E. García-Sánchez, 167–87. Cham: Springer, 2016.
Boudreau, J. Donald, Eric J. Cassell, and Abraham Fuks. "A Healing Curriculum." *Medical Education* 41 (2007) 1193–1201.
Bouteneff, Peter. *Beginnings: Ancient Christian Readings of the Biblical Creation Narratives*. Grand Rapids: Baker, 2008.
———. "Christ and Salvation." In *The Cambridge Companion to Orthodox Christian Theology*, edited by M. Cunningham and E. Theokritoff, 93–106. Cambridge: Cambridge University Press, 2008.
Breck, John. "Bioethical Dilemmas and Orthodoxy." *St. Vladimir's Theological Quarterly* 42 (1998) 171–88.
———. "Orthodox Bioethics in the Encounter between Science and Religion." In *Science and the Eastern Orthodox Church*, edited by D. P. Buxhoeveden, G. Woloschak, and C. Knight, 119–30. Farnham, UK: Ashgate, 2011.
———. *The Sacred Gift of Life: Orthodox Christianity and Bioethics*. Crestwood, NY: St. Vladimir's Seminary Press, 2010.
Bretherton, Luke. *Hospitality as Holiness: Christian witness amid moral diversity*. Hampshire, UK: Ashgate, 2010.
———. "Tolerance, Education and Hospitality: A Theological Proposal." *Studies in Christian Ethics* 17 (2004) 80–103.
Brincat, Cynthia A. "How Medical Training Mangles Professionalism: The Prolonged Death of Compassion." In *Professionalism in Medicine: Critical Perspectives*, edited by D. Wear and J. M. Aultman, 199–210. New York: Springer, 2006.
Bruce, S. M., H. M. Conaglen, and John V. Conaglen. "Burnout in Physicians: A Case for Peer-Support." *Internal Medicine Journal* 35 (2005) 272–78.
Brüning, Alfons, and Evert van der Zweerde. *Orthodox Christianity and Human Rights*. Leuven: Peeters, 2012.
Bucur, Bogdan. "'The Feet that Eve Heard in Paradise and Was Afraid': Observations on the Christology of Byzantine Hymns." *Philosophy and Theology* 18 (2006) 3–26.

Budiani-Saberi, D. A., and F. L. Delmonico. "Organ Trafficking and Transplant Tourism: A Commentary on the Global Realities." *American Journal of Transplantation* 8 (2008) 925–29.

Burks, Derek J., and Amy M. Kobus. "The Legacy of Altruism in Health Care: The Promotion of Empathy, Prosociality and Humanism." *Medical Education* 46 (2012) 317–25.

Burt, Robert A. "Legal Reform and Aging: Current Issues, Troubling Trends." In *What Does It Mean to Grow Old? Reflections from the Humanities*, edited by T. R. Cole and S. Gadow, 99–113. Durham: Duke University Press, 1986.

Cahill, Lisa Sowle. "Embodying God's Image: Created, Broken, and Redeemed." In *Humanity Before God: Contemporary Faces of Jewish, Christian, and Islamic Ethics*, edited by W. Schweiker, M. A. Johnson, and K. Jung, 55–77. Minneapolis: Fortress, 2006.

———. "Religion and Theology." In *Methods in Medical Ethics*, edited by J. Sugarman and D. P. Sulmasy, 73–90. 2nd ed. Washington, DC: Georgetown University Press, 2010.

———. *Theological Bioethics: Participation, Justice, and Change*. Washington, DC: Georgetown University Press, 2005.

Callahan, Daniel. "Death, Mourning, and Medical Progress." *Perspectives in Biology and Medicine* 52 (2009) 103–15.

———. "End-of-Life Care: A Philosophical or Management Problem?" *The Journal of Law, Medicine & Ethics* 39 (2011) 114–20.

———. *The Roots of Bioethics: Health, Progress, Technology, Death*. Oxford: Oxford University Press, 2012.

———. *The Troubled Dream of Life: In Search of a Peaceful Death*. New York: Simon & Schuster, 1993.

———. *What Price Better Health? Hazards of the Research Imperative*. California/Milbank Books on Health and the Public. Berkeley: University of California Press, 2003.

Camenisch, Paul F. "Gift and Gratitude in Ethics." *The Journal of Religious Ethics* 9 (1981) 1–34.

Cameron, N. M. de S. "A Theological Mandate for Medicine." In *The Changing Face of Health Care: A Christian Appraisal of Managed Care*, edited by J. F. Kilner, R. D. Orr, and J. A. Shelly, 35–44. Grand Rapids: Eerdmans, 1998.

Campbell, C. S. "Bioethics and the Spirit of Secularism." In *Secular Bioethics in Theological Perspective*, edited by E. E. Shelp, 3–18. Dordrecht: Kluwer, 1996.

Card, Claudia. "Gratitude to the Decent Rescuer." In *Perspectives on Gratitude*, edited by D. Carr, 99–111. London: Routledge, 2016.

Carel, Havi, and Ian James Kidd. "Epistemic Injustice in Healthcare: A Philosophical Analysis." *Medicine, Health Care and Philosophy* 17 (2014) 529–40.

Carr, David. "Counting Blessings: Towards A Spiritual Conception of Gratitude." In *Perspectives on Gratitude*, edited by D. Carr, 169–81. London: Routledge, 2016.

Casiday, Augustine. "Church Fathers and the Shaping of Orthodox Theology." In *The Cambridge Companion to Orthodox Christian Theology*, edited by M. Cunningham and E. Theokritoff, 167–87. Cambridge: Cambridge University Press, 2008.

Cassell, Eric J. *The Nature of Suffering and the Goals of Medicine*. Oxford: Oxford University Press, 1991.

Cavanagh, Michael E. "Rediscovering Compassion." *Journal of Religion and Health* 34 (1995) 317–27.
Charlton, Blake, and Abraham Verghese. "Caring for Ivan Ilyich." *Journal of General Internal Medicine* 25 (2010) 93–95.
Charon, Rita. "Narrative Medicine: Attention, Representation, Affiliation." *Narrative* 13 (2005) 261–70.
Chryssavgis, John. "Orthodox Spirituality and Social Activism: Reclaiming Our Vocabulary, Refocusing Our Vision." In *The Orthodox Churches in a Pluralistic World: An Ecumenical Conversation*, edited by E. Clapsis, 130–38. Geneva: WCC Publications, 2004.
———. "The Spiritual Way." In *The Cambridge Companion to Orthodox Christian Theology*, edited by M. Cunningham and E. Theokritoff, 150–63. Cambridge: Cambridge University Press, 2008.
———. "The World of the Icon." *Phronema* 7 (1992) 35–43.
Churchland, Patricia S. "Human Dignity from a Neurophilosophical Perspective." In *Human Dignity and Bioethics*, edited by E. D. Pellegrino, A. Schulman, and T. W. Merrill, 99–121. Washington, DC: President's Council on Bioethics, 2008.
Ciobotea, Daniel. "The Tasks of Orthodox Theology Today." *St. Vladimir's Theological Quarterly* 33 (1989) 117–26.
Ciulinaru, Costel. "The Anthropology of the Holy Fathers." *Scientific Journal of Humanistic Studies* 3 (2011) 182–89.
Clapsis, Emmanuel. "The Boundaries of the Church: An Orthodox Debate." *Greek Orthodox Theological Review* 35 (1990) 113–27.
———. "The Challenge of a Global World." In *The Orthodox Churches in a Pluralistic World: An Ecumenical Conversation*, edited by E. Clapsis, 47–66. Geneva: WCC Publications, 2004.
———. "Ethnicity, Nationalism and Identity." In *Orthodox Churches in a Pluralistic World: An Ecumenical Conversation*, edited by E. Clapsis, 159–73. Geneva: WCC Publications, 2004.
Clark, David. "From Margins to Centre: A Review of the History of Palliative Care in Cancer." *The Lancet Oncology* 8 (2007) 430–38.
———. "'Total Pain,' Disciplinary Power and the Body in the Work of Cicely Saunders, 1958–1967." *Social Science and Medicine* 49 (1999) 727–36.
Clément, Olivier. *On Human Being: A Spiritual Anthropology*. New York: New City, 2000.
———. "Orthodoxy and Politics." *Sourozh* 56 (1994) 1–6.
———. "Purification by Atheism." In *Orthodoxy and the Death of God: Essays in Contemporary Theology*, edited by A. M. Allchin, 22–39. London: Fellowship of St. Alban and St. Sergius, 1971.
———. "Science and Faith." *St. Vladimir's Seminary Quarterly* 10 (1966) 120–27.
———. "Witness in a Secular Society." *Sourozh* 36 (1989) 4–16.
Cohen, Joachim, and Luc Deliens, eds. *A Public Health Perspective on End of Life Care*. Oxford: Oxford University Press, 2012.
Cole, Thomas R. "The 'Enlightened' View of Aging: Victorian Morality in a New Key." In *What Does It Mean to Grow Old? Reflections from the Humanities*, edited by T. R. Cole and S. Gadow, 115–30. Durham: Duke University Press, 1986.

Comte-Sponville, André. "Compassion." In *A Small Treatise on the Great Virtues: The Uses of Philosophy in Everyday Life*, translated by C. Temerson, 103–17. New York: Holt, 2001.

Connelly, Julia E. "The Avoidance of Human Suffering." *Perspectives in Biology and Medicine* 52 (2009) 381–91.

———. "The Whole Story." *Literature and Medicine* 9 (1990) 150–61.

Conrad, Peter. *The Medicalization of Society: On the Transformation of Human Conditions into Treatable Disorders*. Baltimore: Johns Hopkins University Press, 2007.

Costache, Doru. "Christian Worldview: Understandings from St Basil the Great." *Phronema* 25 (2010) 21–56.

Coulehan, Jack. "'A Gentle and Humane Temper': Humility in Medicine." *Perspectives in Biology and Medicine*, 54 (2011) 206–16.

Craig, David M. "Everyone at the Table: Religious Activism and Health Care Reform in Massachusetts." *Journal of Religious Ethics* 40 (2012) 335–58.

Crow, Gillian. "Orthodox Vision of Wholeness." In *Living Orthodoxy in the Modern World*, edited by A. Walker and C. Carras, 7–22. Crestwood, NY: St. Vladimir's Seminary Press, 1996.

Cunningham, Mary B., and Elizabeth Theokritoff. "Who Are the Orthodox Christians? A Historical Introduction." In *The Cambridge Companion to Orthodox Christian Theology*, edited by M. Cunningham and E. Theokritoff, 1–18. Cambridge: Cambridge University Press, 2008.

Cyprian, Archimandrite. "Christian Gratitude: A Fundamental Hallmark of Orthodox Spirituality." *Orthodox Tradition* 20 (2003) 13–25.

Daniels, Alan H., J. Mason DePasse, and Robin N. Kamal. "Orthopaedic Surgeon Burnout." *Journal of the American Academy of Orthopaedic Surgeons* 24 (2016) 213–19.

Daniels, Norman. *Just Health: Meeting Health Needs Fairly*. Cambridge: Cambridge University Press, 2008.

Davidson, Adam, and Alex M. Wood. "The State of Psychological Research into Gratitude and the Need for More Interdisciplinary Collaboration." In *Perspectives on Gratitude*, edited by D. Carr, 215–28. London: Routledge, 2016.

Davies, Oliver. *A Theology of Compassion: Metaphysics of Difference and the Renewal of Tradition*. Grand Rapids: Eerdmans, 2001.

Davis, Carol M. "What Is Empathy, and Can Empathy Be Taught?" *Physical Therapy* 70 (1990) 707–11.

Davis, Nancy J., and Robert V. Robinson. "Are the Rumors of War Exaggerated? Religious Orthodoxy and Moral Progressivism in America." *American Journal of Sociology* 102 (1996) 756–87.

Davis, Nancy J., and Robert V. Robinson. "Religious Orthodoxy in American Society: The Myth of a Monolithic Camp." *Journal for the Scientific Study of Religion* 35 (1996) 229–45.

Del Canale, Stefano, et al. "The Relationship between Physician Empathy and Disease Complications: An Empirical Study of Primary Care Physicians and Their Diabetic Patients in Parma, Italy." *Academic Medicine* 87 (2012) 1243–49.

Demetrios, Archbishop. "The Challenge of Pluralism. The Orthodox Churches in a Pluralistic World." In *The Orthodox Churches in a Pluralistic World: An Ecumenical Conversation*, edited by E. Clapsis, 1–10. Geneva: WCC Publications, 2004.

Dennett, Daniel C. "How to Protect Human Dignity from Science." In *Human Dignity and Bioethics*, edited by E. D. Pellegrino, A. Schulman, and T. W. Merrill, 39–59. Washington, DC: President's Council on Bioethics, 2008.
Dolff, Scott N. "The Obligation to Give: A Reply to Tanner." *Modern Theology* 21 (2005) 119–39.
Dos Anjos, Marcio Fabri. "Medical Ethics in the Developing World: A Liberation Theology Perspective." *The Journal of Medicine and Philosophy* 21 (1996) 629–37.
Dougherty, Charles J., and Ruth Purtilo. "Physicians' Duty of Compassion." *Cambridge Quarterly of Healthcare Ethics* 4 (1995) 426–33.
Dresser, Rebecca. "Human Dignity and the Seriously Ill Patient." In *Human Dignity and Bioethics*, edited by E. D. Pellegrino, A. Schulman, and T. W. Merrill, 505–12. Washington, DC: President's Council on Bioethics, 2008.
Dugdale, Lydia S. "Conclusion: Toward a New Ethical Framework for the Art of Dying Well." In *Dying in the Twenty-First Century: Toward a New Ethical Framework for the Art of Dying Well*, edited by L. S. Dugdale, 173–91. Cambridge: MIT Press, 2015.
Duraisingh, Christopher. "Christian Mission in a Pluralistic World." In *Orthodox Churches in a Pluralistic World: An Ecumenical Conversation*, edited by E. Clapsis, 207–18. Geneva: WCC Publications, 2004.
Dwyer, James. "How to Connect Bioethics and Environmental Ethics: Health, Sustainability, and Justice." *Bioethics* 23 (2009) 497–502.
———. "What Is Wrong with the Global Migration of Health Care Professionals?" *Hastings Center Report* 37 (2007) 36–43.
Eck, Diana L. "The Christian Churches and the Plurality of Religious Communities." In *Orthodox Churches in a Pluralistic World: An Ecumenical Conversation*, edited by E. Clapsis, 11–21. Geneva: WCC Publications, 2004.
Eckenwiler, Lisa, Christine Straehle, and Ryoa Chung. "Global Solidarity, Migration and Global Health Inequity." *Bioethics* 26 (2012) 382–90.
Eibach, Ulrich. "Protection of Life and Human Dignity: The German Debate between Christian Norms and Secular Expectations." *Christian Bioethics* 14 (2008) 58–77.
Ekstrom, Laura W. "Liars, Medicine, and Compassion." *The Journal of Medicine and Philosophy* 37 (2012) 159–80.
Emmons, Robert A. "Is Gratitude Queen of the Virtues and Ingratitude King of the Vices?" In *Perspectives on Gratitude*, edited by D. Carr, 141–53. London: Routledge, 2016.
Emmons, Robert A., and Teresa T. Kneezel. "Giving Thanks: Spiritual and Religious Correlates of Gratitude." *Journal of Psychology and Christianity* 24 (2005) 140–48.
Engelhardt, H. Tristram. "Christian Bioethics in a Post-Christian World: Facing the Challenges." *Christian Bioethics* 18 (2012) 93–114.
———. "Conflicting Moralities and Theologies: The Culture Wars in Bioethics Reexamined." *Christian Bioethics* 8 (2002) 3–8.
———. *The Foundations of Bioethics*. Oxford: Oxford University Press, 1986.
———. *The Foundations of Christian Bioethics*. Lisse, Netherlands: Swets & Zeitlinger, 2000.
———. "Orthodox Approach to Bioethics." In *Living Orthodoxy in the Modern World*, edited by A. Walker and C. Carras, 108–30. Crestwood, NY: St. Vladimir's Seminary Press, 1996.

———. "Orthodox Christian Bioethics: Medical Morality in the Mind of the Fathers." In *Religious Perspectives in Bioethics*, edited by J. F. Peppin, M. J. Cherry, and A. S. Iltis, 21–30. London: Taylor & Francis, 2009.

———. "Why Ecumenism Fails: Taking Theological Differences Seriously." *Christian Bioethics* 13 (2007) 25–51.

Fagley, Nancy S. "The Construct of Appreciation: It Is So Much More than Gratitude." In *Perspectives on Gratitude*, edited by D. Carr, 70–84. London: Routledge, 2016.

Falk, Richard. "Religion and Globalization." In *The Orthodox Churches in a Pluralistic World: An Ecumenical Conversation*, edited by E. Clapsis, 67–76. Geneva: WCC Publications, 2004.

Farmer, Paul. *Pathologies of Power: Health, Human Rights, and the New War on the Poor*. Berkeley: University of California Press, 2003.

Farrell, Laura, et al. "Autoethnography: Introducing 'I' into Medical Education Research." *Medical Education* 49 (2015) 974–82.

FitzGerald, Kyriaki K. "Hospitality: Keeping a Place for the 'Other.'" *Greek Orthodox Theological Review* 56 (2011) 161–77.

Fitzgerald, Patrick. "Gratitude and Justice." *Ethics* 109 (1998) 119–53.

Fixmer-Oraiz, Natalie. "Speaking of Solidarity; Transnational Gestational Surrogacy and the Rhetorics of Reproductive (In)Justice." *Frontiers* 34 (2013) 126–64.

Flores, Glenn. "Doctors in the Movies." *Archives of Disease in Childhood* 89 (2004) 1084–88.

———. "Mad Scientists, Compassionate Healers, and Greedy Egotists: The Portrayal of Physicians in the Movies." *Journal of the National Medical Association* 94 (2002) 635–58.

Florovsky, George. *Bible, Church, Tradition: An Eastern Orthodox View*. Belmont, MA: Nordland, 1972.

Fortounatto, Mariamna, and Mary B. Cunningham. "Theology of the Icon." In *The Cambridge Companion to Orthodox Christian Theology*, edited by M. Cunningham and E. Theokritoff, 136–49. Cambridge: Cambridge University Press, 2008.

Frakes, Chris. "When Strangers Call: A Consideration of Care, Justice, and Compassion." *Hypatia* 25 (2010) 79–99.

Fuks, Abraham, James Brawer, and J. Donald Boudreau. "The Foundation of Physicianship." *Perspectives in Biology and Medicine* 55 (2012) 114–26.

Fuks, Abraham, et al. "Narratives, Metaphors, and the Clinical Relationship." *Genre* 44 (2011) 301–13.

Furin, Jennifer, et al. "A Novel Training Model to Address Health Problems in Poor and Underserved Populations." *Journal of Health Care for the Poor and Underserved* 17 (2006) 17–24.

Gadow, Sally. "Frailty and Strength: The Dialectic of Aging." In *What Does It Mean to Grow Old? Reflections from the Humanities*, edited by T. R. Cole and S. Gadow, 235–43. Durham: Duke University Press, 1986.

Gallagher, Romayne. "Compassion Fatigue." *Canadian Family Physician* 59 (2013) 265–67.

Ganguli-Mitra, Agomoni, and Nikola Biller-Andorno. "Vulnerability in Healthcare and Research Ethics." In *The SAGE Handbook of Health Care Ethics: Core and Emerging Issues*, edited by R. Chadwick, H. ten Have, and E. M. Meslin, 239–51. Los Angeles: SAGE, 2011.

Gawande, Atul. *Being Mortal: Medicine and What Matters in the End.* New York: Metropolitan, 2014.

Gelernter, David. "The Irreducibly Religious Character of Human Dignity." In *Human Dignity and Bioethics*, edited by E. D. Pellegrino, A. Schulman, and T. W. Merrill, 387–405. Washington, DC: President's Council on Bioethics, 2008.

Gennadios, Metropolitan of Sassima. "'God, in Your Grace, Transform the World': An Orthodox Approach." *The Ecumenical Review* 56 (2004) 285–94.

Gert, Bernard. *Common Morality: Deciding What to Do.* Oxford: Oxford University Press. 2007.

Gert, Bernard, Charles M. Culver, and K. Danner Clouser. *Bioethics: A Systematic Approach.* Oxford: Oxford University Press, 2006.

Gill, Robin. *Health Care and Christian Ethics.* New Studies in Christian Ethics 26. Cambridge: Cambridge University Press. 2006.

Glick, Shimon M. "The Empathic Physician: Nature and Nurture." In *Empathy and the Practice of Medicine: Beyond Pills and the Scalpel*, edited by H. M. Spiro et al., 85–102. New Haven: Yale University Press, 1993.

Gold, Katherine J., Ananda Sen, and Thomas L. Schwenk. "Details on Suicide among US Physicians: Data from the National Violent Death Reporting System." *General Hospital Psychiatry* 35 (2013) 45–49.

Goodwin, Michele. *Black Markets: The Supply and Demand of Body Parts.* Cambridge: Cambridge University Press, 2006.

Granek, Leeat, et al. "Nature and Impact of Grief Over Patient Loss on Oncologists' Personal and Professional Lives." *Archives of Internal Medicine* 172 (2012) 964–66.

Groopman, Jerome E. *How Doctors Think.* Boston: Houghton Mifflin, 2007.

Gulliford, Liz, and Blaire Morgan. "An Empirical Exploration of the Normative Dimensions of Gratitude." In *Perspectives on Gratitude*, edited by D. Carr, 199–214. London: Routledge, 2016.

Gunson, Darryl. "Solidarity and the Universal Declaration on Bioethics and Human Rights." *Journal of Medicine and Philosophy* 34 (2009) 241–60.

Guo, Qiaohong, and Cynthia S. Jacelon. "An Integrative Review of Dignity in End-of-Life Care." *Palliative Medicine* 28 (2014) 931–40.

Guroian, Vigen. *Ethics after Christendom: Toward an Ecclesial Christian Ethic.* Grand Rapids: Eerdmans, 1994.

———. *Life's Living Toward Dying: A Theological and Medical-Ethical Study.* Grand Rapids: Eerdmans, 1996.

———. "Seeing Worship as Ethics: An Orthodox Perspective." *The Journal of Religious Ethics* 13 (1985) 332–59.

———. *Tending the Heart of Virtue: How Classic Stories Awaken a Child's Moral Imagination.* Oxford: Oxford University Press, 1998.

Gustafson, James M. *Treasure in Earthen Vessels: The Church as a Human Community.* Library of Theological Ethics. Louisville: Westminster John Knox, 2009.

Hafferty, Frederic W. "Beyond Curriculum Reform: Confronting Medicine's Hidden Curriculum." *Academic Medicine* 73 (1998) 403–7.

———. "Cadaver Stories and the Emotional Socialization of Medical Students." *Journal of Health and Social Behavior* 29 (1988) 344–56.

———. *Into the Valley: Death and the Socialization of Medical Students.* New Haven: Yale University Press, 1991.

Hafferty, Frederic, and Ronald Franks. "The Hidden Curriculum, Ethics Teaching, and the Structure of Medical Education." *Academic Medicine* 69 (1994) 861–71.

Hafler, Janet P., et al. "Decoding the Learning Environment of Medical Education: A Hidden Curriculum Perspective for Faculty Development." *Academic Medicine* 86 (2011) 440–44.

Haight, Roger. "Jesus and the World Religions." *Modern Theology* 12 (1996) 321–44.

Halpern, Jodi. *From Detached Concern to Empathy: Humanizing Medical Practice*. Oxford: Oxford University Press, 2001.

———. "What Is Clinical Empathy?" *Journal of General Internal Medicine* 18 (2003) 670–74.

Hamalis, Perry T. "Eastern Orthodox Ethics." *The International Encyclopedia of Ethics*. Blackwell, 2013. 1525–35.

Hamalis, Perry T., and Aristotle Papanikolaou. "Toward a Godly Mode of Being: Virtue as Embodied Deification." *Studies in Christian Ethics* 26 (2013) 271–80.

Harakas, Stanley S. "The Church and the Secular World." *Greek Orthodox Theological Review* 17 (1972) 167–99.

———. "Eastern Orthodox Christianity, Bioethics." In *Encyclopedia of Bioethics*, edited by S. G. Post, 2:691–97. 3rd ed. New York: Macmillan Reference USA, 2004.

———. "The Integrity of Creation and Ethics." *St. Vladimir's Theological Quarterly* 32 (1988) 27–42.

———. *Health and Medicine in the Eastern Orthodox Tradition: Faith, Liturgy, and Wholeness*. New York: Crossroad, 1990.

———. *Living the Faith: The Praxis of Eastern Orthodox Ethics*. Minneapolis: Light & Life, 1992.

———. "Orthodox Christianity in American Public Life: The Challenges and Opportunities of Religious Pluralism in the Twenty-First Century." *Greek Orthodox Theological Review* 56 (2011) 377–97.

———. "'Rational Medicine' in the Orthodox Tradition." *Greek Orthodox Theological Review* 33 (1988) 19–44.

———. "Reflections on Authority in Ethics." *St. Vladimir's Theological Quarterly* 48 (2004) 355–73.

———. Review of *At the Roots of Christian Bioethics: Critical Essays on the Thought of H. Tristram Engelhardt Jr.*, edited by Ana S. Iltis and Mark J. Cherry. *Logos* 52 (2011) 376–79.

Harrington, Michelle, and Daniel P. Sulmasy. "Spiritual Preparation." In *Dying in the Twenty-First Century: Toward a New Ethical Framework for the Art of Dying Well*, edited by L. S. Dugdale, 87–106. Cambridge: MIT Press, 2015.

Harrison, Nonna Verna. *God's Many-Splendored Image: Theological Anthropology for Christian Formation*. Grand Rapid: Baker, 2010.

———. "Gregory of Nyssa on Human Unity and Diversity." In *Studia Patristica Vol 41, Orientalia; Clement, Origen, Athanasius; the Cappadocians; Chrysostom*, 333–44. Leuven: Peeters, 2006.

———. "The Human Person as Image and Likeness of God." In *The Cambridge Companion to Orthodox Christian Theology*, edited by M. Cunningham and E. Theokritoff, 78–92. Cambridge: Cambridge University Press, 2008.

Hatzinikolaou, Nikolaos. "From Ethics of Dilemmas to Theology of Transcendence." *St. Vladimir's Theological Quarterly* 54 (2010) 165–88.

Heitman, Elizabeth. "Cultural Diversity and the Clinical Encounter: Intercultural Dialogue in Multi-ethnic Patient Care." In *Theological Analyses of the Clinical Encounter*, edited by G. P. McKenny and J. R. Sande, 203–23. Dordrecht, Netherlands: Kluwer Academic, 1994.

Henry, Stephen G., Richard M. Zaner, and Robert S. Dittus. "Moving beyond Evidence-Based Medicine." *Academic Medicine* 82 (2007) 292–97.

Hergott, Lawrence. "The View from Fiesole." *JAMA* 310 (2013) 147–48.

Hettema, Theo L. "Autonomy and Its Vulnerability: Ricoeur's View on Justice as a Contribution to Care Ethics." *Medicine, Health Care and Philosophy* 17 (2014) 493–98.

Heyd, David. "Jewish Perspective on Vulnerable Groups: Women and Children." In *Religious Perspectives on Human Vulnerability in Bioethics*, edited by J. Tham, A. Garcia, and G. Miranda, 203–14. Dordrecht, Netherlands: Springer, 2014.

Hierotheos, Metropolitan of Nafpaktos. "Christian Bioethics: Challenges in a Secularized Europe." *Christian Bioethics* 14 (2008) 29–41.

Hilfiker, David. "Allowing the Debilitated to Die—Facing Our Ethical Choices." *NEJM* 308 (1983) 716–19.

———. "Are We Comfortable with Homelessness?" *JAMA* 262 (1989) 1375–76.

———. "Unconscious on a Corner . . ." *JAMA* 258 (1987) 3155–56.

Hinshaw, Daniel B., et al. "Spiritual Issues in Suffering: Creating a Dialogue between Clergy and Palliative Care Providers." *Progress in Palliative Care* 19 (2011) 7–14.

Hobbs, T. R. "Hospitality in the First Testament and the 'Teleological Fallacy.'" *Journal for the Study of the Old Testament* 26 (2001) 3–30.

Hodges, Brian D., et al. "Medical Education . . . Meet Michel Foucault." *Medical Education* 48 (2014) 563–71.

Hoffmann, Willem A. "Benefit-Sharing." In *Encyclopedia of Global Bioethics*, edited by H. ten Have, 246–56. Cham: Springer, 2016.

Hoffmaster, Barry. "What Does Vulnerability Mean?" *Hastings Center Report* 36 (2006) 38–45.

Holmes, Cheryl L., et al. "Harnessing the Hidden Curriculum: A Four-Step Approach to Developing and Reinforcing Reflective Competencies in Medical Clinical Clerkship." *Advances in Health Sciences Education* 20 (2015) 1355–70.

Hooker, Claire. "Understanding Empathy: Why Phenomenology and Hermeneutics Can Help Medical Education and Practice." *Medicine, Health Care and Philosophy* 18 (2015) 541–52.

Hughes, Glenn. "The Concept of Dignity in the Universal Declaration of Human Rights." *Journal of Religious Ethics* 39 (2011) 1–24.

Huntington, Samuel. "The Clash of Civilizations?" *Foreign Affairs* 72 (1993) 22–49.

Illingworth, Patricia, and Wendy E. Parmet. "Solidarity for Global Health." *Bioethics* 26 (2012) ii–iv.

Imber, Jonathan B. "Doubting Culture Wars." *Society* 38 (2001) 31–37.

Imhof, Arthur E. "From the Old Mortality Pattern to the New: Implications of a Radical Change from the Sixteenth to the Twentieth Century." *Bulletin of the History of Medicine* 59 (1985) 1–29.

Institute of Medicine. *Dying in America: Improving Quality and Honoring Individual Preferences Near the End of Life*. Washington, DC: National Academies Press, 2015.

Jackelen, Antje. "The Image of God as Techno Sapiens." *Zygon* 37 (2002) 289–302.

Jaeggi, Rahel. "Solidarity and Indifference." In *Solidarity in Health and Social Care in Europe*, edited by R. ter Meulen, W. Arts, and R. Muffels, 287–308. Dordrecht, Netherlands: Kluwer, 2001.

Jeffreys, Derek S. "The Influence of Kant on Christian Theology: A Debate about Human Dignity and Christian Personalism." *Journal of Markets and Mortality* 7 (2004) 507–16.

Jennings, Bruce. "Reconceptualizing Autonomy: A Relational Turn in Bioethics." *Hastings Center Report* 46 (2016) 11–16.

Jillions, John A. "Orthodox Christianity in the West: The Ecumenical Challenge." In *The Cambridge Companion to Orthodox Christian Theology*, edited by M. Cunningham and E. Theokritoff, 276–91. Cambridge: Cambridge University Press, 2008.

Johnson, Michael A., Kevin Jung, and William Schweiker. "Introduction." In *Humanity Before God: Contemporary Faces of Jewish, Christian, and Islamic Ethics*, edited by W. Schweiker, M. A. Johnson, and K. Jung, 1–16. Minneapolis: Fortress, 2006.

Jones, D. Gareth. *The Peril and Promise of Medical Technology*. New International Studies in Applied Ethics. Bern: Peter Lang, 2013.

Jones, John D. "The Church as Neighbor: Corporately and Compassionately Engaged." *In Communion* 66 (2013) 13–25.

———. "Opening the Doors of Compassion: Cultivating a Merciful Heart." *In Communion* 64 (2012) 4–20.

Jonker, Evert. "Learning the Spirit of Human Dignity: A Practical Theological Exploration." *Scriptura* 95 (2007) 224–40.

Jonsen, Albert R. *The Birth of Bioethics*. Oxford: Oxford University Press, 1998.

Kaczor, Christopher R. *A Defense of Dignity: Creating Life, Destroying Life, and Protecting the Rights of Conscience*. Notre Dame: University of Notre Dame Press, 2013.

Kariatlis, Philip. "'Dazzling Darkness': The Mystical or Theophanic Theology of St. Gregory of Nyssa." *Phronema* 27 (2012) 99–123.

Kass, Leon R. "Defending Human Dignity." In *Human Dignity and Bioethics*, edited by E. D. Pellegrino, A. Schulman, and T. W. Merrill, 297–331. Washington, DC: President's Council on Bioethics, 2008.

———. *Life, Liberty and the Defense of Dignity: The Challenge for Bioethics*. San Francisco: Encounter, 2002.

Kateb, George. *Human Dignity*. Cambridge: Belknap Press of Harvard University Press, 2011.

Kattan, Assaad E. "Hermeneutics; A Protestant Discipline for an Orthodox Context?" *Theological Review: The Near East School of Theology* 23 (2002) 47–57.

———. *Shiraa' Fi Uyoun Mustadira; Dirasat Fi Fikr Almutran George Khodr ‹A Sail in Round Eyes; Studies in the Thought of Metropolitan George Khodr*. Beirut, Lebanon: An-nour COOP, 2012.

Katz, Jay. *The Silent World of Doctor and Patient*. New York: Free Press, 1984.

Kearney, Richard, and James Taylor, eds. *Hosting the Stranger: Between Religions*. New York: Continuum International, 2011.

Khalil, Atif. "The Embodiment of Gratitude (*Shukr*) in Sufi Ethics." *Studia Islamica* 111 (2016) 159–78.

———. "On Cultivating Gratitude (*Shukr*) in Sufi Virtue Ethics." *Journal of Sufi Studies* 4 (2015) 1–26.

Khodr, George. "The Church and the World." *St. Vladimir's Theological Quarterly* 13 (1969) 33–51.

———. *The Ways of Childhood*. Orthodox Christian Profiles Series. Crestwood, NY: St. Vladimir's Seminary Press, 2016.

Khushf, George. "Illness, the Problem of Evil, and the Analogical Structure of Healing: On the Difference Christianity Makes in Bioethics." *Christian Bioethics* 1 (1995) 102–20.

Kidder, Tracy. *Mountains beyond Mountains: The Quest of Dr. Paul Farmer, a Man Who Would Cure the World*. New York: Random House, 2003.

Kirk, David. "Hospitality: The Essence of Eastern Christian Lifestyle." *Diakonia* 16 (1981) 104–17.

Koenig, John. *New Testament Hospitality: Partnership with Strangers as Promise and Mission*. 1985. Reprint, Eugene, OR: Wipf & Stock, 2001.

Kolbet, Paul R. "Torture and Origen's Hermeneutics of Nonviolence." *Journal of the American Academy of Religion* 76 (2008) 545–72.

Konstan, David. "The Freedom to Feel Grateful: The View from Classical Antiquity." In *Perspectives on Gratitude*, edited by D. Carr, 41–53. London: Routledge, 2016.

Körtner, Ulrich H. J. "Human Dignity and Biomedical Ethics from a Christian Theological Perspective." *HTS Teologiese Studies/Theological Studies* 67 (2011).

Koterski, Joseph. "Human Nature from a Catholic Perspective." *American Journal of Economics and Sociology* 71 (2012) 809–39.

Kraynak, Robert P. "Human Dignity and the Mystery of the Human Soul." In *Human Dignity and Bioethics*, edited by E. D. Pellegrino, A. Schulman, and T. W. Merrill, 61–82. Washington, DC: President's Council on Bioethics, 2008.

Kuper, Ayelet, Cynthia Whitehead, and Brian David Hodges. "Looking Back to Move Forward: Using History, Discourse and Text in Medical Education Research: AMEE Guide No. 73." *Medical Teacher* 35 (2013) e849–60.

Labi, Kwame Joseph. "Injustice and Prophetic Evangelism." In *Orthodox Churches in a Pluralistic World: An Ecumenical Conversation*, edited by E. Clapsis, 189–91. Geneva: WCC Publications, 2004.

Lammers, Stephen E. "The Medical Futility Discussion: Some Theological Suggestions." In *Secular Bioethics in Theological Perspective*, edited by E. E. Shelp, 115–28. Dordrecht, Netherlands: Kluwer Academic, 1996.

Landau, Richard L. ". . . And the Least of These Is Empathy." In *Empathy and the Practice of Medicine: Beyond Pills and the Scalpel*, edited by H.M. Spiro et al., 103–9. New Haven: Yale University Press, 1993.

Lantham, Stephen R. "Pluralism and the 'Good' Death." In *Dying in the Twenty-First Century: Toward a New Ethical Framework for the Art of Dying Well*, edited by L. S. Dugdale, 33–46. Cambridge: MIT Press, 2015.

Larchet, Jean-Claude. *The Theology of Illness*. Crestwood, NY: St. Vladimir's Seminary Press, 2002.

Lash, Archimandrite Ephrem. "Biblical interpretation in worship." In *The Cambridge Companion to Orthodox Christian Theology*, edited by M. Cunningham and E. Theokritoff, 35–48. Cambridge: Cambridge University Press, 2008.

Lasker, Shamima Parvin. "Surrogacy." In *Encyclopedia of Global Bioethics*, edited by H. ten Have, 2760–67. Cham: Springer, 2016.

Lateef, Fatimah Abdul. "From Data to Stories: Humanizing Medicine in the Age of Technology." *Education in Medicine Journal* 6 (2014) 50–55.

Lauritzen, Paul. "Listening to the Different Voices: Toward a Poetic Bioethics." In *Theological Analyses of the Clinical Encounter*, edited by G. P. McKenny and J. R. Sande, 151–69. Dordrecht, Netherlands: Kluwer Academic, 1994.

Lawler, Peter Augustine. "Modern and American Dignity." In *Human Dignity and Bioethics*, edited by E. D. Pellegrino, A. Schulman, and T. W. Merrill, 229–52. Washington, DC: President's Council on Bioethics, 2008.

Lebacqz, Karen. "Dignity and Enhancement in the Holy City." In *Transhumanism and Transcendence: Christian Hope in an Age of Technological Enhancement*, edited by R. Cole-Turner, 51–62. Washington, DC: Georgetown University Press, 2011.

———. "Empowerment in the Clinical Encounter." In *Theological Analyses of the Clinical Encounter*, edited by G. P. McKenny and J. R. Sande, 133–47. Dordrecht, Netherlands: Kluwer Academic, 1994.

———. "The Weeping Womb: Why Beneficence Needs the Still Small Voice of Compassion." In *Secular Bioethics in Theological Perspective*, edited by E. E. Shelp, 85–96. Dordrecht, Netherlands: Kluwer Academic, 1996.

Leder, Drew. "Toward a Phenomenology of Pain." *Review of Existential Psychology and Psychiatry* 19 (1984) 255–66.

Lee, Patrick T., and Robert P. George. "The Nature and Basis of Human Dignity." In *Human Dignity and Bioethics*, edited by E. D. Pellegrino, A. Schulman, and T. W. Merrill, 409–33. Washington, DC: President's Council on Bioethics, 2008.

Legrand, Susan B., and Jessica B. Heintz. "Palliative Medicine Fellowship: A Study of Resident Choices." *Journal of Pain and Symptom Management* 43 (2012) 558–68.

Lemna, Keith. "Human Ecology, Environmental Ecology, and a Ressourcement Theology; *Caritas in Veritate* in the Light of Philip Sherrard's Theandric Anthropology." *Logos* 14 (2011) 133–54.

London, Alex John. "Justice and the Human Development Approach to International Research." *Hastings Center Report* 35 (2005) 24–37.

Lossky, Vladimir. *In the Image and Likeness of God*. Crestwood, NY: St. Vladimir's Seminary Press, 1985.

———. *The Mystical Theology of the Eastern Church*. London: J. Clarke, 1976.

Loudovikos, Nicholas. "Nations in the Church: Towards an Eschatological Political Anthropocentrism?" *International Journal for the Study of the Christian Church* 12 (2012) 131–47.

Louth, Andrew. "The Church's Mission: Patristic Presuppositions." *Greek Orthodox Theological Review* 44 (1999) 649–57.

———. *Introducing Eastern Orthodox Theology*. Downers Grove, IL: InterVarsity, 2013.

———. "The Orthodox Dogmatic Theology of Dumitru Staniloae." *Modern Theology* 13 (1997) 253–67.

———. "The Patristic Revival and Its Protagonists." In *The Cambridge Companion to Orthodox Christian Theology*, edited by M. Cunningham and E. Theokritoff, 188–202. Cambridge: Cambridge University Press, 2008.

Lu, Michael Chunchi. "Why It Was Hard for Me to Learn Compassion as a Third-Year Medical Student." *Cambridge Quarterly of Healthcare Ethics* 4 (1995) 454–58.

Lubardic, Bogdan. "Orthodox Theology of Personhood: A Critical Overview (Part 1)." *The Expository Times* 122 (2011) 521–30.

———. "Orthodox Theology of Personhood: A Critical Overview (Part 2)." *The Expository Times* 122 (2011) 573–81.

Lupu, Dale, et al. "Few U.S. Public Health Schools Offer Courses on Palliative and End-of-Life Care Policy." *Journal of Palliative Medicine* 16 (2013) 1582–87.
Lustig, B. A. "Reform and Rationing: Reflections on Health Care in Light of Catholic Social Teaching." In *Secular Bioethics in Theological Perspective*, edited by E. E. Shelp, 31–50. Dordrecht, Netherlands: Kluwer Academic, 1996.
Lynn, Joanne. "Travels in the Valley of the Shadow." In *Empathy and the Practice of Medicine: Beyond Pills and the Scalpel*, edited by H. M. Spiro et al., 40–53. New Haven: Yale University Press, 1993.
Macaleer, R. Dennis. *The New Testament and Bioethics: Theology and Basic Bioethics Principles*. Eugene, OR: Pickwick, 2014.
MacIntyre, Alasdair C. *After Virtue: A Study in Moral Theory*. 3rd ed. Notre Dame: University of Notre Dame Press, 2007.
Macklin, Ruth. "Bioethics, Vulnerability, and Protection." *Bioethics* 17 (2003) 472–86.
———. "Dignity Is a Useless Concept." *BMJ* 327 (2003) 1419–20.
———. *Double Standards in Medical Research in Developing Countries*. Cambridge: Cambridge University Press, 2004.
Mantzarides, Georgios I. "Globalization and Universality: Chimera and Truth." *Christian Bioethics* 8 (2002) 199–207.
Marcel, Gabriel. *The Existential Background of Human Dignity*. Cambridge: Harvard University Press, 1963.
Marcum, James A. "Reflections on Humanizing Biomedicine." *Perspectives in Biology and Medicine* 51 (2008) 392–405.
Marmot, Michael. "Dignity and Inequality." *Lancet* 364 (2004) 1019–21.
Martin, Paul. "Poetry as Theology: An Orthodox Perspective." *Greek Orthodox Theological Review* 52 (2007) 145–95.
Martinsen, Kari. *Care and Vulnerability*. Oslo: Akribe, 2006.
Mavroforou, A., A. Giannoukas, and E. Michalodimitrakis. "Alcohol and Drug Abuse among Doctors." *Medicine & Law* 25 (2006) 611–25.
May, William F. "The Medical Covenant: An Ethics of Obligation or Virtue?" In *Theological Analyses of the Clinical Encounter*, edited by G. P. McKenny and J. R. Sande, 29–44. Dordrecht, Netherlands: Kluwer Academic, 1994.
McConnell, Terrance. "Gratitude's Value." In *Perspectives on Gratitude*, edited by D. Carr, 13–26. London: Routledge, 2016.
McCullough, Michael E., et al. "Is Gratitude a Moral Affect?" *Psychological Bulletin* 127 (2001) 249–66.
McKenny, G. P. "Physician-Assisted Death: A Pyrrhic Victory for Secular Bioethics." In *Secular Bioethics in Theological Perspective*, edited by E. E. Shelp, 145–58. Dordrecht, Netherlands: Kluwer Academic, 1996.
Mendiola, M. M. "Overworked, but Uncritically Tested: Human Dignity and the Aid-in-Dying Debate." In *Secular Bioethics in Theological Perspective*, edited by E. E. Shelp, 129–43. Dordrecht, Netherlands: Kluwer Academic, 1996.
Meyendorff, John. "Orthodox Theology Today." *St. Vladimir's Theological Quarterly* 13 (1969) 77–92.
———. "Unity of the Church—Unity of Mankind." *The Ecumenical Review* 24 (1972) 30–46.
Mizrahi, Terry. *Getting Rid of Patients: Contradictions in the Socialization of Physicians*. New Brunswick, NJ: Rutgers University Press, 1986.

Montgomery, Kathryn. *How Doctors Think: Clinical Judgment and the Practice of Medicine*. Oxford: Oxford University Press, 2006.

Morowitz, Harold J. "The Pre-Med as a Metaphor of Antipathy." In *Empathy and the Practice of Medicine: Beyond Pills and the Scalpel*, edited by H.M. Spiro et al., 70–75. New Haven: Yale University Press, 1993.

Munteanu, Daniel. "Cosmic Liturgy: The Theological Dignity of Creation as a Basis of an Orthodox Ecotheology." *International Journal of Public Theology* 4 (2010) 332–44.

Muzur, Amir, and Hans-Martin Sass, eds. *Fritz Jahr and the Foundations of Global Bioethics: The Future of Integrative Bioethics*. Vienna: Lit, 2012.

Nasr, Seyyed Hussein. "Standing Before God: Human Responsibilities and Human Rights." In *Humanity Before God: Contemporary Faces of Jewish, Christian, and Islamic Ethics*, edited by W. Schweiker, M. A. Johnson, and K. Jung, 299–320. Minneapolis: Fortress, 2006.

Navone, John. "Divine and Human Hospitality." *New Blackfriars* 85 (2004) 329–40.

Neuhaus, Richard J. "Human Dignity and Public Discourse." In *Human Dignity and Bioethics*, edited by E. D. Pellegrino, A. Schulman, and T. W. Merrill, 215–28. Washington, DC: President's Council on Bioethics, 2008.

Newman, Louis E. "Talking Ethics with Strangers: A View from Jewish Tradition." *The Journal of Medicine and Philosophy* 18 (1993) 549–67.

Noble, Ivana, and Tim Noble. "Hospitality as a Key to the Relationship with the Other in Levinas and Derrida." *Auc Theologica* 6 (2016) 47–65.

Normand, Charles. "Setting Priorities in and for End-of-Life Care: Challenges in the Application of Economic Evaluation." *Health Economics, Policy and Law* 7 (2012) 431–39.

O'Rourke, Meghan. "Doctors Tell All and It's Far Worse Than You Think." *The Atlantic*, November 2014.

Oechsle, Karin, et al. "Relationship between Symptom Burden, Distress, and Sense of Dignity in Terminally Ill Cancer Patients." *Journal of Pain and Symptom Management* 48 (2014) 313–21.

Ofri, Danielle. *What Doctors Feel: How Emotions Affect the Practice of Medicine*. Boston: Beacon, 2013.

Olson, Daniel V. A. "Dimensions of Cultural Tension among the American Public." In *Cultural Wars in American Politics: Critical Reviews of a Popular Myth*, edited by R. H. Williams, 237–58. New York: de Gruyter, 1997.

Oreopoulos, Dimitrios G. "Compassion and Mercy in the Practice of Medicine." *Peritoneal Dialysis International* 21 (2001) 539–42.

Owens, Dorothy M. *Hospitality to Strangers: Empathy in the Physician-Patient Relationship*. Atlanta: Scholars, 1999.

Palmer, Parker J. *The Company of Strangers: Christians and the Renewal of America's Public Life*. New York: Crossroad, 1981.

Papanikolaou, Aristotle. "Byzantium, Orthodoxy and Democracy." *Journal of the American Academy of Religion* 71 (2003) 75–98.

———. "Eucharistic Ontology: Maximus the Confessor's Eschatological Ontology of Being as Dialogical Reciprocity." *Modern Theology* 28 (2012) 155–56.

———. *The Mystical as Political: Democracy and Non-radical Orthodoxy*. Notre Dame: University of Notre Dame Press, 2012.

———. "Orthodoxy, Postmodernity, and Ecumenism: The Difference That Divine-Human Communion Makes." *Journal of Ecumenical Studies* 42 (2007) 527–47.

———. "Personhood and Its Exponents in Twentieth-Century Orthodox Theology." In *The Cambridge Companion to Orthodox Christian Theology*, edited by M. Cunningham and E. Theokritoff, 232–45. Cambridge: Cambridge University Press, 2008.

Paul, David, Shaun C. Ewen, and Rhys Jones. "Cultural Competence in Medical Education: Aligning the Formal, Informal and Hidden Curricula." *Advances in Health Sciences Education* 19 (2014) 751–58.

Payne, Daniel P. "The Challenge of Western Globalization to Orthodox Christianity." In *Orthodox Christianity and Contemporary Europe*, edited by J. Sutton and W. van den Bercken, 135–44. Leuven: Peeters, 2003.

———. "The 'Relational Ontology' of Christos Yannaras: The Hesychast Influence on the Understanding of the Person in the Thought of Christos Yannaras." In *St. Gregory Palamas: Orthodox Theology and Orthodox Philosophy Revisited*, edited by C. Athanasopoulos. London: J. Clarke (forthcoming).

Pellegrino, Edmund D. "The Lived Experience of Human Dignity." In *Human Dignity and Bioethics*, edited by E. D. Pellegrino, A. Schulman, and T. W. Merrill, 513–39. Washington, DC: President's Council on Bioethics, 2008.

———. "Toward a Reconstruction of Medical Morality." *AJOB* 6 (2006) 65–71.

Pelluchon, Corine. "Taking Vulnerability Seriously: What Does It Change for Bioethics and Politics?" In *Human Dignity of the Vulnerable in the Age of Rights: Interdisciplinary Perspectives*, edited by A. Masferrer and E. García-Sánchez, 293–312. Cham: Springer, 2016.

Pence, Gregory E. "Can Compassion Be Taught?" *Journal of Medical Ethics* 9 (1983) 189–91.

Pentiuc, Eugen J. *Jesus the Messiah in the Hebrew Bible*. New York: Paulist, 2006.

Peschel, Richard E., and Enid Peschel. "Selective Empathy." In *Empathy and the Practice of Medicine: Beyond Pills and the Scalpel*, edited by H.M. Spiro et al., 110–20. New Haven: Yale University Press, 1993.

Peters, Rebecca Todd. *Solidarity Ethics: Transformation in a Globalized World*. Minneapolis: Fortress, 2014.

Petryna, Adriana. *When Experiments Travel: Clinical Trials and the Global Search for Human Subjects*. Princeton: Princeton University Press, 2009.

Pinker, Steven. "The Stupidity of Dignity." *The New Republic* 238, no. 9 (2008) 28–31.

Plekon, Michael. "The Russian Religious Revival and Its Theological Legacy." In *The Cambridge Companion to Orthodox Christian Theology*, edited by M. Cunningham and E. Theokritoff, 203–17. Cambridge: Cambridge University Press, 2008.

Poirier, Suzanne. *Doctors in the Making: Memoirs and Medical Education*. Iowa City: University of Iowa Press, 2009.

———. "Medical Education and the Embodied Physician." *Literature and Medicine* 25 (2006) 522–52.

Potter, Van Rensselaer. *Bioethics: Bridge to the Future*. Englewood Cliffs, NJ: Prentice-Hall, 1971.

———. "Bioethics: The Science of Survival." *Perspectives in Biology and Medicine* 14 (1970) 127–53.

———. *Global Bioethics: Building on the Leopold Legacy*. East Lansing, MI: Michigan State University Press, 1988.

Prainsack, Barbara, and Alena Buyx. *Solidarity in Biomedicine and Beyond*. Cambridge: Cambridge University Press, 2017.

Prodromou, Elizabeth H. "Orthodox Christianity and Pluralism: Moving beyond Ambivalence?" In *Orthodox Churches in a Pluralistic World: An Ecumenical Conversation*, edited by E. Clapsis, 22–46. Geneva: WCC Publications, 2004.

Reich, Warren T. "Speaking of Suffering: A Moral Account of Compassion." *Soundings* 72 (1989) 83–108.

———. "The Word 'Bioethics': Its Birth and the Legacies of Those Who Shaped It." *Kennedy Institute of Ethics Journal* 4 (1994) 319–35.

———. "The Word 'Bioethics': The Struggle Over Its Earliest Meanings." *Kennedy Institute of Ethics Journal* 5 (1995) 19–34.

Reiser, Stanley Joel. "Science, Pedagogy, and the Transformation of Empathy in Medicine." In *Empathy and the Practice of Medicine: Beyond Pills and the Scalpel*, edited by H.M. Spiro et al., 121–32. New Haven: Yale University Press, 1993.

Ridenour, Autumn Alcot, and Lisa Sowle Cahill. "The Role of Community." In *Dying in the Twenty-First Century: Toward a New Ethical Framework for the Art of Dying Well*, edited by L. S. Dugdale, 107–30. Cambridge: MIT Press, 2015.

Riffin, Catherine, et al. "Identifying Key Priorities for Future Palliative Care Research Using an Innovative Analytic Approach." *American Journal of Public Health* 105 (2015) e15–21.

Rizzo, Robert F. "Major Issues Relating to End-of-Life Care: Ethical, Legal and Medical from a Historical Perspective." *International Journal of Social Economics* 32 (2005) 34–59.

Robbins, Brent Dean. "Confronting the Cadaver: The Denial of Death in Modern Medicine." *Janus Head* 12 (2005) 131–40.

Roberts, Robert C. "Gratitude and Humility." In *Perspectives on Gratitude*, edited by D. Carr, 57–69. London: Routledge, 2016.

Rolston, Holmes. "Human Uniqueness and Human Dignity: Persons in Nature and the Nature of Persons." In *Human Dignity and Bioethics*, edited by E. D. Pellegrino, A. Schulman, and T. W. Merrill, 129–53. Washington, DC: President's Council on Bioethics, 2008.

Rosel, Natalie. "Growing Old Together: Neighborhood Communality among the Elderly." In *What Does It Mean to Grow Old? Reflections from the Humanities*, edited by T. R. Cole and S. Gadow, 199–233. Durham: Duke University Press, 1986.

Rosen, George. *A History of Public Health*. Baltimore: Johns Hopkins University Press, 1993.

Rosen, Michael. *Dignity: Its History and Meaning*. Cambridge: Harvard University Press, 2012.

Rosenbaum, Edward E. *A Taste of My Own Medicine: When the Doctor Is the Patient*. New York: Random House, 1988.

Rothman, David J. *Strangers at the Bedside: A History of How Law and Bioethics Transformed Medical Decision Making*. New York: Basic Books, 1991.

Rubin, Charles. "Human Dignity and the Future of Man." In *Human Dignity and Bioethics*, edited by E. D. Pellegrino, A. Schulman, and T. W. Merrill, 155–72. Washington, DC: President's Council on Bioethics, 2008.

Rumbold, Bruce, and Samar Aoun. "Bereavement and Palliative Care: A Public Health Perspective." *Progress in Palliative Care* 22 (2014) 131–35.

Russell, Norman. "One Faith, One Church, One Emperor: The Byzantine Approach to Ecumenicity and Its Legacy." *International Journal for the Study of the Christian Church* 12 (2012) 122–30.

Ryan, Maura A. "Beyond a Western Bioethics?" *Theological Studies* 65 (2004) 158–77.

Sacks, Oliver W. *A Leg to Stand On*. New York: Summit, 1984.

Said, Edward W. "The Clash of Ignorance." *The Nation*, October 22, 2001, 11–13.

Saunders, Ben. "Altruism or Solidarity? The Motives for Organ Donation and Two Proposals." *Bioethics* 26 (2012) 376–81.

Saunders, Cicely. "The Evolution of Palliative Care." *Patient Education and Counseling* 41 (2000) 7–13.

Schillmeier, Michael. *Eventful Bodies: The Cosmopolitics of Illness*. Theory, Technology and Society. Burlington, VT: Ashgate, 2014.

Schmemann, Alexander. *For the Life of the World: Sacraments and Orthodoxy*. Crestwood, New York: St. Vladimir's Seminary Press, 1973.

———. "The Task of Orthodox Theology in America Today." *St. Vladimir's Theological Quarterly* 10 (1966) 180–88.

———. "Theology and Eucharist." *St. Vladimir's Theological Quarterly* 5 (1961) 10–23.

Schnackenburg, Rudolf. *The Gospel of Matthew*. Translated by Robert R. Barr. Grand Rapids: Eerdmans. 2002.

Schulman, Adam. "Bioethics and the Question of Human Dignity." In *Human Dignity and Bioethics*, edited by E. D. Pellegrino, A. Schulman, and T. W. Merrill, 513–39. Washington, DC: President's Council on Bioethics, 2008.

Schulman-Green, D. "How Do Physicians Learn to Provide Palliative Care?" *Journal of Palliative Care* 19 (2003) 246–52.

Schweiker, William. "Distinctive Love: Gratitude for Life and Theological Humanism." In *Humanity Before God: Contemporary Faces of Jewish, Christian, and Islamic Ethics*, edited by W. Schweiker, M. A. Johnson, and K. Jung, 91–117. Minneapolis: Fortress, 2006.

Scouteris, Constantine. "Bioethics in the Light of Orthodox Anthropology." In *Proceedings of the 1st International Conference "Christian Anthropology & Biotechnological Progress", of the Orthodox Academy of Crete, in Chania, Greece*, 2002.

Sepúlveda, C., et al. "Palliative Care: The World Health Organization's Global Perspective." *Journal of Pain and Symptom Management* 24 (2002) 91–96.

Shapiro, Jordan, Bin Zhang, and Eric J. Warm. "Residency as a Social Network: Burnout, Loneliness, and Social Network Centrality." *Journal of Graduate Medical Education* 7 (2015) 617–23.

Shell, Susan M. "Kant's Concept of Human Dignity as a Resource for Bioethics." In *Human Dignity and Bioethics*, edited by E. D. Pellegrino, A. Schulman, and T. W. Merrill, 333–49. Washington, DC: President's Council on Bioethics, 2008.

Shelp, Earl E. "Introduction." In *Secular Bioethics in Theological Perspective*, edited by E. E. Shelp, vii–xiv. Dordrecht, Netherlands: Kluwer Academic, 1996.

Sherrard, Philip. *The Eclipse of Man and Nature: An Enquiry into the Origins and Consequences of Modern Science*. West Stockbridge, MA: Lindisfarne, 1987.

Smilansky, Saul. "Gratitude: The Dark Side." In *Perspectives on Gratitude*, edited by D. Carr, 126–37. London: Routledge, 2016.

Soelle, Dorothee. *Choosing life*. Philadelphia: Fortress, 1981.

———. *Suffering*. Philadelphia: Fortress, 1975.

Solbakk, Jan Helge. "Vulnerability: A Futile or Useful Principle in Healthcare Ethics?" In *The SAGE Handbook of Health Care Ethics: Core and Emerging Issues*, edited by R. Chadwick, H. ten Have, and E. M. Meslin, 228–39. Los Angeles: SAGE, 2011.

Spiro, Howard M. "Empathy: An Introduction." In *Empathy and the Practice of Medicine: Beyond Pills and the Scalpel*, edited by H. M. Spiro et al., 1–6. New Haven: Yale University Press, 1993.

———. "What Is Empathy and Can It Be Taught?" In *Empathy and the Practice of Medicine: Beyond Pills and the Scalpel*, edited by H. M. Spiro et al., 7–14. New Haven: Yale University Press, 1993.

Steenberg, Matthew. "The Church." In *The Cambridge Companion to Orthodox Christian Theology*, edited by M. Cunningham and E. Theokritoff, 121–35. Cambridge: Cambridge University Press, 2008.

Stöckl, Kristina. "Modernity and Its Critique in 20th Century Russian Orthodox Thought." *Studies in East European Thought* 58 (2007) 243–69.

Sulmasy, Daniel P. "Dignity and Bioethics: History, Theory, and Selected Applications." In *Human Dignity and Bioethics*, edited by E. D. Pellegrino, A. Schulman, and T. W. Merrill, 469–501. Washington, DC: President's Council on Bioethics, 2008.

———. "The Varieties of Human Dignity: A Logical and Conceptual Analysis." *Medicine, Health Care, and Philosophy* 16 (2013) 937–44.

Svenaeus, Fredrik. "Empathy as a Necessary Condition of Phronesis: A Line of Thought for Medical Ethics." *Medicine, Health Care and Philosophy* 17 (2014) 293–99.

Takakuwa, Kevin M., Nick Rubashkin, and Karen E. Herzig. *What I Learned in Medical School: Personal Stories of Young Doctors*. Berkeley: University of California Press, 2004.

Tarasco Michel, Martha. "Vulnerability: Considerations on the Appropriate Use of the Term in Bioethics." In *Religious Perspectives on Human Vulnerability in Bioethics*, edited by J. Tham, A. Garcia, and G. Miranda, 29–37. Dordrecht, Netherlands: Springer, 2014.

ten Have, Henk. *Global Bioethics: An Introduction*. London: Routledge, 2016.

———. "Global Bioethics and Communitarianism." *Theoretical Medicine and Bioethics* 32 (2011) 315–26.

———. "Potter's Notion of Bioethics." *Kennedy Institute of Ethics Journal* 22 (2012) 59–82.

———. *Vulnerability: Challenging Bioethics*. London: Routledge, 2016.

ten Have, Henk, and Bert Gordijn. "Empathy and Violence." *Medicine, Health Care and Philosophy* 19 (2016) 499–500.

ten Have, Henk, and Jos V. M. Welie. *Death and Medical Power: An Ethical Analysis of Dutch Euthanasia Practice*. Maidenhead, UK: McGraw-Hill, 2005.

ten Have, Henk, and Michele Jean, eds. *The UNESCO Universal Declaration on Bioethics and Human Rights: Background, Principles and Application*. UNESCO, 2009.

ter Meulen, Ruud. "Solidarity, Justice, and Recognition of the Other." *Theoretical Medicine and Bioethics* 37 (2016) 517–29.

ter Meulen, Ruud, Wil Arts, and Ruud Muffels, eds. *Solidarity in Health and Social Care in Europe*. Philosophy and Medicine. Dordrecht, Netherlands: Kluwer, 2011.

Tham, Joseph. "Lessons Learned." In *Religious Perspectives on Human Vulnerability in Bioethics*, edited by J. Tham, A. Garcia, and G. Miranda, 215–24. Dordrecht, Netherlands: Springer, 2014.

Tham, Joseph, Alberto Garcia, and Gonzalo Miranda, eds. *Religious Perspectives on Human Vulnerability in Bioethics.* Advancing Global Bioethics. Dordrecht, Netherlands: Springer, 2014.
Theokritoff, Elizabeth. "Creator and Creation." In *The Cambridge Companion to Orthodox Christian Theology,* edited by M. Cunningham and E. Theokritoff, 63–77. Cambridge: Cambridge University Press, 2008.
Thomasma, David C., and Thomasine Kushner. "A Dialogue on Compassion and Supererogation in Medicine." *Cambridge Quarterly of Healthcare Ethics* 4 (1995) 415–25.
Thursby, Jacqueline S. *Funeral Festivals in America: Rituals for the Living.* Lexington: University Press of Kentucky, 2006.
Trakatellis, Metropolitan Demetrios. "The Orthodox Churches in a Pluralistic World: An Ecumenical Conversation." In *The Orthodox Churches in a Pluralistic World: An Ecumenical Conversation,* edited by E. Clapsis, 1–10. Geneva: WCC Publications, 2004.
Tsang, Jo-Ann, and Stephen R. Martin. "A Psychological Perspective on Gratitude and Religion." In *Perspectives on Gratitude,* edited by D. Carr, 154–68. London: Routledge, 2016.
Tsompanidis, Stylianos. "The Church and the Churches in the Ecumenical Movement." *International Journal for the Study of the Christian Church* 12 (2012) 148–63.
Tucker, Tara. "Culture of Death Denial: Relevant or Rhetoric in Medical Education?" *Journal of Palliative Medicine* 12 (2009) 1105–8.
Turner, Bryan S., and Alex Dumas. "Vulnerability, Diversity and Scarcity: On Universal Rights." *Medicine, Health Care, and Philosophy* 16 (2013) 663–70.
Turoldo, Fabrizio, and Y. Michael Barilan. "The Concept of Responsibility: Three Stages in Its Evolution within Bioethics." *Cambridge Quarterly of Healthcare Ethics* 17 (2008) 114–23.
Tzitzis, Stamatios. "The Ethical and the Legal Aspects of Vulnerability in the Christian Perspective." In *Religious Perspectives on Human Vulnerability in Bioethics,* edited by J. Tham, A. Garcia, and G. Miranda, 53–60. Dordrecht, Netherlands: Springer, 2014.
UNESCO. *Report of the International Bioethics Committee of UNESCO on the Principle of Respect for Human Vulnerability and Personal Integrity.* Paris: UNESCO Publications, 2013.
———. *Universal Declaration on Bioethics and Human Rights.* Paris: UNESCO, 2005.
Vachon, Mary L. S. "Care of The Caregiver: Professionals And Family Members." In *Death, Dying, and Bereavement: Contemporary Perspectives, Institutions, and Practices,* edited by J. Stillion and T. Attig, 379–93. New York: Springer, 2014.
Valliere, Paul. *Modern Russian Theology: Bukharev, Soloviev, Bulgakov: Orthodox Theology in a New Key.* Grand Rapids: Eerdmans, 2000.
———. "Russian Religious Thought and the Future of Orthodox Theology." *St. Vladimir's Theological Quarterly* 45 (2001) 227–41.
Van den Block, Lieve, et al., eds. *Palliative Care for Older People: A Public Health Perspective.* Oxford: Oxford University Press, 2015.
van Hooft, Stan. "The Meaning of Suffering." *Hastings Center Report* 28 (1998) 13–19.
———. "Suffering and the Goals of Medicine." *Medicine, Health Care and Philosophy* 1 (1998) 125–31.

Vassiliadis, Petros. "The Universal Claims of Orthodoxy and the Particularity of Its Witness in a Pluralistic World." In *Orthodox Churches in a Pluralistic World: An Ecumenical Conversation*, edited by E. Clapsis, 192–206. Geneva: WCC Publications, 2004.

Veeresham, Ciddi. "Natural Products Derived from Plants as a Source of Drugs." *Journal of Advanced Pharmaceutical Technology & Research* 3 (2012) 200–201.

Verhey, Allen. *Reading the Bible in the Strange World of Medicine*. Grand Rapids: Eerdmans, 2003.

Vlantis, Giorgos. "The Apophatic Understanding of the Church and Ecumenical Dialogue." *The Ecumenical Review* 62 (2010) 296–301.

Ware, Kallistos. "Orthodox Theology Today: Trends and Tasks." *International Journal for the Study of the Christian Church* 12 (2012) 105–21.

Warraich, Haider. *Modern Death: How Medicine Changed the End of Life*. New York: St. Martin's, 2017.

Wear, Delese, and Joseph Zarconi. "Can Compassion Be Taught? Let's Ask Our Students." *Journal of General Internal Medicine* 23 (2008) 948–53.

Wehr, Kathryn. "Notes & Comments: The Pentecost Liturgy as a Call for Unity and Mission." *St. Vladimir's Theological Quarterly* 59 (2015) 235–44.

Welie, Jos V. M. *In the Face of Suffering: The Philosophical-Anthropological Foundations of Clinical Ethics*. Omaha, NE: Creighton University Press, 1998.

———. "The Relationship between Medicine's Internal Morality and Religion." *Christian Bioethics* 8 (2002) 175–98.

———. "Sympathy as the Basis of Compassion." *Cambridge Quarterly of Healthcare Ethics* 4 (1995) 476–87.

Wheeler, Sondra Ely. "Broadening Our View of Justice in Health Care." In *The Changing Face of Health Care: A Christian Appraisal of Managed Care*, edited by J. F. Kilner, R. D. Orr, and J. A. Shelly, 63–73. Grand Rapids: Eerdmans, 1998.

White, Patricia. "Gratitude, Citizenship and Education." *Studies in Philosophy and Education* 18 (1999) 43–52.

Williams, Simon J. "Chronic Illness as Biographical Disruption or Biographical Disruption as Chronic Illness? Reflections on a Core Concept." *Sociology of Health & Illness* 22 (2000) 40–67.

Wilson, John F., and Frederic W. Hafferty. "Long-Term Effects of a Seminar on Aging and Health for First-Year Medical Students." *The Gerontologist* 23 (1983) 319–24.

Wilson, John F., and Frederic W. Hafferty. "Changes in Attitudes toward the Elderly One Year after a Seminar on Aging and Health." *Journal of Medical Education* 55 (1980) 993–99.

Winslow, G. R. "Minding Our Language: Metaphors and Biomedical Ethics." In *Secular Bioethics in Theological Perspective*, edited by E. E. Shelp, 19–30. Dordrecht, Netherlands: Kluwer Academic, 1996.

Wirtz, Derrick, Cameron L. Gordon, and Juliann Stalls. "Gratitude and Spirituality: A Review of Theory and Research." In *Religion and Spirituality across Cultures*, edited by Chu Kim-Prieto, 287–301. Dordrecht, Netherlands: Springer, 2014.

Wirzba, Norman. "A Priestly Approach to Environmental Theology: Learning to Receive and Give Again the Gifts of Creation." *Dialog* 50 (2011) 354–62.

Yannaras, Christos. *The Freedom of Morality*. Crestwood, NY: St. Vladimir's Seminary Press, 1984.

———. "Human Rights and The Orthodox Church." In *Orthodox Churches in a Pluralistic World: An Ecumenical Conversation*, edited by E. Clapsis, 83–89. Geneva: WCC Publications, 2004.

Yannoulatos, Archbishop Anastasios. *Facing the World: Orthodox Christian Essays on Global Concerns*. Crestwood, NY; Geneva: St Vladimir's Seminary Press/WCC, 2003.

Zaner, Richard M. "Illness and the Other." In *Theological Analyses of the Clinical Encounter*, edited by G. P. McKenny and J. R. Sande, 185–201. Dordrecht, Netherlands: Kluwer Academic, 1994.

———. "On Evoking Clinical Meaning." *Journal of Medicine and Philosophy* 31 (2006) 655–66.

www.ingramcontent.com/pod-product-compliance
Lightning Source LLC
Chambersburg PA
CBHW071247230426
43668CB00011B/1626